BLACKFOOT *ways of knowing*

BLACKFOOT *ways of knowing*

The Worldview of the *Siksikaitsitapi*

by Betty Bastien

Jürgen W. Kremer, editor

Duane Mistaken Chief, language consultant

© 2004 Betty Bastien. All rights reserved.
National Library of Canada Cataloguing in Publication
Second printing 2005

Bastien, Betty, 1948-
    Blackfoot ways of knowing : the worldview of the Siksikaitsitapi / Betty Bastien.

Includes bibliographical references.
ISBN 1-55238-109-9
    1. Siksika philosophy. 2. Siksika language.
    3. Bastien, Betty, 1948-. 4. Knowledge, Theory of. I. Title.

E99.S54B37 2004   191'.089'97352   C2004-900735-1

Published by the University of Calgary Press
2500 University Drive NW Calgary, Alberta, Canada T2N 1N4
www.uofcpress.com

We acknowledge the financial support of the Government of Canada through the Book Publishing Industry Development Program (BPIDP). We acknowledge the support of the Alberta Foundation for the Arts for this published work.

Canada   Canada Council for the Arts   Conseil des Arts du Canada

Title page Illustration: Women hauling wood to Blackfoot camp, ca. 1875. Original artwork by Richard Barrington Nevitt. Glenbow Archives NA–1434–28.

Cover design by Mieka West, page design and typesetting by Dwayne Dobson.
Production by Mike Stickel.

Contents

Foreword

by Pete Standing Alone (*Nii'ta'kaiksá'maikoan*)

It is a great honour to have been part of Dr. Betty Bastien's work, namely *Blackfoot Ways of Knowing*. For the first time in my lifetime, an inquiry into the worldview of the Blackfoot-speaking people has been done by a *Niitsitapiaki*, *Sikapinaki* (Blackeyes Woman), Betty Bastien.

Betty Bastien asked me to participate in the study of the *Niitsitapi* – I not knowing all the questions she might ask.

I suggested that we go to the *Kaaahsinnooniksi* or *Aawaahskataiksi* [ceremonial grandparents]. These are men and women, who have gone through the transfer ceremonies of our spiritual ways of knowing.

I, myself, am one of those *Aawaaahskataiksi*, I was taught by *Naaahsiks*, and they were taught by *Otaawaaahskatawaiksi* and so on.

The federal government and the churches did not succeed in totally destroying our spirituality and our identity, sources of our ways of knowing. Things have changed in the last thirty years since I got involved with the *Ihkanakaaatsiiksi* [All Comrades Society – in this case the Horn Society]. White people were not welcome at *Aakokatssin* [Sundance] then.

Now there are white people who are interested in our spiritual ways.

I was an *Aawaaahsskata* member of the Horn Society.

I was painting faces and giving blessings to his clients when a white couple with their two children came in the teepee to be painted and blessed.

Later I asked the *Iitsskinnaiyi* about his friends, and he said, "They are not my friends; they are tourists travelling through southern Alberta, when they saw the *Aako'ka'tssin* and asked about the teepee in the centre and were told that is where you get your face painted and get blessed, so they went and got painted and blessed."

It has been said that white men have no place in the spiritual world of *Niitsitapi*. I wonder.

This book can be a vehicle for *Niitsitapi* to regain who they are, where they came from, and their identity, and therefore know their place and take their responsibilities in the universe.

Oki, Kita'ahkipohtsi'kaiyis Si'tsi'pssa'tohpowawa Annoh Aamo Kitaiyaa' a'a'ko'kstso'powai.

Nitsiikohtaahsitak Ni No'ohk Ohko'tsitsspomissta'ahs Annohk Aamo Sinnaksinni: *Blackfoot Ways of Knowing*. Annohkai A'ahkaiyistsitsai tais tsi'p Niitsitapiaki – A'mowa Sikapinaki, Betty Bastien – Isstssinnakiwa Niitsipoiyiwa Onno'ohk Anist tssksinni'pi Niipaitapiiysinni.

A'mo, Sikapinaki, Nitsstsima'ahka'k Nita'ahkitsspomssta'ahsi O'tai yak Saaak O'tsistapi'tsiss Niitsitapiwa O'paitapiiysowai.

Niisstowa Niino'ohkannistsi'ta'ki Nita'ahk So'powahtsisatahsinnaan Kaahsinnooniksi, Aamo'ksihk AawaaahskataiksOnno'ohk Annistsskinni'powai Niipaitapiiysinni. Anni'ksisskai Iipommowaiyawa, Ki Isstannisksinnimiyawa Naatowapi.

Niistowa Nitaawaaahska'kowa. Nitaisstama'tsooki Naaahsiks, Kii Osstowawa O'no'ohka'tsiistapaisstama'tso'kowai Oomaaahsowaiks.

Aowka'ksstsimmaiksi Maatohkotssikaaatstomaiksawa Kitsitsitapiiysinnooni, Kit Atsimoyihka'nnoonni, Kii Annik Inna'ahkota-waistamatsotsiiyo'pi. A'kaiyiiksstoko'ohkiitsiwa. Aotsitsk Iiyi'poissttoyiwa Nitsitsiitsinihpi Kanna'kaaatsiiks – Napikowaiks annihk Maatohko'tsitapo htowaiksa Aako'ka'tsinni.

Ki Annohk Napikowaiks Ai'yaitsinna'paisiyawa Natowapi.

Nitaawaaahskakowa – Niiksi Iitskinnaiyiiks, Nitaaahska'ki.

Nitaohpoisskinna'katomowai, Niiksi Iitsskinnaiyiiks,

Ta'msooksi piimma Niiksi Napikowani. Naatsitapi O'ko'sowaiks.

Nitao'ohpoiskinnaiyawa.

Nii'ta'kaiksa'maikoan, Pete Standing Alone, transferring the right to wear a war bonnet to my son Piita Bastien at the Blood Tribe annual celebrations.

Aiksisto'ohpoiskiiyawa, Tsit So'powahtsisatai Miiksi Iitsskinnaiyiiks, "Ta'ahka Miiksi Ki Kso'kowaiks." Ma Iitsskinnaiyiwa, Ta Ni'k, "Nimaatsikso'kowawaiksa, Tourists Nistapssiiyawa. Anno' Iinimmiyawa Aakokatssinni, Iitaistoma'ahkaiyawa. Aisopowahtsisiiyawa, "Tsa Nisstapapiiwa Ammi Ta'tsikiiyakokiiisinni." Iitohkannistaiyawa, "That's where you get your face painted." Anniskai Isstsipihtohpoisskii'iyawa.

Aawaaniyo'p "Napikowaiks, Ihkotsoowaitsinna'paissi Kitatowa'pssinnooni." Tai'kamsookohtaiksimsst [Ka'tannistsiwa?]

Annohk Ammo Sinnakya'tsissi, A'kohko'tsiik Itapso'kapi Ma Ni-itsitapiwa Aissaiyaa'a'k O'tsisstapitsim O'tsiitapiiysinni. A'kohtohkot Otsistapi'tsim Annistsihk Ihpipo'to'tsspisstsi [Kitsiitsitapiiysinnooni, Kit Atsimoyihkannoon].

Translation by: Ai' ai'stahkommi

Preface

by Betty Bastien (*Sikapinaki*)

The book is dedicated to the ancestors and grandparents, to my children and grandchildren, and to future generations who are the daily inspirations for the renewal of our sacred responsibilities.

The need for this work arose a long time ago, but the inspiration and opportunity came with my doctoral studies. As a student of the social sciences, I understood that the scientific approach that I had learnt was embedded in a particular history and carried particular assumptions about the nature of the universe. I had also realized that these scientific assumptions were often contradictory to the understanding of my ancestors. As I began to listen to the conversations of Leonard Bastien, Audrey Weasel Traveller, the late Priscilla Bruised Head, Narcisse Blood, Dr. Pamela (Apela) Colorado, Hunbatz Men, David Peat, and the students of the Bachelor of Social Work Degree Program at the University of Calgary (Yellowhead Tribal Council cohort), these conversations seemed to nurture the soul and inspire me to continue the inquiry. I knew almost immediately that I was on a journey. The journey continues; however, it was the generosity and kindness of these people that made a concept a reality. The purpose of the book is to share my journey with the hope of inspiring others in coming to know their place in the universe – the hope that others will come to know the wisdom of their bodies and listen with their hearts and hear the wisdom of the ancestors. It is my hope that our ancestors and ancients will again have their openly acknowledged place in our ways of being and become apart of our daily living. It is my hope that our educational institutions and social organizations generate the ways of being created by the spiritual connections among all people and that "which is." This is the hope and conviction that balance is a possibility.

The journey that I share in this book is one of "coming home." Coming home means knowing and connecting to the mysterious force, Source of Life, and the essence of one's being and at the same moment the totality of existence. It means coming to know the ancestors, the nurturing knowledge and the transformational pedagogy of our ways of knowing, and understanding that our ways of knowing are not lost, but perhaps it is we, the First Nations peoples, who are lost, as the grandparents have said.

The book is my journey of inquiry into the heart and soul of the Blackfoot world and the wondrous possibility of becoming, once again, keepers of the land, raising our children with the healing wisdom of the ancestors and speaking the sacred words that bring balance into our place. I share the possibility that we have the wisdom and knowledge within each one of us to address the challenges of our societies and the ecological crisis of our communities. It is my hope to support others in their inquiry into indigenous ways of knowing. I believe this is a key that will ensure the continual survival of life on the planet. My story is only a seed in the endeavour. Without those that supported my work, my experience would have remained only an idea.

I would like to acknowledge the ancestors who guided me to the teachers, our grandparents, and *Nii'ta'kaiksámaikoan* (Pete Standing Alone) who, through his wisdom, guidance, and support led me on the path of experiencing the sacred teachings of the cosmos and created the opportunity for "coming home."

I would like to acknowledge the grandparents and ceremonialsts who, through their commitment and responsibility to the sacred world of the ancestors, gave their stories with love and generosity. I am deeply grateful for their gifts, their permission, and their encouragement to share the stories in publication.

They must be acknowledged for carrying the responsibilities for another generation, so they too could survive. They are:

- Pete Standing Alone, Horn Society
- Rosie Red Crow, Horn Society, Medicine Pipe Holder, Motokis Society, Brave Horse Society.
- Adam Delaney, Horn Society, Medicine Pipe Holder.
- Frank Weasel Head, Horn Society, Medicine Pipe Holder.
- Francis First Charger, Horn Society, Medicine, Pipe Holder, Brave Horse Society.

I am truly indebted to the following persons: Dr. Jürgen W. Kremer, who, through his unrelenting support, friendship, guidance, and editorial work, made the possibility of this book a reality. Duane Mistaken Chief, who, through living the traditional teachings and speaking the sacred language of Blackfoot, was able to create the opportunity for me to experience the relationships of an inclusive universe. I would like to express my deep appreciation for his generosity, kindness, and friendship.

I would like to acknowledge the following for making the journey possible. The learning community of the Traditional Knowledge Program, Russell Barsh, and Marie Marule-Smallface for their foresight and commitment to the indigenous ways of knowing.

I would also like to acknowledge Henry Big Throat for the opportunity to learn from the history of the land, the valley, the trees, the river, and the wildlife, and the people in Native American Studies at the University of Lethbridge, who trusted and presented challenges that deepened my inquiry into the sacred world of *Niitsitapi*.

A special acknowledgment and thanks are due to Dr. Pamela (Apela) Colorado, Dr. Busaba Paratacharya, Dr. Daniel Deslauriers, Dr. Gwendalle Cooper, the late Peggy Robins, Dr. Gayla Rogers, Louise

Woodrow, Chantel Molar, Carloyn Lastuka, Tania Big Throat, Walter Hildebrandt, and the Nechi Insititute.

I want to thank the Piikani Nation Chief and Council, the Peigan Board of Education, the Guggenheim Foundation, the Faculty of Social Work at the University of Calgary, and Nechi Institute for their financial contributions.

A unique debt is due to my sister, Babette Bastien, for her unconditional support and her tenacity for working late into the nights and on holidays. I thank my son, Piita, who with humor and insight so often puts the issues of the day into context and provides me with the opportunity to laugh at myself. Special thanks to my dogs Pirate (who has passed) and Wilamin; and my cats Eddie (who has passed) and Ugly for their unconditional loyalty and companionship.

Oki, Kita'ahki'pohtsi'na'ki'tsini'ko'ohpowawa Annohk Aamostsi Sinnaksiiistsi.

A'kaissamitao'taa'a'p Annohk Anni Nistapsinnakssinni Ma'ahk A'potsi'ssi. Nitaomatapsskinnima'tsoko'ohsi my Doctorate, Annikaiyai Tsitsii'i'kato'p Nita'ahkohkotksistsspi'ta'ki Nita'ahkoht Sinnaaksinni. Sootamma'totsisstapi'tsihp Nitsika'ksi'tsii'i'katosi Napissksska'ta'ksinni, A'mi Social Science, Maatohksitsitapissksskatsispa. Nappikowaiks No'oh ka'taiyo'ohkitaisksskatsimiyawa Anno Iitapaisaopi, Ki Niipaitapiiysinni. Ni'towao'k No'mohto'taisksskataki. Sootamma'totsissta'pi'ta'ki Anni Ommaanistaisksskata'kihp Napikowaiks, Otsao'ao'ohkitapitsstapiss Kiipaitapiiysinnooni, Kii Anna'k Issko'ohta'k O'no'ohkannistsskatsihpowa iyi Niipaitapiiysinni – Niitsinnahkotawaistama'tssto'ohkato'pi.

Nitao'mata'pisstsiiwa'tahsi: Aapaomaahkaan (Leonard Bastien); O'pitaami, (Audrey Weasel Traveller; Annam, Naamitapiaki (Priscilla Bruised Head); Kiina'ksap'opa (Narcisse Blood); Dr. Pamela (Apela) Colorado; Hunbatz Men; David Peat; Kii Niiksi Aisksinnima'tsaiksi Social Work, Ammi Mo'ohkinnihtsis (The-Elbow/Calgary) – Aapatohsiisin-

naikowanniawa (from Yellowhead Tribal Council). Ommohtaipoissawa
Niipaitapiiysinni sootamohtsiksistsspi'taki, Kii Niitaitohtso'kimmohs.

Sootamohpiista'pssksinni'p, Nikaomata'psspiyowaa'a'to'ohsi
No'mohtaiyaa'a'k Otsisstapitsihpi. Kii Annihkaiyai Ni'tsiimaiyii'I'ka'kima't
o'ohp Annohksiistsikoi. Aamoksi Matapiiksi Nitsiinihkataiksi, Nitsiiyiksin
i'sto'to'kyawa, No'mohtohko'tomatapaa'a'to'pi.

Noomohtsinnaihp Annohk Ammo Sinnakyatsissi, Matapiwa
Ma'ahko'ohka'tsi'tsi'ksisstsspi'ta'kssowa Ma'ahko'ohka'to'tsisstapitsihs
owai O'mohtsitsipo'to'wahpyawa Anno Iitapaissao'pi, Anno Ksahkoi.
Ma'ahko'ohkitssksinnissa Annik Inna'ahkotawaistama'tsstohkato'pi.

Niino'ohkaiso'ki'taki A'ohko'ohka'tainihkatsima'tahs Anna'k Isski'ki'wa,
Ma'ahko'ohkatsitssko'to'toihpommihtaaniyawa.

Iika'kso'kapiwa, Aamostsihk Iitaisksinnimatssto'ohkyo'pistsi Ma'ahk
o'ohkohpowaistamatsstohkssawa No'ohkannistsi poto'tsspi, kitsiitsitapi-
iysinnooni. No'ohkanistai'tomma'tapaissao'pi A'ahko'ohka'tsitapitsstapissi
Niitsitapiipaitapiiysinni. A'ahko'ohkatohtsa'pao'aohsi Niitsisstsi. Nitsii'i'k
o'ohkannistsi'taki A'kohko'tssksso'kapihsi Niita'paitapiiyao'pi – Ma'ahka'tss-
katsimmipaitapiiyao'si.

Annohk Ammo Sinnakiya'tsissi Miiksistsitsinni'kato'ohp
Nitsskotohkai'si – Niino'ohkatsitapo'ta'ksipoissi Kiipaitapiiysinnooni.
Niitaanistapowaanisto'p "Nitsskota'ahkaiihpi" Nii no'ohkatohkannaiskom
ata'potsistapi'tsissi kiipaitapiiysinnooni – Niima'tssksi'tapitapiiyissinni.

Nistapiwa, No'ohkatskomatapotsistapitsissi Annik Inna'ahkotawaistam
a'tsstohkato'pi.

Ahksi'kamannistsiwa, "Maatonnowawa'tsto'pa Kiipaitapiiysinnoonni,
Kiistonnoon – Niitsitapiiyo'pa – Anniksiyai A'tso'ohsao'p," Anniyai
Aawaani Ommahkitapiiksi.

Annohk, Ammo Sinnakkyatsissi, Miiksist Annistapi,
Nitsskawawakinno'tsihp Kitsiksikaitsitapiiysinnooni, No'ohkanistsipaitapi
iyo'pi. Ahkamma'po'ohkatsitsskaotoi'tsikato'ohp Anno Kitao'ahsinnoonni,
Anno Ksahkoi. A'ahkamma'po'ohkatsitsskomatapo'ohpai Stawatayi
Ko'ko'sinnooniksi Annik Aatsimoyihkaani, So'kapiyi'k, Pommi'kapiiyik.

Nitsiiyiko'ohkanistsi'taki Ihkannaissksinni'p Niitaiyaa'a'kssksso'ka-wa'tao'aopi, Iiso'ksipaitapiiyo'pi.

Niitsii'i'ko'ohkanistsi'ta'ki Nita'ahksspommowa'ahsi Anna'k No'ohka'ta iyaa'a'ksii'I'ka'kimma'tooma Ma'ahk O'tsistapi'tsihs Kiipaitapiiysinnooni.

Tsii'i'k kannistsi'ta'ki A'kohtomanistaikamo'tao'p, Aomanistaiyii'i'ka'ki-ma'to'ohsi Kiipaitapiiysinnooni.

Annohk Ammo Nita'po'tsihpi Sinnakyatsis Nimaatohko'tsi'tapaotsih-pa, Aakaitapi Iitsspommihtaiksi. Aomatsowaitaohkoisspommokoini'ki, Nita'ksika'ksammo'ohkaiksimmihta'to'ohp.

Nomohtsi'ksimmatsi' Annak Iikaiyissaa'a'kiwa, Niitsitapaistama'tsii'ii's, Anniksi Kaaahsinnooniksi, No'ohkawaistama'tsstohkatooma Kiipaitapi-iysinnoonni.

Oki, Ni'ta'kaiksa,maikowan, Nitsii'i'ksinii'i'towawa Niino'ohkanistsspo mmoisspi. Nitsii'i'kso'kaistama'tsok.

Oki, Tsii'I'ka'tsinii'I'towaiyi, Anniksi Awatowa'pssiiksi, Ki Anniksi Aawaaahskataiksi. Ii'i'ksii'i'ka'kimatoomiyawa Annik Ihpipo'towahpiyawa Aatsimoyihkaani. Anniksihkao'kyawa Ihkanaitsina'po'takiiyawa Annihkai "Guggenheim Project."

Niitsii'i'katsinii'i'tsihp Annstsi Nitsiitsinni'koihpiyawa. Nitsii'i'ka'ahki mminnihpiyawa Nita'ahksinnaisi Anohk Ammo Sinnakyatisi. **Kammitst-sihki Pahtsapi, Pahtsisinnaihpi, Niistowa Ni'taitotapihp**.

Niiksi Omahkitapii'i'ksi ihkotohtsiiyana'kowaiyawa O'tsiiyika'kimato'ohsawa Ma'ahkomanistaipo'ohto'ohsi Kiipaitapi-iysinnoonni. A'ahkohtomanistaikamotaosi Kiistonnoon, Ki Anna'k Maanaiyaa'a'kitapiwa.

Ammoksi No'mohtaipoihpiksi Omahkitapii'i'ksi, Anniksiyo'ki:

Nii'ta'kaiksa'maikoani (Pete Standing Alone)
    A'kaotsskinnaiyiwa
Tsiinaki (Rosie Red Crow), A'kainaimihkawa, A'kaotoki,
    Kanna'tsomitawa, A'kaotsskinnaiyiwa.
Mamiyo'ka'kiikin (Adam Delaney), A'kaapa'ksipistawa/
    A'kaotsskinnaiyiwa.

Mi'ksskim (Frank Weasel Head), A'kaotsskinnaiyiwa,
A'kainaimihkawa.

Ninnaisipisto (Francis First Charger), A'kainaimihkawa,
A'kaotsskinnaiyiwa, Kanna'tsomitawa.

Oki, Ammo'ksi Niitsii'i'kspommokiyawa, Ni ta'ahkam sao'ohko't so'po'k
Annisto'p Nitaanist So'ksspommoiyihpi:

Jürgen Kremer, Niiniitap So'ksi'ksokowamawa. Maat Omatsskaoh-
siwa. Aa'a'yaa'a'ksitaksinnaim Ammo Sinnakyatsis, Miistsi O'tsi Nihpi
Ni'pahtsi Sinnaksii'i'st. Nomohtssa'pa'kihp Ammo Sinnakyatsis Nitsii'i'ka'
ahkimminnii'ihpi.

Ai'ai'stahkommi – Otsipaitapiiyi'ihkihtsis Annistsihk Aistam-
ma'tsstohkssii'ihts, Ki Otsitsipowa'to'ohsi Annik Iimaatsimapii'i'k
Ki'tsi'powahsinnooni, No'moht O'tsistapi'tsihp Niitohkannaiksokowamot-
siiyaopi, Matapiwa'k, Iipotawa, Ksahkomma, Kannaomiiyanistsipiksiwa.
"Kita'ahkohtssksinnihp Nitaanistsinnii'i'tsihpi Kinno'ohkso'ksi'kso'kowam-
mo'kssi, Kitaanistsikimmo'kihpi, Ki, Kita'ahsitapiiysinni."

Oki, Ammoksiyaiyi, Niima'tohtsiiyana'kowaiyi Nitanistsspommoihpi:

Anniksi Nitohpokssksinnimatsotsiimaiksi Amii Traditional Knowledge
Program; Pinnapi'tapi (Russell Barsh); Ki, Isstoikamo'saki (Marie Smallface-Marule), Otsii'i'ka'kimma'to'ohsawa Kiistonnoon Noohkanistssks-
satsihpi Niipaitapiiysinni.

Iitsskinnaipo'kawa (Henry Big Throat), Nitsii'i'katsinii'i'towawa.
Annohk Oomi Ni'topissinni, Oistoi Nommohtsi'topi. Anniksi Miistsiiksi,
Anni Nii'i'tahtai, Kyaniksi Kanaomiyanistsipi'kssiiks Iitopiwa
Anni Ksissa'po'ohtsi, Nitsii'i'kohtakaotsistapi'tsihp Niipaitapiiysinni,
Nitsitsspiyaopissi.

Ki Ammiiksi Iit A'paotakiiksi Native American Studies Ammi University of Lethbridge. Miiksit tohtsstskima'kyawa Nitahk A'kyotsistapi'tsis
Niipaitapiiysinni – Niitsitapipaitapiiysinni.

Oki Amoksi Niitsii'i'katsso'ksspommokiyawa, No'ohtsitsiksimatsii'i':

Dr. Pamela (Apela) Colorado, Dr. Busaba Paratcacharya, Dr. Daniel
Deslauriers, Dr. Gwendalle Cooper, Peggy Robins, Dr. Gayla Rogers,

Landscape of my home along the Belly River, my companions Pirate and Wilamin.

Louise Woodrow, Chantelle Marlor, Carloyn Lastuka, Tania Big Throat, Walter Hildebrandt, and the Nechi Insititute.

Nima'tsiksima'tsimaiyi, Piikani Board of Education, the Guggenheim Foundation, Ki Niiksi Faculty of Social Work, Ammi University of Calgary, Noomohtsspommokyawa Ihtaohpommaopi.

Oki Niimatsi'tsspyonowawa, Nississa, Babette Bastien. No'mohtsspommok Nika'kso'kitsihtai'ai's. Toksskai'ai'st Imma'taipanapotakiwa, Ki No'ohkssikopii'i's, Niita'ka'tsspommo'k. Kii, No'ohkowa "Piita (Bastien)." Nitsii'i'kaikya'ahpi'ksisto'to'k, Iimakom aisinnasii'i'ni'ki. Oki, Niimaatsaipo'towawa Nitohpoosiima, "Ugly," Nitoomitaamiksi, "Pirate" (A'kaohka'psiwa/has passed on), Ki, Wilamin. Sootamiitapa'komimmokyawa, Maataiyamimo'kaiksa.

Translation by: Duane Mistaken Chief, Sr.

Blackfoot *(Siksikaitsipowahsin)* Pronunciation Key

by Duane Mistaken Chief, Sr.

Recognizing the difficulty in reading and pronouncing the Blackfoot words in the text of this book, the following pronunciation key has been assembled in an effort to assist the reader. The following are very simple guidelines that will enable you to pronounce most words adequately; they do not require knowledge of linguistic rules. This "key" is not based on standard linguistic practices. If the reader wishes to undertake a more detailed linguistic analysis of the Blackfoot Language – often referred to as *Niitsipowahsinni* by Blackfoot people – other materials should be accessed (e.g., Donald Frantz and Norma Jean Russell's, *Blackfoot Dictionary of Stems, Roots, and Affixes*). Most letters in the written Blackfoot language are pronounced the same as they are in English. The following list gives pronunciation guidance for those letters pronounced differently from English.

a   is pronounced similarly but shorter and less drawn out, as in "alternator." A good rule to follow is that the two are similar in pronunciation, but the double "*a*" signifies that the "*a*" is more drawn out, e.g., *Aawapssp* – "eye."

a'   with a glottal stop is pronounced the same as the single "a," however stopped abruptly in the throat. Oftentimes, the glottal stop is described to be like a swallowed "*t*." For instance, " [The] person is drunk," in Blackfoot would be said in the following manner: "**Aawa'**tsi."

aa   is pronounced as a drawn-out short "*a*" in the English language, as in: "**Baa baa** black sheep...." For example: *Aawapssp* – "eye."

aaa This is one of the possible combinations of double vowels and a single vowel which modify pronunciation. For example, "*Naaamai.*" This indicates that the first two letters are drawn out, followed by a third (same) letter, which is pronounced briefly in addition. The "**aa**" is pronounced distinctly in a drawn-out fashion, followed by the second "**a**," also distinctly pronounced, although much shorter. In each case the "**a**" and "**aa**" are still pronounced as indicated in the previous parts of the key. They are only pronounced in quick but smooth succession. The same rule applies to other letters written in the same sequence.

ah spelling in Blackfoot is pronounced as in the German "ach," as in "**Ach**tung." Example: *Ahkooomohkasin* – "vow."

ai in Blackfoot is similar to the "*a*" in "**a**lley." Example: *Siksik**ai**tsitapi.*

ay The difference between "**ai**" and "**ay**" in Blackfoot words is that in the "**ay**" the "*y*" modifies the pronunciation after the "*a*" as in the "*y*" in "**y**ikes." So it would be equivalent to pronouncing a short "*a*," as in "**a**bout," followed quickly by a "*y*" as in "**y**ikes." Examples: *Ninn**ay**awa* – "authority," *Kimmapiiyipitssinni* – "values."

i is pronounced similar to the "*i*" in "**ti**n" in English. We can find an example of this in the term, "*inna'kotsiiysin*," – a word often associated with the English term, "respect."

ih in Blackfoot, is pronounced similar to the "*iss*," in the word "Sw**iss**," however with a very slight "*ish*" tendency. Example: *Aatsimoy**ih**kaan* – "sacred way of speaking."

ii is pronounced similar to the double "*ee*" in "**see**n," as in *Piit*, which means, "come in." The double vowels denote the drawing out of that particular letter.

iiy This letter combination is pronounced as a long "*e*," as in "**Lee**," followed quickly by a "*y*," as in "**y**es." See "**ay**," for similarity. Example: *Niipaitap**iiy**sinni* – "lifeworld of *Niitsitapi.*"

o in the Blackfoot language is pronounced similar to the "*o*" in the English word "**do**." For example, "*Koitapiiisin*" – "receiving a gift."

o' with a glottal stop is pronounced as an "*o*" in "**o**ats." We see this in the Blackfoot word, "*Kommo'tsissta'pi*," which means "cylindrical case." This example shows both the "*a*" and "*o*" glottal.

oh is pronounced similarly, except the "*o*" (short "*o*") modifies the German "**Ach**tung," to "**Och**tung." or in the town name "Ochtrup." The "**ch**" portion is not pronounced any differently; it is only modified by the "*a*" or "*o*" accordingly. Example: Kiitom**oh**piipotokoi – "what you have been put here with."

oo in Blackfoot is pronounced as in the double "*oo*" in the English words "n**oon**" and "s**oon**." For example, "*Kokonnoon*" – "our home." As in the cases of the "*a*" and "*i*," the doubling denotes that the letter is drawn out.

y As in the "*y*" in "**y**ikes." Example: *Kakyosin* – "understanding" (see glossary for contextual explanation).

' All glottal stops indicate the abrupt stopping of the pronunciation in the throat.

On the March.

Blackfoot camp on the march with horse and dog travois. ca. 1875. Original artwork by
Richard Barrington Nevitt. Glenbow Archives NA–1434–30.

1. Context

1. Introduction

As educator and scholar, I believe that the time has come to break the cycle of dependency and to assert the tribal paradigms of Indigenous cultures through affirmative inquiries based on culturally appropriate protocols. Any such inquiry must be designed to explore solutions to contemporary problems from within tribal interpretations. *Ao'tsisstapitakyo'p*[1] means "to be cognizant and to discern the tribal connections"; it refers to our sacred science and thus to the way to connect with our relations once again experientially through our ways of knowing. These ways of knowing are premised on seeking understanding of the complex levels of kinship relations that constitute a cosmic world of balance and harmony. Indigenous ways of knowing are the tribal processes that align *Niitsitapi* [lit. "real people," i.e., Indigenous people] with their alliances from which all knowing and knowledge is obtained. This way of knowing is of a different nature than the knowledge generated using cross-cultural or alien perspectives developed by Eurocentred sciences.

> Knowledge from a cross-cultural perspective must become a caricature of the culture in order for it to be validated as science or knowledge. Borrowing from the imagery of Frantz Fanon, the study of colonized peoples must take on a "lactification" or whitening in order for the produced knowledge to be palatable to the academy. The consequences of such cross-cultural production

---

1 See the glossaries at the end of the book for translations and explanations of Blackfoot terms.

of knowledge have been ongoing neo-colonialism within the discipline of psychology. (Duran & Duran 1995, 4)

The use of traditional ways of knowing among tribal cultures constitutes the initial and essential step in breaking the cycles of dependency. In this fashion, Indigenous people connect to the sacred, to their alliances, and to the knowledge that is generated for balance, free of dependency. This creates independence because it is self-sufficient and balanced, based on years of intimate observations of the web of place, community, and cycles of time passing.

The primary purpose of this book is the articulation of the ontological responsibilities of *Siksikaitsitapi* identity so that they can have impact within the current educational system. The structure and processes of *Siksikaitsitapi* epistemologies and pedagogy are constituted through the lived process of these ontological responsibilities. I believe that the current focus of Indigenous inquiry must be on healing the genocidal effects of colonialism. *Siksikaitsitapi*, among other *Niitsitapi* cultures of the world, continue to experience genocide, which begins by destroying the foundations of Indigenous science and knowledge. Reaffirming our ancient ways of knowing is essential for the generation of knowledge that is healing and unites the people with their alliances, regenerative ways of being, and an aware relationship with the natural world. This book focuses on the *Siksikaitsitapi* ways of knowing by identifying the basic responsibilities of the *Siksikaitsitapi*, i.e., the responsibilities that maintain the connection to ancestral ways of knowing. They are the essence of our distinct ways of being and have prevented the complete annihilation of *Siksikaitsitapi*.

The responsibility of seeking knowledge is fundamental to the identity of *Niitsitapi*. Knowledge is generated for the purpose of maintaining the relationships that strengthen and protect the health and well being of individuals and of the collective in a cosmic universe. In this respect, seeking knowledge is a fundamental responsibility for contributing to the collective good. *Ao'tsisstapitakyo'p* ["we have come to understand"] is the process of coming to know. *Aissksinihp* means "we know it to be like that."

Both words refer to a level of understanding and presence within the web of alliances and responsibilities that is different from merely knowing.

This book covers three major aspects of *Siksikaitsitapiipaitapiiyssin* [the Blackfoot way of life]. First, it identifies the responsibilities that make up tribal *Siksikaitsitapi* identity. Second, it identifies how these responsibilities are taught and how the people learn them. Third, it identifies how these responsibilities are maintained through ceremonies.

This affirmative inquiry is a contribution to the reconstruction of processes and structures that have been part of the educational and human development processes of *Siksikaitsitapi* in the past *for the present-day educational system*. The traditional protocol I followed provided an opportunity for *Kaaahsinnooniksi* [our grandparents] to fulfill their roles and responsibilities to pass on knowledge to the next generation. As a result, the text carries on the traditional knowledge handed down through the generations by way of oral tradition. Sacred science and tribal responsibilities are all part of the same process. If the children are to learn who they are through knowing their responsibilities, then these teachings must come from *Kaaahsinnooniksi*. The heart of knowing *Siksikaitsitapi* sacred science consists of knowing the tribal responsibilities.

The purpose of my inquiry was to gather information that would help reaffirming and reconstructing the traditional *Siksikaitsitapi* ways of knowing in an alien educational environment, i.e., the Eurocentred educational system. The reconstruction of these ways of knowing must begin with how *Siksikaitsitapi* understand the world, that is, their ontological stance. The nature of being, *Kipaitapiiyssinnooni* [our way of life] is at the heart of this reconstruction. Within *Siksikaitsipoyi* ontology, spiritual energies permeate the cosmic universe from *Ihtsipaitapiiyopa* [the Source of Life]. These energies manifest in physical form, and from them *Niitapaissao'pi* [the nature of being] is created. Based on this ontological view, we can establish how knowledge is understood and what the process of *Kakyosin* [coming to know] is. The process of knowing is based on the interrelationships of natural alliances. Knowledge is generated through these relationships. Spiritual energies are the ultimate substance of the universe from which all life forms originate (*Ihtsipaitapiiyopa*), including knowledge. Furthermore, they are found in every aspect of a cosmic universe (a reality of interrelationship); *Siksikaitsitapi* is constituted through the spiritual connections that make up their identity. These relationships are reciprocal by nature, and thus it is possible to generate knowledge by renewing these relationships. The nature of being is conceived within and originates from these relationships.

Ontological responsibilities of *Siksikaitsitapi* are the beginning of affirming and reconstructing ways of knowing. These fundamental responsibilities must be renewed by coming to know the natural alliances. They are, so to speak, the essence of Being, and by renewing them *Siksikaitsitapi* will have access to their ways of knowing. The alliances are the conduit through which we generate knowledge. They are the way in which we participate and engage with the natural order. In partnership with our alliances, we can affirm, recover, and restore the balance that is necessary for health, prosperity, and long life.

Being these responsibilities, *Siksikaitsitapi* become aligned with the natural order of a cosmic universe. In aligning themselves with cosmic energies, they are connecting with the universal intelligence or *Ihtsipaitapiiyo'pa* [Source of Life]. This creates the possibility of accessing a web of kinship alliances that make up our universe. In connecting with these alliances, *Siksikaitsitapi* must first come to know how to approach these relationships. By learning how to approach them, we come to know the patterns of relationships among the natural order. They embody the knowledge and processes necessary for *Siksikaitsitapi* to live in harmony with the natural order, the basis of our knowledge, and, subsequently, for the survival of a cosmic universe, *Niipaitapiiyssin*. Ontological responsibilities constitute the relationships that create the being of *Siksikaitsitapi*. *Niipaitapiiyssin* means, in essence, renewing and maintaining balance among alliances in this universe from *Ihtsipaitapiiyo'pa*. Alliances are kinship relationships. Kinship means that *Siksikaitsitapi* survival is dependent upon the cosmic order and that our existence is based on knowing and learning our alliances.

Reconstructing *Siksikaitsitapi* ways of knowing is a process of recreating and affirming alliances with knowledge coming from *Ihtsipaitapiiyo'pa*, *Akaitapiwa* [the ancestors and guides], and a cosmic universe of natural relations. This process of coming to know (*Kakyosin*) occurs through the spiritual connection with the alliances. My own process of connecting to the alliances of *Kipaitapiiyssinnooni* [our way of life] started by connecting with *Niitsi'powahsinni* [the words that carry the breath of the ancestors] and by coming to know the ancestors through ceremony, offerings, sacrifice, and mediation. Meditation and prayer are the roots of the process of coming to know. Knowing is communicating with the natural and cosmic world of *Siksikaitsitapi* and integrating the knowledge that transpires from these relationships into one's own being. This knowledge is alive. Knowing results from being aware, observant, and reflective. *Kakyosin* creates and reveals the living knowledge of a cosmic universe. It is living because it is generated from the relationships among the knowledge from *Ihtsipaitapiiyo'pa*, *Akaitapiwa*, the cosmic universe and myself. The knowledge exists as long as the relationships with the alliances continue and changes as these relationships change.

Knowledge that is generated from these relationships can only be understood and acquired through living and communicating with the natural and cosmic alliances. As a result, the understanding of the knowledge and wisdom that *Kaaahsinnooniksi* transferred to me through *Nitaisstammatsokoyi* ["what I have been shown or instructed"] is only achieved through my experiences; the depth of my own knowledge is relative to understanding my place and responsibility among the alliances. The process of my journey in connecting with the ways of knowing and coming to know who I am can be shared with those who are searching for their identity. My story can help them to reclaim their traditional ways of knowing and reconstructing the healing knowledge that is generated and created by this process.

When individuals reconstruct the traditional ways of knowing, it means they are reclaiming the tribal alliances of *Siksikaitsitapi*. They are renewing the traditional knowledge that unites and strengthens the natural and cosmic worlds. This will generate ways of being that balance *Niipaitapiiyssinni* [our way of life]. I began this reconstruction during my inquiry while studying the traditional manner of teaching and learning. I initiated this process with *Kaaahsinnooniksi* who had been keepers of medicine pipes and bundles. And secondly, with those ancestral guides who have protected the integrity of the ceremonies, and, finally, with the natural and cosmic alliances living in the pipes and bundles. This way I began to connect with the alliances and initiate my personal process of reconstructing and reclaiming tribal ways of knowing.

This book discusses traditional forms of learning that form the basis for the development of a *Siksikaitsitapi* studies program premised on our particular epistemology and pedagogy (as well as *Niitsitapi* epistemologies and pedagogies in general). This objective supports the desire of *Kaaahsinnooniksi* who had expressed the need to begin teaching children the language and felt the desire to see them begin thinking in the way of *Siksikaitsitapi*. The book has its origins in other projects that I had the good fortune of being a part of. It is my hope that it will contribute to our ongoing efforts to decolonize by way of cultural affirmation.

Part I provides some necessary historical context. Part II focuses on my journey of retraditionalization through my personal work and the various educational and research projects I have been involved with. Part III discusses the responsibilities that make up *Siksikaitsitapi* identity and describes how they are acquired and ceremonially maintained. Part IV contains a concluding discussion of Indigenous self-affirmation in the context of genocidal histories. At the very end of the book, the reader will find glossaries to help with Blackfoot terminology.

2. *Innahkootaitsinnikaˈtoˈpi Siksikaitsipoyi* – History of the Blackfoot-Speaking Tribes

2.1 **Introductory Remarks**

It is beyond the scope of this text to provide a *Siksikaitsitapi* auto-history; yet, it does seem necessary to provide the reader with some cursory historical information. My brief overview is provided with the following caveat from *Kaaahsinnooniksi* [grandparents]:

> There have been many people who have written about us. These people are known for writing stories about Indians. Ewers, Schultz, Middleton, Wissler, Cobert, and others. White people wrote these books. We did not dispute them. What we are doing today is talking about how our life has been transferred. We don't have to say, let's go to that person and ask for that advice. We, collectively, we are going to discuss our way of life and give advice.
>
> As we are sitting here listening to each other speak, our words come from our hearts, from the way we live. In other words, we didn't borrow our knowledge from anybody. What we are talking about is something we know. White people would say, we heard it from the horse's mouth.

While it may also be necessary to provide a *Siksikaitsitapi* auto-history following traditional protocols, this has not been the focus of my conversations with *Kaaahsinnooniksi*. Readers should keep their cautionary statement in mind as I give this brief overview. The subsequent sections include a critical reading of the sources, yet this reading is neither complete as critique nor is it even intended to provide the level of historico-critical discourse mandatory within a Eurocentred approach. The historical overview provides a more external or bridging perspective in preparation of documentation generated by following traditional protocols for affirmative inquiry. The analysis of cross-cultural communication and miscommunication has not been part of the current endeavour; on the contrary, it attempts in its central parts to supercede the dichotomy of "good subjects" vs. "bad subjects" as choices for colonized people (Dion-Buffalo & Mohawk 1994) by asserting the "non-subject" option of discourse, i.e., affirming *Siksikaitsitapi* ways of knowing, while still remaining accessible to the dominant discourse.

2.2 *Iitotasimahpi Iimitaiks* – The Era of the Dog or the Time of the Ancestors (Pre-Eighteenth Century)

The history of the *Siksikaitsitapi*, their origins, and sacred knowledge and science are the fabric from which their identity is woven. The breach from these sacred ways originated with colonialism. In consequence, the need arises to affirm and, as necessary, to reconstruct an identity from the fabric that holds the sacred ways of the ancestors. The children of the *Siksikaitsitapi* must once again learn the sacred ways of their ancestors. Learning the sacred ways is learning the traditional forms of knowing. The children must know where *Siksikaitsitapi* come from as this is the source of finding one's place in the universe and knowing one's relatives.

The origins of the ancestors are preserved in stories that have also been recorded by ethnographers, e.g., Ewers (1958, 3). In the beginning of the world was water. *Napi*, the Old Man, sent down four animals to find out what was beneath the surface water. First the duck, then the otter, then the badger. They didn't come up with anything. Finally the muskrat came up with earth between his paws. Old Man took this small lump of mud and blew upon it, and it continued to grow until it became the earth. *Napi* travelled about the earth making mountains, rivers, lakes, grasses, roots, berries, timber, animals, and birds. From a lump of clay, he made himself a wife. Together, the Old Man and the Old Woman determined how they should live.

The above narration reveals the distinct relationship between the people, environment and geography, and the animal and plant worlds. The stories and legends of *Napi* address the origins and existence of *Siksikaitsipoyi* culture as well as the geographical features of their territory. This can easily be seen in many of *Napi*'s adventures that are associated with specific locations in Alberta (Kehoe 1995, 9). They are legends explaining their cultural significance. As an example, the Old Man River flowing between the Peigan Reserve in Alberta is said to be the Old Man's Gambling Place (Ewers 1958, 4). Other places associated with his adventures include "Old Man's Sliding Place," "Rolling Stone Creek," and "Tongue Flag River" (Kehoe 1995, 9).

Siksikaitsitapi traditionally inhabited the Great Plains area. Early explorers estimated the population to be 30,000 to 40,000 (McClintock 1992, 5). Upon contact in 1691, *Siksikaitsitapi* occupied a vast area bordered to the north by the North Saskatchewan River; to the west by the Rocky Mountains; to the east by the Sweet Grass hills and central Saskatchewan; and to the south, the Yellow Stone River (Kehoe 1995, xiii). *Siksikaitsitapi* all speak the same language and are comprised of four tribes: The South Peigan (*Aamsskaapipiikani*) located in Montana, the North Peigan (*Aapatohsipiikani* or *Skinnii Piikani*), presently in Canada, the Blood (*Kainai* or *Aapaitsitapi*), and the Blackfoot (*Siksika*).

The two Peigan tribes were originally one. Their *Niitsitapi* names (*Otsiitsitapiinihkasimmowaistsi*) refer to their locations after they split into two tribes. The *Aamsskaapipiikani* located in Montana, and the *Aapatohsipiikanni* or *Skinnii Piikani* (North Peigan) are located in Canada. I am told that the name "Peigan" is the English pronounciation of the *Siksikaitsitapi* word *Piikani*, meaning "poorly dressed" or "torn robes" (Ewers 1958, 5) or "robes that are worn and thin from wear." *Skinnii* refers to the place that they occupy. It means "to live at the edge," referring to the mountains (P. Standing Alone, personal communication, October 1997). The name *Piikani* was likely the tribe's name prior to contact.

The English name "Blood Tribe" has several possible explanations. It is reported to have come from the Kutenai. Members of the tribe were said to have massacred a small group of Kutenai and were returning home with bloodstained faces and hands (Ewers 1958, 7). Another explanation for the name *Aapaitsitapi* comes from the Cree who gave them this name because of the *Aapaitsitapi* ceremonial use of sacred red paint on faces and hands. However, according to P. Standing Alone (personal communication, April 1998), the name *Aapaitsitapi* came from the misinterpretation of the *Siksikaitsipoahsin* or Blackfoot word that describes the weasel's winter coat, *Aapaa* (*Api*, meaning "white"). The colour of the weasel coat changes from the winter to the summer season, and thus the name of the weasel changes corresponding to these seasonal changes. "Blood" is mistranslated from *Aapaitsitapi*, the white phase or pelt of the weasel or real people (the word was mistakenly connected to *Aaapan* [blood]). The *Kainai* (Many Chiefs/ *Aakainawa*) have used the weasel's coat for their clothing and other household items, thus they were referred to as the weasel people by other groups (P. Standing Alone, personal communication, April 1998). White weasel pelt shirts were a prized possession of the *Aapaitsitapi*, *Kainai*, or Blood.

"*Siksika*" literally translates to "Blackfoot people." It has been speculated that they were named by the Crees because of their black feet (maybe as a result of the many prairie fires that coated their moccasins with blackened earth, or perhaps they may have dyed their moccasins black). Some unclarity remains as to the origins of the different *Siksikaitsitapi* names (Ewers 1958, 5–6).

In the Eurocentred literature (anthropology, ethnography, mythology, etc.), *Siksikaitsitapi* are described as independent "Stone Age people" who dominated the northwestern plains with their military power (Ewers 1958, vii). Ewers (1958, 7) argues that *Siksikaitsitapi* adopted the horse, metal tools, and weapons in the early eighteenth century. It is also reported that *Siksikaitsitapi* migrated from the area around Lake Winnipeg. On the other hand, Kroeber argues that they may be regarded "as ancient occupants of the northern plains" (Potvin 1966, 5). One indication of this long-standing occupancy is that sacred places and creation stories (involving Old Man *Napi*) mark the boundaries of *Siksikaitsitapi* territory.

The basic belief system of *Siksikaitsitapi* includes belief in the spiritual nature of the sun, constellations, birds, animals, waterfowl, etc. and their ability to communicate some of their sacred knowledge to humans. While praying and fasting, the sacred powers may be received through dreams and daytime visions (see also Ewers 1958, 17 & 162). It was not only the animals and birds that gave sacred knowledge to *Siksikaitsitapi*, but also the sky beings, such as *Ksisstsi'ko'm* [Thunder] who gave *Niinaimsskaahkoyinnimaan*, the Thunder Medicine Pipe Bundle. Beaver and otter are two potent underwater beings and *Ksisskstakyomopistaan* [the Beaver Bundle] is said to be the oldest among *Siksikaitsitapi* (see also Ewers 1958, 17–18). *Siksikaitsitapi* understand that with the knowledge of these sacred powers comes the ability to call upon them for protection, and the bundles and pipes are a major source of protection through their balancing power. As a result, *Siksikaitsitapi* relate to the natural forces with respect, the fundamental premise of their ethical and moral conduct. Balance is recognized as the natural law of the cosmic universe, and respect is based on this law (I use the term "cosmic universe" to reference *Siksikaitsitapi* understandings of reality emanating from *Ihtsipaitapiiyopa*, the Source of Life). This law is acknowledged in the thought patterns and organizational behaviour of *Siksikaitsitapi*. The pipes and bundles form the societies that shape the organizational behaviour of the people. Balance is the mission of the *Siksikaitsitapi* culture, and through the organization of societies, balance is manifested in the values, norms, and roles of the people. Striving for balance becomes the motivation of life and the impetus for all relationships. Thus we see that relationships are connections with cosmic beings creating alliances. They constitute the foundation for what, in Eurocentred terms, would be call *Siksikaitsitapi* ontology, epistemologies, and pedagogy. We talk about it as *Kipaitapiiyssinnooni* [our way of life], the *Siksikaitsitapi* lifeworld which we seek to understand, *Paitapiiyssin* [lit. "up(right) life," as in "up and living," "alive and walking around as physical beings," the processes of our way of life].

The holistic interrelationship or mutual reflection of the various aspects of *Niipaitapiiyssin* (such as ontology, epistemologies, and cosmology) are the basis for traditional forms of knowing and are necessary for the cultural production of contemporary *Siksikaitsitapi* societies. The knowledge and the forms of teaching and learning are embedded in the ways of the ancestors that we can understand today as epistemologies and pedagogical theories and practices. Ceremonies are a way to make present, teach, and demonstrate through origin stories the life of the ancestors, the natural laws of universe and relationships, the moral and ethical conduct of the people, and the essence and respectful approach to the alliances of the bundles. The legends and stories of these bundles and ceremonies are the connection to *Siksikaitsitapi* knowledge, customs, and rituals. They constitute the pedagogical foundations for acquiring knowledge that is a way of life, just as knowing is a way of being. Both mutually reflect and are conditioned upon each other as they are embodied in the ways of relating to and participating in a world designed for balancing the cosmic world in which we live.

As a result, *Siksikaitsitapi* organize themselves according to their observations of the natural world and the understanding of their relationship with the environment. The natural world with its various resources are experienced as interrelated in a manner that respects all its beings – whether the wide-open grass plains for the buffalo, or other four-legged animals, or forested hills for shelter, or timbered river valleys for winter camps, or roots, berries, and plants. Anthropologists and ethnographers have also noted this. Kehoe (1995, xiv), for example, states that the ways of the bison were very similar to those of the *Siksikaitsitapi*. Similarly, the *Siksikaitsitapi* culture changed as the environment changed. Technological changes were incorporated into the culture just as environmental and other natural changes were incorporated within the context of creation. All was regarded as imbued with *Ihtsipaitapiiyo'pa* [Source of Life], which is inherent in all of life and also works as cause for change. *Ihtsipaitapiiyo'pa* is powerful and is always acknowledged and respected in every aspect of living. The power of *Ihtsipaitapiiyo'pa* was and is maybe most obvious to outsiders when they observe the *Siksikaitsitapi* relationship to the dog, which is their close companion and partner. (The relationship with the horse is similar.) These relationships illustrate the context in which *Siksikaitsitapi* adapted to technological changes and their manifestation in the societal structure. The advent and welcoming of dog and horse illustrate how *Siksikaitsitapi* culture is premised on balance.

The pre-horse era among *Siksikaitsitapi* is referred to as *Iitotasimahpi Iimitaiks*, "dog days." Eurocentred researchers report that they presumably organized themselves in small travelling hunting bands described as economic and political units (Ewers 1958; Kehoe 1995). They journeyed throughout their territory seasonally as guided by their economic activities and ceremonies. The literature also reports that *Siksikaitsitapi* gathered annually in the summer for the *Ookaan*, a ceremony sponsored by a Holy or Medicine Woman (Ewers 1958; Kehoe 1995; Taylor 1989, 19). Other gatherings for ceremonial purposes, such as *Niinaimsskaahkoyinnimaan* [Medicine Pipes] and *Ksisskstakyomopisstaanistsi* [Beaver Bundles], are not discussed in the literature.

In the era of *Iitotasimahpi Iimitaiks*, the *Siksikaitsitapi* travelled on foot with their companion, the dog. Researchers (e.g., Ewers 1958, 7–10) believe that they marched in small groups following the buffalo over the grasslands. Each family was responsible for its own teepee and supplies. It is estimated that the dog could drag a load of seventy-five pounds on a wooden travois. Able-bodied men flanked the march, and the women and children were in the centre, some distance away from the dogs. Lodges were small due to the weight limits of what dogs could pull.

The dog was given grave respect because it was seen as the companion of humankind possessing *I'ta'kiwa* ["has a spirit"] and consciousness. The gifts that dogs give are loyalty, and even their lives, in order to protect their *Siksikaitsitapi* partners. In addition, dogs can see those ghostly beings who did not make it to *Omahksspa'tsikoi*, the Sand Hills (the place where the dead live). It will give a specific bark that will alert the *Siksikaitsitapi* to the fact that a ghost has entered their midst. Sometimes *Ma, mo'ta'k* [the spirit] may leave the body of an alive person and travel to visit favorite places or people. On these occasions, dogs will alert their companions to such a presence.

Ewers (1958) claims that *Siksikaitsitapi* did not have the *Ookaan* during *Iitotasimahpi Iimitaiks*, but that they did have *Ksisskstakyomopisstaan* [Beaver Bundle]. When food was scarce, the *Siksikaitsitapi* called upon *Iiksissksta'kyo mo'pisstaiksi* [the Beaver Bundle holders] to open the bundle and perform the ceremony to call the buffalo, just as *Ksisskstaki*, the Beaver, instructed them to do. *Maa, Iimopisstawa*, the Keeper, and his wife would sing the songs that would charm the direction of the wind and drive the buffalo toward camp. In exchange, *Ksissksta'kyo mo'pisstaiksi* would receive the choice cuts from the buffalo kill. This ceremony is one of the forms of alliances whereby *Siksikaitsitapi* engage in traditional ecological relationships to honour and renew mutual dependency. *Ksissksta'kyo mo'pisstaiksi* would acknowledge these alliances through songs, and they would sing to drive the buffalo toward camp. This invocation alludes to the complexity of the natural relationships and alliances within a holistic nature of *Niipaitapiiyssinni* [cosmic universe].

Certain *Siksikaitsitapi* have always been distinguished because of their special abilities. They may have had the power to call on *Iiniiwa*, the buffalo, or to heal the sick. They may have had outstanding war records and swiftness of foot as well as physical stamina. These important characteristics helped them to sustain themselves in relationship to the natural world. Ewers (1958, 17) assumes that the buffalo was hunted by extremely good runners, who could overtake buffalos (or enemies). These special gifts gave confidence and integrity to the *Siksikaitsitapi*.

2. 3 *Ao'ta'sao'si Ponokaomita* – The Era of the Horse (Eighteenth Century to 1880)

Horses were probably introduced to the Plains tribes around 1630, when they were abducted from other *Niitsitapi* charged with taking care of them for the Spaniards. Through gifts, barter, and thefts the horse made its way to *Siksikaitsitapi* approximately a hundred years later (Potvin 1966, 12).

However, *Siksikaitsitapi* have stories that tell of an earlier encounter with the horse (Narcisse Blood, personal communication, September 1966).

Ewers (1958, 22 & 23) reports that *Aamsskaapipiikani* first encountered the horse when it was ridden by one of their enemies, the Shoshonis. They managed to kill the horse with an arrow in the belly. Initially, *Siksikaitsitapi* named the horse *Iimitaa* [big dog] and later renamed it *Ponokaomita* [elk dog]. They now could journey much longer, and travel was less tiresome. Horses made food easier to obtain while hunting, making them much more valuable than dogs. The transfer of ceremonial bundles was facilitated as a result of these changes, and a closer relationship developed among the various medicine societies (Potvin 1966, 15). It also supported the initiation of individuals into social and military societies. For example, when Red Crane, *Kainaikowan*, acquired the Long Time Medicine Pipe, *Misommahkoiyinnimaan*, for the second time, he gave away sixty horses in the transfer (P. Standing Alone, personal communication, November 1996). In addition to easing the creation of bonds among the ceremonial societies through transfers, the horse also made it possible to travel to other *Niitsitapi* camps much more frequently. *Ponokaomita*, the horse, provided the mechanism and the opportunity to accumulate wealth. It also generated more time for social, recreational, and ceremonial activities. Young boys were well adapted to riding by the ages of six or seven, and in their teens they were expected to join the tribal hunts (Potvin 1966, 30). These changes increased the unity and the strength of the *Siksikaitsitapi* Confederation (Potvin 1966, 15).

Europeans characterized *Siksikaitsitapi* mounted on the horse as "a powerful nation."

> War is more familiar to them than other nations.... In their in roads into the enemies' country, they frequently bring off a number of horses, which is their principal inducement in going to war. (Potvin 1966, 13)

According to anthropologist Robert Lowie, horses represented wealth (Potvin 1966, 15). Such interpretations reflect European values of aggression and accumulated property. However we may interpret its meaning, it is clear that horses did have a tremendous impact on *Siksikaitsitapi* culture and society, which, according to Ewers (1955, quoted in Potvin 1966), probably happened around 1790. According to Grinnell (1962, 243 & 244), *Ponokaomita* not only changed *Siksikaitsipoyi* attitude or need for war, but it also changed their attitude towards the accumulation of property and generated the idea of warfare for territory. Such warring and capturing of horses from other tribes is estimated to have occurred over a seventy-five to eighty-year span.

The *Siksikaitsitapi* interpretation of the terms "warring" and "capturing of horses for the accumulation of property" is *Naamaahkaan* [coup]. *Naamaahkaani* is a custom that requires the physical and spiritual characteristics to which *Siksikaitsitapi* men aspired. It complements their mission of balance, integrity, and bravery. The term "coup," which means, "blow" (Grinnell 1962, 245) and "to take a trophy from an enemy" (Frantz & Russell 1989, 347), is attributed to the French traders and trappers. A direct translation of the Blackfoot word *Naamaahkaan* is the phrase "to strike the enemy." I am told that the actual behaviour meant touching the enemy or going inside his home where his horse was tied and taking the horse (P. Standing Alone, personal communication, May 1998). It does not mean merely attacking the body of the enemy. In practice, the coup was executed by approaching the enemy close enough to strike or to touch him with something held in hand. The characteristics required for *Naamaahkaani* included bravery, physical courage, lack of fear, and daring (Grinnell 1962, 245). For example, a man might ride over and knock down an enemy who is on foot (the horsemen could not be shot or receive a lance at close range). The taking of horses was also considered *Naamaahkaan*, as were the capture of a shield, bow, gun, war bonnet, war shirt, or medicine pipe (Grinnell 1962, 245–48). Warriors usually provided proof of their statements through possession of these items. On special occasions *Naamaahkaan* was performed in public and during ceremonies (Grinnell 1962, 246). The practice of *Naamaahkaan* was clearly a collective agreement among the tribes. *Ponokaomita* and *Naamaahkaan* became integral parts of the *Siksikaitsitapi* culture through the annual ceremonies of the *Kanatsomitaiksi* [Brave Horse Society] and *Iitskinnaiyiiks* [Horn Society]. In this way, *Siksikaitstapi* continued the sacred ways of their ancestors as they responded to changes.

Horses were incorporated into the social and religious practices of *Siksikaitsitapi*. They were seen as sacred animals and became central to their dreaming (Potvin 1966, 55). P. Standing Alone (personal communication, November 1997) described dreams generally as an aspect of receiving knowledge, with some dreams having visionary significance. Dream knowledge usually takes the form of information, guidance, or warning and is frequently only meant for the dreamer (Taylor 1989, 160). Potvin (1966, 55) quotes A. M. Josephy's apt description:

> The plains had always been a place for dreams, but with the horses more so. Something happens to a man when he gets on a horse.... There seems never to have been a race of plains horsemen that was neither fanatically proud or religious. The Plains Indians were both.

According to the stories told, horses were gifts from *Ksisstsi'kȯm* [Thunder], from *Sooyiitapiiks* [water spirits] or from *Ipissowaasi* [Morning Star]. Horses were derived from the same sources as all *Siksikaitsitapi* sacred possessions. They were seen as having supernatural powers that allowed them to perform unusual feats and gave them exceptional endurance. Horses that recovered from seemingly mortal wounds or escaped battle unscathed were perceived to have "secret power" (Potvin 1966, 56, 57). Ethnographers saw the "horse medicine cult" as a secret society surrounded by mystery with the rituals possibly resembling the *Niinaimsskaipasskaan* [Medicine Pipe Dance] (Potvin 1966, 56–57). They report that members of the society practiced a ritual designed to aid the healing of horses or humans; however, most of the time they dealt with the capture and handicapping of enemy horses.

Pre-contact culture quickly eroded under the influence of European technology and materialism, which was introduced over a relatively short period of time during the eighteenth century. By way of gun and Christianity, European materialism quickly permeated *Siksikaitsipoyi* culture. The people demonstrated their ability to adapt to these new influences as they became the most feared tribes in the colonized plains (Ewers 1958). However, in adapting to the influences of European materialism, their own system of spirituality began to deteriorate, leading to unprecedented changes in their way of life, which continue to this day.

During this period of transition, it is reported that, with the use of gun and horse, *Siksikaitsitapi* had intensified their warring with other tribes and increased their wealth through participation in the fur trade. These changes began to alter fundamental relationships in the *Siksikaitsitapi* world. The shift from harmony and the sacredness of life to materialism began the breach with the sacred. This is most obvious in the relationship with *Iiniiwa* [the bison]. Traditionally, *Iiniiwa* is seen as a gift from *Ihtsipaitapiiyopa*, and it is a part of the ceremonies as well as a staple food for subsistence. The relationship with the bison shifted from a ceremonial and subsistence relationship to one of commercial use.

The demise of the *Iiniiwa* changed the overall *Siksikaitsitapi* relationships of alliances with all beings of the natural world. As these relationships were altered, the traditional responsibilities and alliances between *Siksikaitsitapi* and *Iiniiwa* were also changed. The entire *Siksikaitsitapi* universe was affected. It was a violation of the natural laws of *Niipaitapiiysinni* [the cosmic universe] or the *Niitsitapi* lifeworld, the interdependence and interconnectedness of life. One breach affects all other alliances. In the natural world of alliances, the physical manifestations of life are derived from connections with *Ihtsipaitapiiyopa*. This shift in relationship with fur-bearing animals introduced the beginnings of imbalance in the *Siksikaitsitapi* way of life. The perception and connection to the sacred had been altered, as history after the demise of the buffalo illustrates.

2. 4 *Ao'maopao'si* – From when we settled in one place (1880) to today

The destruction of the buffalo was almost complete by 1880. This began a series of events that almost annihilated *Siksikaitsitapi*, with the reservation era being the last major effort by governments to control and render the people dependent. *Siksikaitsitapi*, like all other *Niitsitapi*, were placed on separate reservations with severe restrictions. Legislation and policies of this era forced the placement of children in residential schools for most of their childhood and adolescent years; it limited ceremonial practices and the use of *Niitsi'powahsinni* [Blackfoot language]; migration patterns and economic pursuits were now completely controlled by colonial forces. These restrictions, coupled with their severance from their natural alliances, such as with *Iiniiwa*, accentuated and increased the split within the sacred world of *Siksikaitsitapi*, and, in turn, accelerated their adoption of European materialism.

On the reserves, *Niitsitapi* began to live as they were taught by the Indian Agents (Department of Indian Affairs) and the missionaries. The *Treaty of 1867* formalized the boundaries of the reserves. In 1920 and 1930, the Government of Canada enacted two sections as part of the *Indian Act* that enforced the compulsory attendance at missionary-operated residential schools by *Niitsitapi* children. These practices led them further away from their alliances with the natural order. In the past, the people taught the young children their responsibilities of being *Niitsitapi*. Now children began to perceive the ways of *Niitsitapi* as obsolete and irrelevant. Most of the children no longer spoke the language, and the old people no longer told the stories of the grandparents. Repressive legislation prohibited dances and ceremonies in the 1920s and 1930s. Ceremonial bundles were confiscated or sold to museums by missionaries and police. The absence of these sacred bundles is reflected in the following observation by Clark Wissler, who, after a fourteen-year absence, returned to living with *Aamsskaapipiikani*:

I found the once noted chief and medicine man, Brings Down the Sun, in a small poor lodge on the outskirts of the camp [the Sun-lodge camp of 1917], unnoticed and seemingly unknown to the younger generation of the Blackfoot. He had come from his home in Alberta to attend ... and lead in the ceremonials of the Sun-lodge.... The young men were engaged in a baseball game by the side of Sun-lodge.

Comes Down the Sun had this to say to the younger generation:

Young men, come forth and help us! You now have homes of your own and should do your share in keeping up the worship of the Sun. You no longer are helpers, but sit idly by and seem willing to abandon all of our old religious customs. While we live we should keep up our religion. You seem to care only for whiskey, gambling and horse racing. (Quoted in McClintock 1992, 507)

Although much seems lost in translation, the above quotation captures the shift from a consciousness emanating from and connected with *Ihtsipaitapiiyopa*, to the consciousness of materialism. It is the beginning of an era of imbalance and colonization. Their effects are as evident in contemporary society as they were almost a century ago.

Siksikaitsitapi experienced starvation with the disappearance of *Iiniiwa* during "the starvation winter" of 1883–84. Other fur-bearing animals depended upon for subsistence were also getting rare. Epidemics of small-pox (1869–70) and influenza devastated the populations. As an example, the 1836 diphtheria and 1837 smallpox epidemics reduced the *Siksika* by six to seven thousand people (Hildebrandt et al. 1996, 18). The harsh climates of sub-zero weather with the lack of proper shelter now proved to be insurmountable for *Siksikaitsitapi*. Finally, there was the whiskey trade. All these factors, in conjunction with isolation and segregation, contributed to the near extinction of *Siksikaitsitapi* in the nineteenth century. Their traditional knowledge had been altered with this shift toward Christianity and materialism. This also changed the mission of *Siksikaitsitapi* society. The influence of Europeans values and the perception of land as a commodity began to permeate and disrupt the traditional value system. Land became a valuable commodity for settlers and government. As a result, all *Niitsitapi* territory shrank to small parcels of land called "reserves." *Siksikaitsitapi*, near starvation, had now been herded onto these reservations and were kept alive with government rations (McClintock 1992, 508).

The environment had changed drastically over time: *Iiniiwa* was gone, the seasonal hunts were a thing of the past, and seasonal gatherings for ceremonies no longer took place. The small reserves, with the absence of game, the prohibition of ceremonies, the loss of language, and the children in residential school, left the survivors with the belief that *Niitsitapi Oopaitapiiyssoowaiyi*, the way of life of *Niitsitapi*, was no longer a necessity for survival.

In 1763 the *Royal Proclamation* established the procedure for obtaining land. Its rules for acquiring First Nations lands later became the basis of Aboriginal rights. The *Proclamation* recognized Aboriginal title to lands not already colonized (Brizinski 1993, 151). It also outlined an apartheid system between settlers and Indians. It was originally established to protect the First Nations from exploitation by European settlers. As a result, non-Natives had to pay penalties for trespassing. This policy was reversed in 1885 and now the Natives could not leave their reserves unless given a pass. Although this pass system was not law, York (1990) reports that the Royal Canadian Mounted Police enforced it as though it had been legislated.

During this painful process, Aboriginal peoples internalized the expropriation of their lands that had been justified by the government with "public interest," "national interest," and "common good" arguments (Boldt 1993; York 1990). Boldt (1993, 67) describes this as an artificial construct used to create the illusion that a natural homogeneity of interests exists and that governmental policies are designed to promote these interests.

Some of the details of the expropriation process are worth remembering. The appropriation of First Nations lands began in 1822 with the practice of individual payments, primarily used to entice starving people to sell their land and to instill the idea of individual ownership. In 1850 the *Lands Act* was passed. It stated that lands occupied by First Nations were to be held in trust and protected from taxes (these sections continue to be a part of the present *Indian Act*). In 1857, the *Act for the Gradual Civilization of Indians* was passed by Parliament. This legislation effectively eroded much of the communal and collective consciousness of the tribes through the enfranchisement criteria and through the opportunity to own land in fee simple. In 1869 the *Act for the Gradual Enfranchisement of Indians* was passed. It was designed to remove traditional tribal leadership and to set up a government based on municipal laws and the Euro-centred concept of "majority rule." Until this time traditional leadership had been based on values that produced harmony, respect, and integrity through consensus.

In 1884, the *Indian Advancement Act* outlined the training of tribal leaders for the implementation of municipal structures and processes. Government agents were now authorized to dispose of chiefs and councils resisting the government and practicing their beliefs and values. The government also introduced the "location ticket." This was the allotment of Indian reserves, where each person would receive a piece of land if they could demonstrate that they understood the concept of private property. It was used as a standard for "being civilized" in accordance with the *Indian Advancement Act*. The government also began using the proceeds from land sales to enforce assimilationist policies. The First Nations were told that they would lose more lands if they did not begin to farm. In 1889 the government was empowered to lease and sell tribal lands not in use for farming or ranching and to use the proceeds from sales to carry out its objective of assimilation. Under this system, individual *Niitsitapi* were given forty acres to farm, whereas settlers were farming up to 160 acres at that time. The emphasis was on root crops. The objective for this type of farming was to keep the First Nations people busy with tedious work and to distract them from their ceremonies, dances, and other gatherings. Under the *Indian Advancement Act* "vagrancy" was prosecuted by government agents. Technology was poor by the standards of the day, and First Nations farmers did not have control over their own produce (Buckley 1992, 54–62).

These policies and practices were designed "to advance and civilize the Indian people." This meant the destruction of pre-contact conditions and traditional ways of life. In the seventeenth and eighteenth centuries, the Europeans found that

> the Indians in general exceed the middling stature of Europeans.... Their constitution is strong and healthy, their disorders few.... The Indians are in general free from disorders; and an instance of being subject to dropsy, gout or stone, never came within their knowledge. (York 1990, 77)

Today government officials often point to the decrease in disease rates among Canadian Aboriginals. The decline, however, has been agonizingly slow and is outweighed by deaths from accidents, violence, alcohol, drugs, fires, and suicides. For example, in 1964, 22 percent of all Aboriginal deaths were the result of accidents and violence. This figure has since increased to 35 percent and is one of the worst in the world (York 1990, 77). Aboriginal people are also four times more likely to be murdered than non-Natives. The death rate among Canadian Aboriginals from accidents and violence exceeds most rates in the Third World and almost anywhere in the industrial world. This compares to only 5 percent of deaths due to accidents and violence among non-Natives (York 1990, 77–78). The *Indian Act* with its restrictions on Native people's autonomy, and the patchwork of tiny reserves on infertile land, has locked them into a cycle of unemployment, overcrowding, poor health, and dependence on welfare (York 1990, 79).

In spite of overwhelming genocidal forces, resistance persists to this day. *Siksikaitsitapi* still cling to the traditional beliefs and practices. As demonstrated in the following example, *Aawaaahsskataiksi* [ceremonial grandparents] who pursue their customs had to become secretive and highly protective of their traditions in order to survive as who they are – *Niitsitapi*. Despite the difficulties, they remained *Siksikaitsitapi* by annually renewing their responsibilities through the *Aako'ka'tssin* [Sundance].

Mad Wolf had this to say:

> It has been our custom ... to honour the Sun God. We fast and
> pray that we may lead good lives and act more kindly to each other.
> I do not understand why the white men desire to put an end to
> our religious ceremonials. What harm can they do to our people?
> If they deprive us of our religion, we will have nothing left, for we
> know no other that can take its place.... We believe that the Sun
> God is all powerful, for every spring he makes the trees bud and the
> grass to grow. We see these things with our eyes, and therefore, we
> know that all life comes from him. (McClintock 1992, 508)

McClintock (1992, 509) comments: "Their unselfish and patriotic lives, devoted to the welfare of their tribe, rise before me in strange and painful contrast with the rich and powerful of my race." The strength of the *Siksiakaitsitapi* ceremonialists and their ceremonies are captured in these words. It ensures the continued survival of *Niitsitapipaitapiiyssinni* (the *Niitsitapi* lifeworld). Their strength is living the circle. Understanding the natural law of the cosmos means the "circle comes around." This is living in the consciousness that everything is connected and has consequences (Wub-e-ke-niew 1995, xiv). Government and businesses had made every effort to seduce *Niitsitapi* to forfeit this principle (Boldt 1993; York 1990). Such efforts continue to this day.

The prophecies of many tribes (such as the Hopi and Maya) speak of a new era to come (Kremer & Gomes 2000). One of the characteristics of Indigenous culture is the understanding of the cycles of time. Prophecies among grandparents, elders, and spiritual leaders speak of a time of renewal that will bring a second great flowering of the Americas. No matter how we may interpret these prophecies, it is clear that this is a time of great change. According to the Mayan people, the present timecycle

My Grandmother, *Siipiinamayaki*, Josephine Plain Eagle, with brother, *Otsskoi Ka'ka'tosi*,
Elmer Bastien, in 1946.

will come to an end on December 21, 2011 (Gonzalez & Kremer 2000). Another prophecy speaks of the time when a new fire – the Seventh Fire – will be lit (Peat 1994, 217).

I understand my own work in the context of these prophecies. Reaffirming and reconstructing *Siksikaitsitapi* ways of knowing is renewal as well as part of our ongoing resistance to colonial and genocidal forces; making them part of government-regulated education is mandatory. Language and ceremonies are the essential foundations from which they can begin to understand and experience anew the philosophies, principles, and social and normative systems of our ancestors and the ancients. Language and prayer establish and maintain the emotive and kinship connections that are at the heart of being *Siksikaitsitapi*. They are the key ways through which to access the knowledge, wisdom, sentiments, and meaning of *Niitsitapiipaitapiiyssin*. According to the teachings contained in the prophecies, the ceremonies have protected our science. This means that it is imperative to affirm our traditional knowledge and to reconstruct *Siksikaitsitapi* ways of knowing in new arenas, such as education. This will allow our children to live by them.

The prophecies also state that the time will come when the White Brother will look to the Red Brother for guidance. Now we have to teach a world community about the responsibilities of humanity in a universe of alliances as we understand it.

3. Cultural Destruction – Policies of Ordinary Genocide

Raphael Lemkin coined the term "genocide" in 1944, when he wrote in *Axis Rule in Occupied Europe* that

> … generally speaking, genocide does not necessarily mean the
> immediate destruction of a nation, except when accomplished
> by mass killings of all members of a nation. It is intended rather
> to signify a coordinated plan of different actions aiming at the

destruction of essential foundations of the life of national groups, with the aim of annihilating the group themselves (quoted from Davis & Zannis 1973, 9).

Canadian governmental policies constituted a coordinated plan to disrupt and destroy the essential foundations of *Niitsitapiipaitapiiyssin*, and the resultant actions fit this definition of genocide. They were an attempt to destroy a holistic way of relating to the world by disrupting the process of maintaining the alliances central to the *Niitsitapi* way of life and identity through ceremony, language, and traditional instruction.

Colonization can be described as a process that disconnects tribal people from their kinship alliances. After the initial physical violence, it becomes a process that is slow, insidious, and often abstract in nature. The explicit or implicit objective is to alter the identity, the self, and the sense of humanity of the colonized. This is done by redefining identity, self, and humanness as abstractions instead of defining them through the specific lived realities of natural alliances. It is through the use of these abstractions that the experiences and minds of the colonized are altered. This process changes the consciousness of tribal peoples as it changes the world in which they live. It has created unprecedented conditions of dependency by virtue of the destruction of kinship alliances and the emergence of isolated, individualistic selves. Such dependency is found in the Third World conditions in which Aboriginal people find themselves in Canada (Clarke 1990; Bolaria 1991; Royal Commission on Aboriginal Peoples 1996).

J. S. Frideres describes the process and its results clearly:

Land that was eventually set aside for Indians was selected because it was away from the main routes of travel, not suitable for agricultural development, and lacking in visible natural resources such as mineral wealth. The result has been that most reserves have not had an adequate ecological basis for their existence as self-sufficient

communities.... Indians have not enhanced their economic status
or relative position in the Canadian class system. (Bolaria 1991, 116)

The above conditions of dependency are a systemic part of the Canadian
polity. They are accepted and legitimized within a fundamentally racist
system. The politics of assimilation and integration became the
justification and the intellectual arguments for designing theories,
structures, and mechanisms for rendering a people dependent
and inferior. Racist assumptions have been instrumental for the
perpetuation and mystification of the paternalistic policies, the cloak
of cultural genocide that governs Aboriginal people. They grew from
the notions that Native people were heathens, primitive, and lazy. Such
prejudices provided the Canadian government with the moral and civic
responsibility and justification to ban and destroy essential features of
tribal practices.

The following examples illustrate cultural genocide as experienced by
Canadian Indians. In 1889, the Royal Canadian Mounted Police urged
the Department of Indian Affairs to clearly define cultural practices so that
ceremonies could be made illegal.

If you will, by the Departmental instructions, or through the Indian
Commissioner, clearly define what dances, if any, the Indians are to
be allowed to participate in, either on or off Reserves, the police will
endeavour to enforce your legislation. (Titley 1986, 167)

In 1889, Sam Steele, Superintendent of the Royal Canadian Mounted
Police, after visiting *Kainawa Ot Akokatssowai* [the *Kainai* Sundance]
the previous year, wrote to his superiors urging them to discourage
this ceremony:

Old warriors take this occasion of relating their experiences of
former days, counting their scalps and giving the number of horses
they were successful in stealing. This has a pernicious effect on the

young men; it makes them unsettled and anxious to emulate the deeds of their forefathers. (Titley 1986, 165)

The Oblates were most instrumental in advancing the idea that paganism was a problem among Indians. Father J. Hugonard wrote to Commissioner Laird in 1903 stating:

I am convinced that Christianity and advancement, and paganism and indolence cannot flourish side by side; one or the other has to give away; paganism, dancing and indolence are most natural to the Indian, who has no thought for the morrow. (Titley 1986, 167)

The above policies and practices were designed to alter the consciousness of tribal people in Canada by destroying the foundation of their tribal ways.

They were forced to develop the type of personality that is seen as successful within a Christian and Eurocentred culture. The colonizers projected their own cultural fears of "primitivism" or "heathenism" upon Indigenous peoples. Average Canadians are probably not even aware of this projection, nor are they aware of the genocidal effect of the policies resulting from these fears. The majority of Canadians support these policies because of the manner in which the Eurocentred societies have defined the concept of "culture." However, from an Indigenous perspective, it appears as an abstract system of meanings through which reality is apprehended and a social order is established (Urban 1991, 1). This set of abstractions can be manipulated and controlled in a way *Ni-itsitapi* knowledge cannot. An isolated, individualistic and dissociated self is easier to manipulate than a self connected with fellow humans and the natural world through ceremonial alliances. Because of an entirely different understanding of self, colonizers can convince themselves and their citizens that Indigenous peoples can be assimilated without any serious adverse consequences. It is only the Native's reluctance or refusal to join the colonizer's society that stands in the way. From an Indigenous perspective, this is a twofold illusion. First, *Niitsitapi* culture is not an abstraction but is rooted in the concrete relationships of tribal people to their world. Second, the abstract culture of European conception cannot perceive Indigenous tribes as culture. Aboriginal tribes, on the other hand, can only see the Eurocentred abstractions and dissociations as illusions, imbalance, pathology, and lack of culture.

From a European perspective, tribal people need to be civilized and assimilated by developing so-called autonomous selves. This and similar understandings have categorically regarded Aboriginal people as inferior and, consequently, in need of improvement justifying assimilation policies. The need for assimilation is part of the racist conceptualization of who First Nations people are and should be. It reveals equality as illusion, and mention of equality and justice is only made in the context of assimilation or development, not in the context of settlers and Indigenous peoples. The objective is to alter tribal peoples' culture, society, and identity. The resultant policies and practices are advancing genocide while ideological statements deny and ignore their impact or blame any deficiencies on *Niitsitapi*, the victims.

It is crucial for Indigenous people experiencing the effects of these genocidal policies to articulate and express their experiences in their own voices and not through the interpretations of Eurocentred academics and historians. I will discuss this particular issue at greater length toward the end of the book. Healing from the impact of colonization and genocide means strengthening our personal and cultural voice. Thus we affirm who we are as First Nations people.

The concept of cultural genocide implies the destruction of a peoples' belief system, meaning in the case of Indigenous peoples the destruction of concrete kinship relationships that are crucial for the survival of who they are, whether *Siksikaitsitapi* or another tribe. For example, residential school policies and practices were designed for the destruction and disruption of the life-sustaining kinship relationships of tribal peoples. The destruction of these kinship relations were essentially done by targeting the following: keeping young people away from ceremonies, prohibiting the use of First Nations languages, enforcing a Christian belief system, and treating each pupil as an individualistic monad. The intent is to destroy the purpose, meaning, and life-sustaining relationships of a people. Chrisjohn describes this in the following way:

> Consequently, the phrase "cultural genocide" is an unnecessary ellipsis: cultural genocide is genocide. In any intellectually honest appraisal, Indian Residential Schools were genocide. If there are any serious arguments against this position, we are ready to hear them.
>
> "Ordinary genocide" is rarely, if at all, aimed at the total annihilation of the group; the purpose of the violence (if the violence is purposeful and planned) is to destroy the marked category (a nation, a tribe, a religious sect) as a viable community capable of self-perpetuation and defence of its own self-identity. If this is the case, the objective of the genocide is met once (1) the volume of violence has been large enough to undermine the will and resilience of the sufferer, and to terrorize them into surrender to the superior power and into acceptance of the order it imposed; and (2) the marked group has been deprived of resources necessary for the continuation of the struggle. With these two conditions fulfilled, they are at the mercy of their tormentors. They may be forced into protracted slavery, or offered a place in the new order on terms set by the victors – but which sequel is chosen depends fully on the conquerors' whim. Whichever option has been selected, the perpetrators of the genocide benefit. They extend and solidify their power, and eradicate the roots of the opposition. (Chrisjohn et al. 1994, 30)

The concrete relationships of *Niitsitapi* are to the land, animals, time, stars, sun, and to each other, but hundreds of years of Europeanizing history have colonized these relationships and they have become abstractions. Detachment and disassociation are evident in the dispiritualization of these concepts and relationships. They make genocide possible and allow denial afterward. Similarly, the abstracted definition of "culture" fails to perceive the culture of concrete relationships among *Niitsitapi* and thus negates it. Abstracted definitions as used in laws, policies, schools, and social science theories legitimize the dispiritualized perception of the natural world. Enforcing their use destroyed the alliances central to *Niitsitapi* concepts of self. The colonizers who formulated racist theories and designed genocidal policies were and are detached from the conditions of Aboriginal people. Such distance is a characteristic of ordinary genocide. Davis and Zannis (1973, 32 & 180) describe such acts of genocide as polite and clinical and conclude that the systematic liquidation of Indigenous culture and society leaves First Nations people with neither the resources to build again nor even the public sympathy to perpetuate their memory.

Through the processes of racism just described, the characteristics and potentialities of First Nations children are calibrated. More often this means the expectation of failure from early on, rather than any realistic hopes of becoming *Kaaahsinnooniksi* or *Aawaahsskataiksi* [elders or ceremonial grandparents]. Suicide among young people is a symptom of this situation. Among Canadian Aboriginals under the age of twenty-five, suicides occur six times the national rate compared to non-Natives. In fact, one-third of all deaths among Native teenagers are suicides (York 1990, 97). The mortality rate among the entire Canadian Aboriginal population is four times the national rate. Racist characteristics projected onto First Nations people lead to feelings of uselessness and estrangement. These factors need to be considered as underlying causes for illness and death among Natives (Bolaria 1991, 116). Children inevitably interpret their formative years, their early childhood socialization, and the educational experience within the racist context they live in. *Niitsitapi* children are denied their own interpretations of a world of cosmic alliances. Racism has produced interpretations of life that most likely result in an identity based on powerlessness and debilitation. This ensures the continuity of generation after generation of tribal children shaped into an identity that has its roots in colonialism rather than in the power and beauty of their own natural alliances.

I remember driving to work on a cold snowy morning one late November. The temperature was minus 23 degrees Celsius. I passed two little children, barely three feet tall, who were not more than seven or eight years old. They were waiting on the road for the school bus. With plastic boots and no hats or gloves, they were not dressed for the elements. As I admired the tenacity and perseverance of their parents and these children, I remembered the generations of children who have surivived residential school. Perseverance has been the mark of our survival. Each *Niitsitapi* generation that has survived the genocidal policies has drawn from the strength derived from our ancestors and our connections with the natural alliances.

Blackfoot medicine pipe bundle on a tripod, ca. 1875. Original artwork by Richard Barrington Nevitt. Glenbow Archives NA–1434–34.

II. Tribal Protocol and Affirmative Inquiry

4. *Niinnohkanistssksinipi* – Speaking Personally

This book is a document of my personal retraditionalization as it expresses itself in my work in the field of education. This ongoing process is embedded in community and builds upon past projects. It has also become the seed for more recent projects. The being/knowing of *Siksika itsitapiipaitapiiyssin* [Blackfoot way of life] calls for descriptions from my personal history as necessary background to understand the way in which I am able to give *Kaaahsinnooniksi* voice.

Let me begin by sharing a story told in 1996 in one of my classes by Narcisse Blood, *Kainaikoan*, a *Iipommowa*. He, in turn, had heard it from Pablo Russell, a student of the traditional ways. Although short, the story has many lessons about who we are as *Siksikaitsitapi* and what our relationship to the natural world is:

> Once there was a *Siksikaitsitapi* who was hunting in the foothills
> and mountain area. He had but one horse. In those days people
> usually had different horses for different functions. Usually, a
> hunter would have a hunting horse and another with which to
> pack the kill. However, this man had but one horse. He was a poor
> man. He was very fortunate, though, for on this day he had a kill.
> He had cut up the meat and packed it on his horse. Also, he had
> left enough for a good meal for the coyotes or wolves. On the way
> back home, he ran into a pack of wolves. He knew the wolves were
> on their way to the remains of his kill. A little later, he ran into an

Old Wolf, who was having a hard time keeping up with the pack. The hunter stopped and offered the choicest cut to the Old Man and told him, "By the time you get there, there may be nothing left for you to eat." As it was a cold winter and everyone was hungry, he replied, "I am in a hurry, those ahead are hungry. I need to get there because they will not start without me. You see, I am the grandfather. You will receive a gift for your generosity." Later, the hunter was very fortunate in his hunting expeditions and as a result had many horses.

The story teaches about the natural law of reciprocity. Here we learn to respect others and our environment. We learn about the connections with our relatives with whom we co-habit the land. The story is grounded in the observation of nature, the foundation upon which the science of our people builds. It is the way we come to know our relatives and alliances, and this is how we learn our reciprocal responsibilities and how to maintain balance. This science is significantly different from Eurocentred scientific practices. Both have careful observations at their core; however, the context for the observations (how they are held and what is observed) is entirely different. Instead of a concern with replicability or experimentation for the sake of technological development and progress, *Niitsitapi* science is part of a holistic practice of balancing ourselves within our environment. Nature always tries to be in balance, and it is in this balance that life is strengthened and renewed. It is because of this observation that the lives of *Niitsitapi*, of all First Nations peoples, can best be understood as striving for balance. At an early age, every child learns that our lives are interdependent and interconnected with nature, that we are part of alliances that we actively need to engage in. In this view, we are all simultaneously creating. We breathe in the same air that our ancestors breathed. Earth, air, water, and heat from the sun are continuously renewed. This process gives us *Kiipaitapiisinnooni*, our way of life, and our connections with our ancestors. We understand the meaning of life as renewal. It is through renewal that we breathe the same air as our ancestors. These complex relationships of mutual renewal consist of the interconnecting life force in every rock, animal, plant, bird, and human being. Modern physics, for example, is only beginning to understand these lessons and the rich relationships that make up the universe, but these are the very things that our ancestors learned as children, as Narcisse Blood's story illustrates.

The story also speaks of good fortune as a consequence of kindness and generosity. Children are taught to live in this way. The focus is on connections with others and with the world in which they live. How we behave has consequences for our own self, our family, and often for our tribe. How to be and how to live with others in the world is one of the initial teachings in the development of any child. Honouring interconnectedness, kindness, and generosity are the fundamental lessons for *Siksikaitsitapi* as well as all other *Niitsitapi* children.

The story is still told today; I heard it not that many years ago. But now the children are changing. Today, *Kaaahsinnoonniksi*, ceremonial grandparents and elders, are saying, "The children do not listen. Before we finish talking, they answer us and say 'I know, I know.' They must be very smart to know what we are going to say even before we say it." Another complaint of theirs is, "The children tell us what to do. If we ask them to do something for us, they say, 'Buy me this and then I will do it.'" Children no longer see the connection to *Kaaahsinnooniksi* and how *Kiipaitapiiyssinnooni*, our cultural way of life, is handed down through the grandparents. They no longer understand that listening to *Kaaahsinnooniksi* and elders is essential for their personal and human development as *Niitsitapi*. And neither do they understand that the grandparents are the carriers of the traditions and knowledge of our responsibilities in being *Siksikaitsitapi*. As a result, the grandparents say, "We do not understand the young people, *Maanitapiwa*, the new people, our children."

The young people are truly new people. They no longer know the language, they have not experienced the old people talking, and therefore they have not had the opportunity to hear the words of the ancestors. These new people have been moving further away from *Kiipaitapiiyssinnooni*.

What has happened? The responsibilities that make up the identity of *Niitsitapi* have been central to child-rearing and educational practices in pre-colonial times. However, with the advent of colonization, these practices have largely been replaced by secular educational practices based on European thought. The idea of "development," instead of renewal and balancing, is now used along with the colonizer's child educational systems.

From an Indigenous perspective, it is crucial to heal the impact of colonization and genocide as we come to the end of a large astronomical cycle (as reflected in the Mayan and other calendars). This means that the renewal of the responsibilities that connect children to their ancestors and to the natural world must, once again, become part of any tribal educational process. It is these responsibilities, however each Indigenous culture specifically may understand them, that are essential if tribes are to survive the forces of genocide and if they are to honour the sacred alliances of their ancestors. It is through ancestral sacred knowledge that tribal children have a place in the universe from which to build a future for themselves. Otherwise, they will only be in reaction to the circumstances of colonialism. The children must experience their connections with the natural world for themselves in order to begin to integrate the ways of their ancestors. This process begins with "self" or the identity, which is based on knowing and living the traditions. Living the traditions is knowing your relatives and relating to them as it is taught through the oral traditions of the people. These traditions embody the sacred teachings about cosmology, history, the sciences, sacred organization, and language; they constitute the tribal responsibilities that generate specific tribal identities.

Such precepts are specific to each *Niitsitapi* culture, and, consequently, tribal cultures have different epistemologies. Each epistemology is linked to the precepts of its culture in intricate ways; the interrelationships of precepts form its conception of reality. Epistemology, or the specific Aboriginal way of knowing, is the foundation upon which each tribal society builds its web of knowledge.

BLACKFOOT WAYS OF KNOWING

Tribal people's knowledge is based on thousands of years of observation and participatory relationship with the natural world, their places of settlement or seasonal migrations. Greg Cajete (1994, 42) writes that "spirituality evolves from exploring and coming to know and experience the nature of the living energy moving in each of us, through us, and around us. The ultimate goal of Indigenous education was to be fully knowledgeable about one's innate spirituality." Nature as living energy is the foremost assumption and understanding of any Indigenous epistemology. It is understood as the source from which all life originates and from which all knowledge is born. *Ihtsipaitapiiyopa* ["that which gives life"] is the *Siksikaitsitapi* term expressing this understanding.

Generally speaking, Indigenous knowledge is generated through an epistemology emphasizing dynamic transformation and a form of logic that transcends Eurocentred reason and rationality. It is found in ceremonial practices of tribal peoples; knowledge that is scientific in nature (meaning that it follows an explicit protocol available to a community of inquirers for repetition) is exchanged (Kremer 1996). Inquiry is founded upon knowing the "self" in relationship to the alliances that form one's natural order. The meaning of research, knowledge, and truth is profoundly different from Eurocentred thought and goes beyond rational explanations that attempt to reduce unfathomable mysteries of nature to a finite set of laws that grant order to the cosmos (Knudtson & Suzuki 1992, 10). *Niitsitapi* epistemologies are founded upon generating and creating knowledge premised on the goal of existing in harmony with the natural world. They allow tribal individuals to turn inward unto the self, toward an inner space. This inner space is synonymous with "the source," "Spirit," "the self" or "being" (Battiste & Barman 1995, 103). Indigenous epistemologies, the resultant *Niitsitapi* knowledge, and the communal and individual responsibilities of Indigenous people reflect each other and are consistent with each other in their roots.

Tribal responsibilities are based upon the natural laws of the cosmic universe as perceived by each people, and they form their natural world. They can never be abstracted from *Ihtsipaitapiiyopa*, energies, or forms to which they refer (Peat 1994, 177). They are not abstract ideas that would allow the manipulation of nature. Indigenous natural laws operate as concrete relationships within the cosmos and are the basis for the alliances that form the social order of *Siksikaitsitapi*. They define tribal people as human beings and circumscribe their relationship to the underground people, the star people, the winged people, and to the four-legged. The natural world is inscribed with meaning regarding the origin and unity of all life.

Narcisse Blood's story is a specific example of the intricate interplay between ancestral knowledge of natural alliances, a particular way of knowing and understanding, and the resultant balancing. It is a story woven into and from the cultural knowledge that *Siksikaitsitapi* carry. I want to share my personal story of how I came to lose my connection to this knowledge and my cultural way of inquiring and being present during the process of the colonization that First Nations peoples are suffering. I also want to tell you how I began to reconnect, recover, and reaffirm my heritage. This book is the continuation of that story and discusses how I have reconstructed *Siksikaitsitapi* ways of knowing, not just for myself, but also for my work in the arena of an educational system that came to us not by choice, but by force of colonization.

As a young child I had no question as to who I was. I was *Sikapinaki* (Blackeyes Woman), and I lived with my parents and siblings. We lived near the Oldman River in a log house. We had a dog named Roy, who was family. We also had horses, chickens, and pigs. My favorite pastime was playing with siblings. As children, we had many chores to attend to on a daily basis: cleaning house, washing dishes, taking care of the younger siblings, getting water, feeding the chickens, and sometimes getting firewood. As a family, we were extremely busy in providing the basic necessities for survival and in enjoying the company of our relatives.

My grandmother was a significant part of my life in those early years. I loved her and enjoyed visiting with her. My visits were very special because I was her companion. I was included in all her plans, and she often conferred with me. I felt valued and respected for who I was.

I am standing beside my brother *Otsskoi Ka'ka'tosi*, Elmer Bastien, and my sister *Kaatsikmoinihyaki*, Blandine Bastien[R], at the Sacred Heart Residential School.

At seven years of age, I went to the Sacred Heart Catholic residential school, where I remained until I was twelve. Home visitations included weekends, holidays, and two months in the summer. In the earlier years of my residential school experience, we went home only two weekends a month. Outside of these visitations and with the exception of playtime during those five years, I did not have any social, familiar, or cultural relationships. The classroom seemed sterile most days. Often the content of the course material was irrelevant to what I wanted to learn. I found myself daydreaming of past happy times or talking to my neighbour. Both were frowned upon, and as a result, I would be sent to bed early or had to recite the rosary. However, one of the most painful memories was learning the English language. I knew some basic words in English but could not converse in it. I remember not knowing what was said in the classroom, especially when I was spoken to. I remember the shrill voice of the Grey Nun that seemed to penetrate into my very existence. I felt anxious and afraid and often confused. Later, feelings of humiliation and shame seemed to engulf me during these experiences. Other children may have felt like I did. I remember that some of the children would wet their pants when asked to read in front of the class. At the time I could not understand how they could humiliate themselves in this way. I now better understand the feelings of terror that they must have experienced and their inability to communicate the anxiety. I remember that terror and anxiety seemed constant in those early school years.

The residential school created a vacuum or a void in the development of my *Aapatohsipiikanni* or *Piikani* self. Instead of support for an identity based on familial and cultural relationships, it provided a sterile environment that was based on incomprehensible rules and authority. It prescribed an alien normative order enforced through degrading and humiliating orders. My adaptation to the rules of the residential school became the basis of my behaviour and of my identity. Survival meant conforming to the colonial rules of authority and becoming dependent on them.

Initially, in order to understand the English language and to follow the rules of conduct, I had coped with the situation by observing others and emulating their behaviour. This began a process of looking outside of myself to identify appropriate behaviour – behaviour determined by the rules of colonialism instituted by the Catholic Church and the Canadian government. They determined the basic coordinates of my developing identity and behavioural repertoire.

However, I have other residential school memories. To this day I think fondly of playing with other children in the playground. The missionaries had constructed a fence for the children, and one cardinal rule was never to leave the yard area for any reason whatsoever. We were threatened with corporal punishment. Exceptions were made during the spring and fall, when we went for long walks down the road. These walks were usually on weekends after Sunday lunch, and they are among the happiest experiences of residential school. We picked beautiful small pebbles and flowers or little things that were out of the ordinary. I remember enjoying the countryside, the wide-open spaces, and the wind blowing gently, whispering secrets I could not understand. Another memory I have is of fresh-cooked yeast bread with a chunk of butter, which we received as rewards after cleaning pots and pans in the kitchen. During these earlier years of residential school, I acquired a consistent need to follow the rules of my superiors in order to feel accepted and to avoid humiliating disapproval.

Neither the residential school nor my early childhood experiences prepared me for the questions I began to have as I grew into a young woman. That was when I first noticed the huge differences between the neighbouring towns and the reserve. Compared to the two nearest communities, our reserve was in a desperate condition. The segregation between the two areas was just as striking. I remember going to Fort Macleod with my grandmother and parents to purchase groceries and other household necessities. Occasionally, my father had to have a tire or parts of his machinery repaired, which often took some time. On these occasions I discovered that some of the merchants would not allow me to use their bathroom. Sometimes, when I was with one of my younger siblings, we would sneak into the bus depot and crawl under one of the stalls to use the bathroom.

Around that time I began to question the prevalent stereotypes of "Indian" people. I had heard "Indians" associated with the characteristics of being lazy, dirty, drunk, and dumb. I realized that the residential school program was designed to instill a particular work ethic. "Idle souls are the devil's workshop," I was told. Another objective of the residential school regime was cleanliness. As children, we cleaned the school from morning to bedtime. Chores were done intermittently throughout the day. The stereotypes that I heard about seemed to contradict my own experiences as a pupil. Also, both my parents worked extremely hard. In the springtime, I would not see my father for days, as he would be up early seeding his farm to return hours after I had retired. However, as I grew older, I began to see evidence that supported the stereotypes of the dominant society. I began to look for ways to understand these seemingly contradictory pieces. Why is the poverty among Indians so great? What is it that makes us Natives? Why are we so different from the non-Natives? I entered university with these questions.

This book is the result of my attempts to find answers to these questions. My search led me to a profound personal and academic inquiry into traditional *Siksikaitsitapi* ways of knowing. I came to realize that to know only within Eurocentred forms of education amounted to the annihilation of the traditional knowledge and the sacred science of Indigenous people. My biography is a good example of how this happens.

5. Traditional Knowledge in Academe

Needless to say, the education I received did not answer my questions about poverty and difference. There certainly was no adequate answer to the question of what makes us Natives who we are. My questions only intensified after surviving the frustrations of obtaining my initial degree. I had received three scholarships during the four-year program and made history among my own tribe by being the first *Pikanaki* or for that matter *Pikannikowan* to complete a university degree. Nonetheless, the experience was disappointing because my own expectations of gaining some understanding of the conditions in which First Nations people live was not fulfilled. I was left with the need to acquire more knowledge, thinking that perhaps then I would gain deeper understanding of the causes for the condition in which others and I lived. By this time I had realized that the knowledge I had acquired was irrelevant for the questions I was trying to answer. I had wanted to apply the knowledge and understanding that I gained from university to my own community and the contradictions I was observing; however, this was not possible.

I realized that the research skills I had acquired were not appropriate for the investigation of issues of central importance to Indigenous peoples. In the fall of 1976, after my graduation, I took a ten-day alcohol counsellor training program at the Nechi Institute of Alcohol and Drug Education in Alberta. The course was based on experiential learning of the cultural philosophies and traditions of Indigenous peoples. I found the experience to be totally engaging. The commitment of the trainers was inspiring and enlightening. The trainees shared their pain, anger, fear, humor, and spirituality. Since early childhood this was my first experience of authenticity, humility, and honesty in a tribal community. I began to feel human again. It connected me to my own feelings and emotions, to my love for people, and to the strength of my own connections with *Ihtsipaitapiiyopa*, the sacred powers of mystery. These experiences created in me an awareness of the dissociated self within myself. Kremer (1994, 61), who introduced the concept of "dissociative schismogenesis," describes the disease process for an Indigenous person as the knowing of the Eurocentric perspective:

> This process is the abstract core of the empiricist and rationalist worldview which is an attempt to align the world to *man's* will (needless to say, an imperialistic endeavor on all counts). The consciousness process of the modern mind is thus labeled as an escalating process which ... will lead to intolerable stress and

eventual breakdown…. Dissociative schismogenesis is the stilling and killing of those aspects of being human which are needed to be whole or in balance. Dissociative schismogenesis is the increasing unconsciousness of our participation in the phenomena.

Looking back, I see how I moved further and further away from my tribal connections as I continued further and further in my formal education. Fortunately I had experienced family connections during my childhood on which I was able to draw as I began a profound search for my identity. By returning to *Siksikaitsitapi* ways of knowing, I began to understand how to apply the knowledge that I had acquired during my formal education and my life experiences to pressing issues such as the dismal failure of Native children in the Eurocentred educational system.

At that time I began to work with Dr. Pamela (Apela) Colorado, who had coined the term "Indigenous science." She describes it as

… a state of balance which is at the heart of the universe and the spirit of the science…. The greatest power of Native science lies in the reasons behind the tree's existence…. (1988, 36–38)

This is one of the terms that can be used to describe my journey of connecting with and participating in my tribal responsibilities through the integrity of tribal ceremonies and traditions. Indigenous science refers to the intimate knowledge of *Siksikaitsitapi* alliances that are central for my recovery.

Research, understood as an inquiry using traditional protocols, is a journey of relating, participating, and understanding my relatives. This text cannot possibly capture this journey in its entirety, nor can it capture the spirits and ancestors who guided these processes, nor does it capture the depth of understanding that I have gained within my own tribal alliances. However, the objective of this book is to identify the pertinent concepts that have guided me on this journey and to present them as a model for tribal people who are aware of their colonization and have the desire to reconstruct their tribal responsibilities. I present a model of healing premised on recovering one's tribal idenity through recovering and reclaiming tribal responsibilities. It is my experience that I present as a way of healing from the effects of colonization. The book maps my own process of coming to know. I hope this will support and assist students and teachers who struggle with similar issues on their own path of coming to know.

The process of decolonization entails remembrance, specifically re-membering the teachings of *Kaaahsinnooniksi*, the ways of the ancestors and the ancients. I remembered how my early childhood experiences had connected me to the ways of *Siksikaitsitapi*. But then powerful memories of residential school surfaced. The loss of relationships and the loss of experiences of tribal ways of life became painfully present. In the mirror of my memories I recognized colonial thought, colonial behaviour, and the normative order of colonization. However, these painful memories simultaneously identified lost knowledge that can now be recovered. I can reconstruct the missing pieces for myself personally, and we can do it within an educational system of a different making. The intent of decolo-nization is an essential prerequisite for the engagement with tribal alliances.

This process is not only painful, but also joyful and full of promise and peace. Remembering is an obligatory ingredient for the completion of the past in a manner that is respectful and honours the losses as we honour the strength of the ancestors and acknowledge their gifts to our present generation. Remembering means drawing on the strengths of my own past from which I can carve a future. It is the past that carries us into the future and contributes to the journey of the present. As human beings, we *Siksikaitsitapi* see ourselves as cosmic, because we are intercon-nected, related to all of time and to all that there is. As a result, I continue to experience this miracle of our way of life and the gifts and blessings of *Akaitapiwa* ["the old days people," my ancestors].

The awareness of my own "dis-ease process and dissociation created an experience that was transformative for me. I realized that the four years of university had sharpened my skills in analysis and rational thought. Now I also became aware of my own feelings and began a journey of connecting with the natural world. However, I had yet to realize that my connections with *No'ta'k* [Spirit] had been awakened. While in the Nechi program, I became more passionate about relationships, an awareness that was both liberating and exhilarating. I felt this experience was changing my life. It helped me to nurture a new awareness and a different way of being.

Coming home begins with the self. Here we begin to connect with *Ihtsipaitapiiyopa* [lit. "(that) which causes or allows us to be living"; Source of Life] and develop an understanding of *Ihtsipaitapiiyopi* [how we live through the Source of Life]. Coming home means coming to know the ancestors who are part of the alliances of the natural world. It is through these alliances that we *Siksikaitsitapi*, like all *Niitsitapi*, are connecting to a collective consciousness that is also our access to *Ihtsipaitapiiyopa* – the Source of Life. *Niitsitapi* humanity emerges from this source and determines our ways of knowing. Knowledge and truths flourish through our relationships and our connections with the natural world.

These connections with *Ihtsipaitapiiyopa* and the alliances of the natural world are contextualized in our human experiences that make up a cosmic self woven into tribal relationships. The purpose and meaning of life arises as this self experiences an interconnected world in which every aspect has the potential of giving meaning to life. All that occurs is understood as sacred, meaning all of life is honoured. The honouring occurs through the conscious connection with the natural alliances in a cosmic world. There is no separation between sacred and secular as in the Christian or Eurocentred sense.

I experienced these alliances for the first time in my life when I began to participate in ceremonies. In 1987, as a part of my Indigenous research project, I went to *Aako'ka'tssin*, the Sundance encampment. Beforehand, I had asked my cousin, who was a member of *Iitsskinnayiiks* [Horn Society] for instruction. However, there was no way that I could have been prepared for the experience that I had at *Aako'ka'tssin*. The bundle spoke to me clearly and with much love. This was love I had never experienced in life. There was no uncertainty in the message that

I experienced. The bundle said, "You are home." The feelings and emotions were overwhelming as I received this love. I had the experience of being whole and complete. At this moment, I had a momentous insight that came in the phrase "since time immemorial."

In coming home I had remembered the context for making sense of my personal past and our tribal past. It was a beginning from which to design a future based on my own *Siksikaitsitapi* paradigm. I now saw more clearly what had happened and what needed to be done. I began to reinterpret past experiences in a way that guided me to a fresh understanding. They took on a totally different meaning. I now had the strength to overcome the distorted history of my people and the dissociation of my individualistic self from my ancestors. I now was connecting to the *Siksikaitsitapi* ways of knowing by interpreting my past experiences within the context of the natural world. This gave me the capacity to heal my dissociation as I began to reconstruct my tribal alliances through ceremony. I was no longer an isolated self, but a human being held within the natural and tribal world.

Connecting to ancestors means knowing the ways of *Niitsitapi*, specifically my ancestral ways of *Siksikaitsitapi*. The English translation of the word *Niitsitapi* does not convey the meaning of the word. "Real," as part of the word *Niitsitapi*, refers to "a state of being in connection with the purpose of life," or "journeying with the nature of life." "Life" refers to the "world of *Niitsitapi* and their relationship to a cosmic universe." The concept of "nature" refers to the *Niitsitapi* understanding of the natural laws of a cosmic universe within which they form alliances. These alliances are readily seen in the ceremonial pipes and bundles.

This means that to be *Niitsitapi* is not a given, but is attained through the journey of life. My grandmother would often refer to people who did not possess or aspire to the characteristics valued among the *Siksikaitsitapi* as *Sta'aoi* [ghosts]. Her usage had the connotation of people who were useless in the daily activities of tribal survival. The policies and practices of ordinary genocide have created generations of people who literally function as "ghosts." Such people are referred to as *Ksisstapsi* ["having no real source"], signifying the absence of concerted and tangible efforts toward the collective survival of concrete kin relations that constitute the world of all *Siksikaitsitapi*.

I was looking for a Ph.D. program that would provide support for my process of reconnecting with my tribal alliances, instead of taking me away from my ancestral ways of knowing. The Traditional Knowledge Program at the California Institute of Integral Studies was described as follows:

The mission ... is to protect, strengthen, and perpetuate the crucial knowledge of Indigenous peoples globally. As their ancestors did in the past, tribal people ... share knowledge among themselves. Traditionalists are supported in finding appropriate and protected ways to pass on this knowledge to a world in need, and students are educated in using tools that will allow them to achieve this goal in the contemporary world.

The Traditional Knowledge concentration calls together practitioners of authentic Native mind and life. We are concerned about the ongoing assaults on this precious way of knowing and about the threats to all life forms on the planet. As practitioners of traditional knowledge we uphold and adhere to the original instructions of our cultures, which clearly outline our responsibility for maintaining and reestablishing the integrity of our life-ways and for reversing the destruction of the planet.

As we listen to the cries of our people, our beloved ancestors, and the voices of the Earth's children, our generation is mindful of how serious the losses continue to be. For this reason, the Traditional Knowledge concentration reaches out to traditional people from around the world. Not only are we affirmed by sharing our common story and struggles, but when we gather, we discover that each of us holds a piece of the missing knowledge for each other. Our ancient people had a practice of passing on knowledge of power to kindred traditional people and tribes. This practice ensured that knowledge would not be lost. As we come together, we may find that distant peoples will have a song, chant, or sacred item long lost to the tribe of origin. This is the main reason for coming together.

The concentration does not teach traditional knowledge, but supports traditional people who live with and work for their own people. Students deepen their knowledge by working with their own Elders. (California Institute of Integral Studies promotional brochure)

The Traditional Knowledge program had three residencies per year. These intensives ranged from ten to twelve days and provided the opportunity for exploring the dark and painful history of our personal process of colonization; to learn from other international and national cultures; and to learn from world-leading scientists and grandparents from other traditions. In addition, the residencies had several ceremonialists and healers who conducted and participated in ceremonies with us. The residencies were a laboratory where we practiced Indigenous science and were supported in reconstructing our own tribal identities and, subsequently, to reconstruct our own tribal responsibilities. The next chapter describes that aspect of my work.

6. Cultural Affirmation

While enrolled in my Ph.D. program, I also was part of a series of projects concerned with cultural affirmation. While conducting this work, I participated in ceremonies and visited sacred sites throughout North America seeking guidance and blessings from *Akaitapiiks* and working to maintain the highest level of integrity for my work.

First Nations people in Canada, in preparation to assume the management and administration of their children's services under the authority of provincial Child Welfare authorities, must have their employees trained in social work education. The *Kainai* initiated a two-year social worker diploma education program on the reserve in 1990. The initiative began with an agreement with Mount Royal College in Calgary, Alberta, to offer the Social Work Diploma at Red Crow Community College that is situated on the Kainai Reserve. In recognition of the need for a culturally appropriate and sensitive curriculum, the Red Crow Community College initiated a Social Work Task Force. This book has its earliest origins in my involvement with this group initiated in the spring of 1992. The task force was comprised of First Nations professionals working or teaching in the human service area. Its overall objective was to develop a culturally relevant curriculum for a Bachelor of Social Work Degree Program for *Siksikaitsitapi*. It was given the mandate to develop a social work education program that would be a hybrid of Western methods and traditional knowledge and learning experiences. In the summer and fall of 1992, several meetings were held, and the following tasks were identified:

- a needs assessment for *Siksikaitsitapi*,
- a review of existing human service programs,
- and the development of a proposal to seek funding for the work of the task force.

By the fall of 1992, Ms. Smallface-Marule, President of Red Crow Community College, and members of the Social Work Task Force had formally articulated the following objectives:

1. To identify *Siksikaitsipowahsiistsi* [Blackfoot language words] and concepts that would facilitate an understanding of *Siksikaitsitapi* cultural beliefs, and would subsequently be used for the development of a *Siksikaitsitapi* social work curriculum.
2. To identify appropriate social work skills for First Nations communities.
3. To identify culturally sensitive specialization skills in areas such as alcoholism, child welfare, family violence, etc.

4. To identify distinct *Siksikaitsitapi* concepts to be used in the development of theory and practice for social work curricula.

The task force held a think tank comprised of elders and ceremonialists. The purpose was to have the group address the cultural components of a social work curriculum. These discussions focused on the need to identify a healing process for educators and social workers. The group felt that everybody in the helping and teaching professions must be involved in their own healing process to truly understand the issues facing *Siksikaitsitapi* and their tribal ways.

- The group identified three components that must be included in the process and in the content of the curricula.
- The first was healing through the *Siksikaitsitapi* way of life; this means connecting, understanding, and living *Niitsitapiipaitap iiyssinni* [the ways of *Niitsitapi*].
- The second component was teaching helping professionals their tribal responsibilities in order to have sufficient knowledge and skills in guiding others through the process of healing. This process involves connecting to and living *Niitsitapiipaita piiyssinni*, not just having a cognitive knowledge of it.
- The third component consisted of certain key concepts identified by the group as foundational for curriculum development.

The concepts making up the third component structure the normative roles of *Siksikaitsitapi* society and include:

Aatsimoyihkaan: prayer, sacred way of speaking;
Siimohkssin: cautioning;
Kimmapiiyipitsinni: kindness;
Aistammatsstohksin: teachings;
Ainnakowawa: to respect (related to *Iinniiyim*);

Saam: medicine; can also be translated as "food"
    (*Iisaami* = has medicine, or special powers);

A'pi'pikssin: a process where a person is seeking help for
    self or others. It literally means running around in fear of
    something [and seeking deliverance from danger, hardship,
    etc.]. The act is *A'pi'pikssin*.

These concepts describe the basic responsibilities of *Siksikaitsipoyi*. Any curriculum must be based on affirming and, as necessary, reconstructing *Niitsitapiipaitapiiyssin* and the responsibilities that constitute the identity of *Siksikaitsitapi*.

A year later, in 1993, proposals for funding were submitted to both Indian and Northern Affairs Canada (INAC) and Medical Services Canada. Neither application was funded. Finally, in 1994, Russell Barsh, professor at Native American Studies, University of Lethbridge, assisted the project by writing and submitting a proposal to the Guggenheim Foundation.[2] This led to a two-year funding agreement.

During the two years of working with *Kaaahsinnooniksi* and *Aawaatowapsiiks*, we discussed issues of epistemology, pedagogy, and ontological responsibilities that are manifested in ceremonial practices. All *Kaaahsinnooniksi* had been approached using traditional protocols. In fact, the focus of this book emerged from conversations with these *Kaaahsinnooniksi* from the Kainai and Piikani Reserves who had participated in a previous research project undertaken jointly by Red Crow Community College on the Blood Indian Reserve and by the Native American Studies Department at the University of Lethbridge. Gatherings were held in November 1996 and in March 1997. A total of twenty-one people participated in the day-and-a-half-long dialogues. The *Kaaahsinnooniksi* and *Aawaatowapsiiks* were asked to discuss their relationships with teachers and their own role in the educational system.

---

2 The Guggenheim Foundation provided funding to Red Crow Community College for initial discussions with elders, which took place in 1996–97. This book is a result of these discussions.

The research proposal was premised on affirming and reconstructing the ways of coming to know that constitute ontological responsibilities. For *Niitsitapi*, these are engagement, participation, and connecting people with kin relationships that form their world. These relationships are the ways in which we come to know. They are the basic building blocks of our cosmic universe, our reality. Relationships form the natural world; they include the Above People, the Underwater and Underground People, and those who walk the earth. Knowing your relatives is fundamental to the reality of any *Niitsitapi* and presents the basis of our identity. Relatives shape and form the children's identities through nurturing, strengthening, and renewing their reciprocal and essential responsibilities.

Our ontological responsibilities are the essence of *Niitsitapi* reality because they allow us to form alliances with the natural order. They are inclusive of all relationships and thus include the individual's relationship to knowledge. Knowledge arises in a context of alliances and reciprocal relationships. Implicit is the notion of partnerships that entail obligations or responsibilities on behalf of both parties. In consequence, to seek knowledge is to take on grave responsibilities. Such a quest is founded upon the reciprocal relationship between knower and known. Without taking on these responsibilities, *Niitsitapi* knowledge does not arise, and we fail to come to know.

Following *Niitsitapi* ways of knowing, the subject seeking knowledge engages in inquiry by participating in reciprocal relationships. Therefore, knowing who you are means taking on the responsibility of engaging in these reciprocal relationships. As a result, the pursuit of knowledge means not only to know one's place in a cosmic universe but, by knowing one's relatives, knowing how to relate within these alliances. Knowing one's relatives is the responsibility of knowing. Knowing is thus a circular and reciprocal process. These responsibilities permeate the existence of *Niitsitapi*. They are the foundation of our philosophy, economics, science, government, values, and roles. In essence, they form the normative order of our society designed for the pursuit of well-being, health, prosperity, and, ultimately, the survival of the people. To seek knowledge means to establish and maintain relationships – the essence of the normative order of *Niitsitapi*.

The research project was initially designed to work with grandparents and elders from each of the respective *Siksikaitsitapi* tribes; however, the majority of the participants were *Kainaikowanniya*. The intention of the project was to apply the results to broader social and psychological questions regarding human development and educational theories of *Niitsitapi* and, finally, to incorporate the training needs of *Siksikaitsitapi* students within the curriculum for social work and counselling. Later, as the proposal grew in scope and cultural impact, we, the researchers, were asked to include teachers' education and training.

The research team consisted of bilingual students who were selected from both college and university academic levels. The primary criterion for their selection was their interest in pursuing further studies in *Niipaitapiiyssin*. Data collection occurred through individual visitations with elders, seminars that focused on the research process, and debriefing consultations with elders. And finally, we held convocations with elders, ceremonialists, and grandparents. These visits and gatherings were conducted in *Siksikaitsipowahsin* as the intent of the project was to work within *Niipaitapiiyssin*, necessitating the use of the Blackfoot language, protocol, theoretical orientation, and the traditional knowledge of the people. The methodology was experiential in design. This approach was developed in order to reconstruct the process of *Siksikaitsitapi* ways of knowing. The research process was the critical component of the project. We began by connecting to our ancient ways of knowing. It was only through the researchers' own process of connecting to their tribal ways, and thus being in the consciousness of *Niipaitapiiyssin*, that we began to relate and understand the reconstruction process. The research reflected the traditional cultural process of connecting to the alliances of knowing. Ultimately, the healing process sought by the task force would be identified as the traditional learning practice of *Siksikaitsitapi*. This understanding met the overall goal of the project, which was to strengthen *Niipaitapiiyssin*, our way of life, and community.

The first year's objectives were specifically designed to focus on process and included:

- orienting advanced students from the college and university level;
- building a strong and committed research team;
- visiting with elders and ceremonialists from *Kainai* and *Piikani* tribes, who were knowledgeable about *Niipaitapiiyssin*, thereby establishing a traditional mentor relationship between the student and grandparent;
- facilitating the development of a college of elders and ceremonialists through visits and gatherings; and
- articulating and following the *Siksikaitsitapi* protocol for seeking guidance and understanding of our way of life.

The first year's objectives were accomplished in the following manner:

- a traditional person from *Kainai* introduced *Kaaahsinnooniksi* to the group;
- an offering of tobacco to *Kaaahsinnooniksi* was made prior to our request for help;
- visits and gatherings were held with elders and ceremonialists to establish working relationships;
- a ceremony was requested to begin our work; and
- convocations with elders and ceremonialists were held.

As bicultural researchers, the following tools from both paradigms were used to formulate an approach to inquiry:

- transcription and translation of recorded data with subsequent coding, thematic analysis, and written reports.
- review of the report with selected *Kaaahsinnooniksi* representing the Horn Society, Medicine Pipe Holders, Beaver Bundle Keepers, and the Maotoki Society.

In addition to visiting with the elders, ceremonialists, and grandparents, the research group held bimonthly seminars during this initial phase. They concentrated on decolonization and the reconstruction of the *Siksikaitsitapi* worldview through the use of language and sacred ceremony. The first year was also spent learning the appropriate ways of coming to know by visiting elders and following appropriate cultural protocols. The seminars provided the forum whereby the researchers discussed and debriefed with both a professor from the University of Lethbridge and a grandfather of *Kainai*. Topics discussed in these seminars were essential to our ways of coming to know; they included: listening, respect, intuition, understanding, the power of the word in the language, prayer as way of life. The discussions were always nourishing and elating. However, we also discussed our colonization experiences, which often were concerned with the internalization of racism and sexism in our lives, the painful experiences of dissociation and its effect on our lives, and intergenerational violence of families and communities. The seminars proved to be insightful, enlightening, refreshing, and exhilarating. The honesty and commitment of the research team became evident through the approach to their own learning process and through the manner in which they demonstrated their involvement and commitment to traditional practices (such as attending ceremonies and becoming ceremonialists themselves through initiations).

Pete Standing Alone, *Nii'ta'kaiksámaikoan* [Real-Many-Tumors-Man] of the sacred Horn Society, was our spiritual and methods advisor throughout our process of inquiry. He was a part of our bimonthly seminars and was instrumental in guiding the team in *Siksikaitsitapi* protocol, translation, and explanation of concepts. He helped our individual learning processes in understanding the tribal way of life. As part of this process, the researchers spent many hours talking and visiting late into the nights. It seemed that the greatest gifts came when it wasn't apparent that we were discussing the project.

Throughout the project we as researchers were keenly committed to our own healing process and became acutely aware of our own colonial process. The group, in coming to understand our responsibility as *Siksikaitsitapi*, understood that ceremony, offerings, and sacrifice were integral aspects of coming to know. A *Kanotsisissin* [All-Smoke Ceremony] took place in February 1996. *Aawaaahsskataiksi* from the *Ihkanakaaatsiiksi* [Horn Society], *Niinaimsskaiksi* [Medicine Pipe Holders], *Ksisskstakyomo-pisstaiksi* [Beaver Bundles], and *Maotoki* [Buffalo Women's Society] came to support the project. This ceremony concluded the preparatory phase and initiated our actual work with the ceremonialists and grandparents.

The project was also designed to facilitate the development of a college of *Kaaahssinnooniksi* and *Aawaaahsskataiksi*. Traditionally, they are people who teach, give guidance, and discuss the problems of the day; they are asked for guidance and direction and are responsible for ceremonies. They have the prerequisite experience of ceremonial life (see chapter 15, *Kaaa-hasinnooniksi*), are "qualified" through transfers (*Pomma'ksinni*), and thus have the authority to teach and guide the people. It became evident that they would be the teachers and guides of the project.

During this first year, the following findings were gleaned from the autobiographies of *Kaaahsinnooniksi* and *Aawaaahsskataiksi* as well as from the team of inquirers. Conceptual discussion focused on these issues:

1. *Siksikaitsitapi's* original language (*Siksikaitsipowahsin*) is fundamental to knowing *Niipaitapiiyssin*.
2. The *Siksikaitsitapi's* way of life includes a spiritual dimension, which must be learned in ceremonies and from the land.
3. Children must be given both individual and collective roles and responsibilities from an early age (7–10 years old).
4. Personal growth and healing are centred fundamentally on taking and understanding responsibilities to family, to the people, and to life.
5. The most effective guides, teachers, counsellors, social workers, etc., are individuals who are already learning the path of cultural and spiritual knowledge.

At the second gathering with grandparents and ceremonialists the following suggestions were made:

- There is a need for a *Siksikaitsitapi* language immersion program for preschool or kindergarten levels. (The elders felt that the children must learn to think in *Niitsitapi* first.)
- The teachers of *Siksikaitsitapi* children must learn *Kiipaitapiiyssin*.
- The parents and families of *Siksikaitsitapi* children should learn the language and the way of life with their children so that they can support what their children are learning.
- A survival camp for children and young adults must be established so that they can experience *Kiipaitapiiyssinnooni* and learn to live on and respect the land.

The grandparents and ceremonialists were asked to discuss the relationship between teachers and students. In later convocations they were specifically asked, "What is the relationship a teacher should have with the students and what is the role of the elders in the educational system?" The basic ideas that emerged from these questions were:

First, *niitsi'powahsinni* [language] and *aatsimoyihkaan* [prayer] are the foundations of *Niitsitapiipaitapiiyssin* [seeking to understand life]. Second, that language and prayer are the medium for transmitting the teachings of *Niipaitapiiyssin*.

Children raised with the language know their relationships and understand *Niipaitapiiyssin* because language structures and shapes the experiences of the child. These experiences are the primary knowledge of the tribe, and they form the methods of coming to know the ways of knowing.

In the gatherings with the grandparents, the term "elder" was clarified: "elder" is a word that they, *Kaaahsinnooniksi* and *Aawaaahsskataiksi*, could not relate to; they attributed it to a Eurocentred interpretation. The word appears to have the same connotation as "old people" to the *Kaaahsinnooniksi*. *Kaaahsinnooniksi* are those who are sought to teach new initiates the knowledge and practices of ceremony. *Kaaahsinnooniksi* are those who participated in this project; their words form the basis of my personal journey of retraditionalization as well as this book. *Kaaahsinnooniksi* are those who are asked to teach and advise the young people, the ceremonial societies, and who perform the ceremonies. They are people who have experienced the ceremonial responsibilities of *Niipaitapiiyssin* and have demonstrated their understanding of the way of life through *Pomma'ksinni* [transfers]. "They are people who have maintained their responsibilities through *Pomma'ksinni*," said one of the *Awaaahsskataiksi*.

Kaaahsinnooniksi and *Aawaaahsskataiksi* felt strongly that *Kiipaitapiiyssinnooni* was intact, and that the resources were available to begin language immersion schools for *Siksikaitsitapi* children. They felt that *Kaaahsinnooniksi* had put aside or forgotten their role and responsibility for teaching the children, saying that often they wanted to get paid for guidance, advice, and sharing their knowledge of *Kiipaitapiiyssinnooni*. *Awaaahsskataiksi* who accepted to be a part of the research expressed the need for the project and their participation as traditional knowledge and teachings were being forgotten and children may need to incorporate the traditional forms of learning in this contemporary method of education. They felt that otherwise the teachings might be forgotten by the young people. Our inquiries, they added, are an opportunity for *Kaaahsinnooniksi* to once again take up their responsibilities to teach the children and for the knowledge to be shared by those who have the "authority" to teach.

The educational process for teaching the responsibilities of *Siksikaitsitapi* are carried through the ceremonies. It was explained in this way: "The life of *Siksikaitsitapi* is *Pomma'ksinni* [transfers]. Our life is transferred to us," said one of the *Aawaaahsskataiksi*. "*Pomma'ksinni* is the way knowledge is passed on and the way to maintain balance in a cosmic universe. It is our responsibility as *Siksikaitsitapi* to give back what has been transferred. It is not the way of the people to sit with or keep the knowledge, wisdom, and blessings that have been given to you. As an example, those who have received an education return and become of service to the people. *Kipaitapiiyssinnooni* [our way] is to help, to assist, and help will come from *Ihtsipaitapiiyo'pa*. We have to try hard and work hard. It is good, *Ihtsipaitapiiyo'pa* will help."

"We need not worry," continued one of the other *Aawaaahsskataiksi*. "*Niipaitapiiyssinni* is premised on giving and sharing of knowledge, and through prayer, assisting and helping the group survive. It is giving which strengthens life."

The actions of giving and sharing are contextualized in the fundamental philosophical premises of the mission of life. Balance is created through sharing and giving and, as a result, maintains the reciprocal nature of a cosmic order. Sharing and giving have been observed in the natural order of the universe and are a part of the responsibilities learned in *Pomma'kssinni*. These are examples of tribal responsibilities of people of *Siksikaitsitapi* identity.

Kaaahsinnooniksi also spoke of the critical nature of learning these responsibilities. They said: "Children who are not raised within *Kiipaita-piiyssinnooni* do not understand their role or their responsibilities as *Siksikaitsitapi*. It is important to know these things because these responsibilities are the basis for our decisions and they shape our thought patterns and behaviour. Through the language and the knowledge of our relations, we come to know who we are. As an example, many of the uninitiated do not know how to assist or contribute to the *Ookaan* [Sundance lodge]. It has come to a place and time, where we *Siksikaitsitapi* are afraid of our way and our prayer; we scare each other with it. Many of our people do not know," said one of the *Aawaaahsskataiksi*. Traditionally, the individual was motivated and committed to learn the ways of the people with integrity and humility, both of which are necessary for their journey in understanding life.

This study resulted in the development of a *Siksikaitsitapi* education program. The program is founded upon *Niitsitapi* epistemologies and pedagogy and will identify the essential content and process for reconstructing an educational model for *Niitsitapi*, and *Siksikaitsitapi* in particular. The anticipated long-term effect of such a curriculum is the change of a dependent people to communities premised on self-determination. The curriculum is intended to deconstruct the fundamental belief that Eurocentred knowledge is the foundation of Indigenous people's self-sufficiency. The research is proposing an educational model premised on Indigenous ways of knowing from which people can determine their own destiny and thus acquire self-determination. Self-determination means the power to define oneself and to determine one's destiny.

The curriculum will call various community components together and begin a unifying and healing process for the tribe. Children, educators, parents, and the grandparents will come together in connection with the sacred. Connecting to the sacred is the beginning of once again fulfilling our responsibilities as *Siksikaitsitapi*. And these responsibilities must be observed and expressed daily by carrying out our activities that respect and honour life.

I believe that, through connecting with the sacred, *Siksikaitsitapi* will connect with relatives and ancestors, and that through these relationships they will once again live in harmony and balance.

7. Protocol of Affirmative Inquiry

The traditional approach I used as the basis for this book had four major aspects, namely:

- the guidance by *Aawaaahsskataiksi* of the *Iitsskinaiyiiks* [Horn Society] and my personal ceremonial and spiritual process,
- the preliminary projects described in the previous section,
- the work in my graduate program, and
- the convocation of *Kaaahsinnooniksi* on which the central parts of this book are based.

Following the prerequisite protocols, as they are traditionally defined, was the only way to achieve authenticity for the affirmative inquiry I chose to endeavour in. Overcoming the dichotomous choice of conformity to colonial forces versus opposition to them by, instead, affirming Indigenous identity, values, and ways of knowing requires remembering and implementing these protocols in a painstaking fashion. Such an approach (or methodology, if you wish) is decolonizing in its assertion and affirmation of knowing and knowledge.

Kaaahsinnoona Pete Standing Alone, *Nii'ta'kaiksa'maikoan* [Real-Many-Tumors-Man], was asked to guide the process of my work. Traditional protocols had been used in approaching *Kaaahsinnoona* as a traditional teacher for my dissertation work. Protocol among *Siksikaitsitapi* is the method and process of maintaining good relations, which strengthen the mission of balance. Traditionally, it is *Kaaahsinnooniksi*, those who have lived the ways of life of the people, who teach the young people. Their teachings are based on their alliances with the world of *Siksikaitsitapi*.

Niita'kaiksa'maikoan stated:

> If we didn't know our way of life, we could not help you. We would not be sitting here today. This is how our way of life is passed on.
>
> The way of life is passed on through relationships, especially relationships with *Kaaahsinnooniksi* who have experienced the life of *Siksikaitsitapi*, in the language of our people. The spirits of *Akaitapiwa*, the ancestors, flow through the words of the *Kaaahsinnooniksi*.
>
> We are sitting here because we still use our ways; we put the other aside [meaning the Eurocentred way of life]. We use it, but we are living our ways of life.

I have had *Niita'kaiksa'maikoan*'s advice and guidance since acceptance into my doctoral program. His help has been used throughout the course work and in the design of the inquiry process, the questions, and the protocols that have been used for the materials gathered in this book.

Kaaahsinnooniksi whom I approached at the beginning of my inquiry had knowledge of my own preparation with the ancestors; I was seeking and attempting to understand *Siksikaitsitapi* ways of knowing, the alliances of a cosmic universe, through *Kakyosin* [the essence of knowledge based on observation and understanding embedded in our alliances] and *Ihtsipaitapiiyo'pa*. This preparation included offerings, sacrifice, and ceremony. I sought *Kaaahsinnooniksi* of the Kainai [Blood] Tribe who could identify *Ihpi'po'to'tsspistsi*, the basic ontological responsibilities that constitute *Siksikaitsipoyi* identity. *Kaaahsinnooniksi* are living knowledge – they live the connections and know the alliances of *Kiipaitapiiyssinnooni*. Their experiences, including the time they spent with their teachers, embody the accumulated knowledge that has been passed through the generations. The stories they have shared represent their own relationships to the alliances and their understanding of the knowledge that has been revealed to them. The stories shared in meetings are the living *Siksikaitsipoyi* knowledge told by the teachers of this generation. This is what they mean when they say, "These are our stories." This knowledge has been passed through the generations in the same manner as I learned during the process of *Kakyosin* as part of following protocols for the interdependent alliances. I understand my experience to be a gift from *Kaaahsinnooniksi*, and the teachings I have received will benefit my life. In return, it is my responsibility to share it and give it away.

Kaaahsinnooniksi of four of the *Siksikaitsitapi* ceremonies participated. These ceremonies are *Ao'kaiksi* (sponsors of Sun-Lodge), *Niinaimsskaah-koyinimaan* (Medicine Pipe Bundle), the *Kanakaaatsiiksi* (Society and Bundle Carriers), and *Maotokiiks* (Buffalo Women's Society) ceremonies. *Nii'ta'kaiksa'maikoan* (Pete Standing Alone), *Tsiinaki* (Rosie Red Crow), *Mamiyo'ka'kiikin* (Adam Delaney), *Mi'ksskim* (Frank Weasel Head), and *Ninnaisipisto* (Francis First Charger) are fluent speakers of the language and have undergone the appropriate tribal processes and protocols in order to carry on the ceremonial responsibilities of *Kainai*. Their responsibilities include teaching, performing, and advising in the ceremonial life. As a result, I have established the traditional mentor–student relationship with them. It is a relationship founded upon sincerity and commitment to the way of life of *Siksikaitsitapi*.

Kaaahsinnooniksi often assess whether a student is ready to engage in the responsibilities of the *Siksikaitsitapi* way of life. One *Kaaahsinnoon* said:

> The way I see it now, there are many things I do not tell people because they do not have the right to be told these things. There are some things I would not tell them. I would wait before I told them.

Sincerity and commitment are necessary to begin building a teacher–student relationship with *Kaaahsinnooniksi*. The process of building and connecting are essential components of traditional forms of pedagogy. In this specific affirmative inquiry, I have worked with these *Kaaahsinnooniksi* for three years immersed in the traditional method of learning.

Traditionally, students seek the advice of *Kaaahsinnooniksi*, and the form of proper tribal protocol creates the place where knowledge can have authenticity. Young people thus demonstrate their commitment to learning. Efforts are primarily made by asking questions and visiting with them for long periods of time. However, guided by contemporary Eurocentred educational pedagogy, students often interview *Kaaahsinnooniksi*, and their words are documented to be kept in libraries. This is as troubling as the many sacred bundles that have found their way into museums. Traditionally, the knowledge of the people is not passed on through the written word but orally through those who have experienced the way of life of *Siksikaitsitapi*.

The ways of coming to know or the *Siksikaitsitapi* theory of knowledge is the basis of cultural production. This source of knowledge is the means by which *Siksikaitsitapi* can survive genocide. Their traditional responsibilities are the source of regenerative and creative ways of being, which connect to *Ihtsipaitapiiyo'pa*, the source of the universe. They are the essential ingredients for the people to begin to produce solutions for the socioeconomic problems that have resulted from colonialism. It is the method by which we will become *Siksikaitsitapi* again, allowing us to survive.

A convocation with grandparents formed the basis for the central pieces of this book. It took place on the Kainai Reserve in the boardroom of one of the tribal corporations. One year earlier, I had approached *Kaaahsinnooniksi*, whom I wanted to become involved, in the traditional manner of asking for their guidance and teachings. One week prior to the convocation, I gave them a letter in person formally inviting them to the convocation.

During the preparation for the convocation, I continued to learn more of the traditional ways of my people. As an example, in the planning and preparation of the traditional meal, one of the *Kaaahsinnooniksi* of *Iitsskinnaiyiiksi* and *Maotokiiks* societies came to help me prepare the pemmican. She also had been transferred the responsibilities of making pemmican for the sacred ceremonies of *Iitskinnaiyiiks*. I was able to observe and became a part of the process of making one of the staple traditional foods of our people.

Family also came together to support me on this very special day. My older sister had the dried meat for the pemmican, which she gave to me, and my younger sister prepared and served the meal while I took care of the recording, coffee, and notes.

Upon their arrival, *Naaahsinnaaniksi* were served refreshments. Gifts were given as offerings to the ancestors as a way of asking for their guidance and protection. The *Kaaahsinnooniksi* were familiar with each other: some of them are biologically related, and all are spiritual brothers and sisters as members of *Iitsskinnayiiks* [Horn Society]. They visited and joked among themselves.

The convocation was opened with a prayer from one of *Kaaahsinnooniksi*. I then began by introducing myself formally, stating the purpose and objective of my project. I had prepared a document regarding the confidentially of the participants from which I read. I then asked for permission to record. They agreed to the recording and stated that confidentiality was not an issue. They also said that if I wanted to use their names in the document, this would be appropriate. One of *Kaaahsinnooniksi* said: "It is only when we lie that we would not want to be identified. We will tell you what we know, and it is our responsibility to tell you the things you have asked us."

The aforementioned four *Kaaahsinnooniksi* had participated in the preliminary work. As a result, they supported my dissertation research as well as this book and agreed to be identified in the acknowledgments. Furthermore, they stated that any of the quotations used in the text should have the consent of the participants in order for other authors to use them within the context of tribal interpretation. This tenet is in keeping with tribal protocol and integrity of traditional ways of knowing. One aspect of traditional protocol requires approaching *Kaaahsinnooniksi* and forming a relationship with them. These relationships begin by forming and coming to know the alliances that are the basis of all transactions among *Siksikaitsitapi*. This is the way of life that has been traditionally handed down through the generations in the oral traditions of the tribe.

The traditional forms of teaching have changed as family structures have changed due to the constant influence of the surrounding and dominating contemporary society. One of the *Kaaahsinnooniksi* identified the need to develop *Siksikaitsitapi* methods of teaching that apply to the children of today:

My granddaughter, we have raised her. Now, my great granddaughter, we have raised her. Now, my great granddaughters are at a stage where they don't listen. All they do is watch television. When I want to watch news, then they get mad when I try to change the channel. The television is teaching them. Men and women, now they go outside the home to work. I wonder how much time do they have to talk and sit with their children. They have to do what needs to be done at home, then they drive away again. We have to work. That is why we don't have that much time to spend with our children compared to the past. That is why I am saying, you people, you must educate the children about our way of life.

Prior to European contact, children learned the ways of *Siksikaitsitapi* by participating in the familial and tribal structures and processes. Children in contemporary society are often isolated and their parents do not spend much time with them. These new conditions create a need for the articulation of *Siksikaitsitapi* methods of teaching and learning in the present educational system.

The existing educational system on the reserves must begin to address the responsibilities of *Niitsitapi*. The questions posed to *Kaaahsinnooniksi* address the basic philosophical and behavioural knowledge of *Siksikaitsitapi* epistemologies. They relate to the responsibilities of participating in ceremony, and they address the specific ontological responsibilities that express the normative structure. This inquiry addresses how these responsibilities are learned and maintained through participation in pedagogical ceremonies. The answers to the questions verbalize the framework for the human development and educational processes that are the foundation for teaching sacred science and traditional ways of knowing. They provide the outline for a *Siksikaitsitapi* studies program, which will replace the genocidal and colonial forms of our existing educational system.

Kaaahsinnooniksi were pleased with the preparation and organization for the gathering of information. After the refreshments and the opening prayer, the convocation proceeded with the questions. I had chosen open-ended questions that allowed *Kaaahsinnooniksi* to give whatever information they felt was necessary and appropriate. They determined the depth of knowledge that was given. They appeared to be comfortable with the setting, even though they had not previously participated in an environment where they were taped. These particular *Kaaahsinnooniksi* have rigorously followed the oral tradition and its methods of teaching. They felt that the time had come to participate in a project that was designed to help young people in coming to know who they are. The teachings that are ordinarily given are the stories that can be referred to as the "common knowledge" in coming to know.

The *Kaaahsinnooniksi* were asked to respond to the following questions:

1. What should a person know in order to begin to participate in ceremonies? What should one do to participate in ceremonies; how do people prepare themselves for participating in ceremonies? What is essential for participating in ceremonies?
2. How is a person taught these very important ways of being for participating in ceremonies? How do the ceremonies help them learn these responsibilities?
3. Who teaches the individual? How does the individual learn?

The responses were taped and *Kaaahsinnooniksi* were initially asked to speak in both languages, *Siksikaitsipowahsin* and English. My reason for asking them to speak in English was to have the *Kaaahsinnooniksi* do their own translation. However, they chose to speak only in their language. This presented a formidable challenge. I had had previous experience in translating *Siksikaitsipowahsin* into English and therefore knew of the difficulty of articulating the interdependent relationships of the philosophical and concrete processes of our way of life using English concepts. English words simply cannot convey words contextualized in relationships with the sacred. *Siksikaitsipowahsin* is the expression of our sacred language that carries the breath of *Ihtsipaitapiiyopa* [Spirit], which is experienced in speaking. Some of my discussions below will illustrate this. For example, the English word "prayer" is used to convey the meaning of *Aatsimoyihkaan*, the sacred way of speaking that is one and the same as the good life – the way of the people. Both a good heart and the living of a good life are the basis for maintaining harmony and balance. *Aatsimoyihkaan* is a concept that is often referred to by *Kaaahsinnooniksi*. It is used in many different ways, each circumstance connecting to a particular meaning and relationship. The translation loses this aspect of the language. "Prayer" has the more limited meaning of "to ask for" and is problematic because of its Christian connotations. (This concept has been used in the language section [chapter 13] of the document to illustrate the holistic nature of the culture and way of being that is fundamental to the good heart.)

To increase the accuracy of translations and interpretations *Niita'kaik'-samaikoan* (Real-Many-Tumors-Man) reviewed them. (I fully understand the language but am not a fluent speaker.) He checked the translated interpretations and provided feedback. He stated that *Kaaahsinnooniksi*'s words are difficult to translate into English, however,

> ... the transcripts do carry the message of the grandparents. It is difficult to translate the context and meaning of their message in English. The teachings must be done in *Siksikaitsipowahsin*.

He also commented that it is important to remember that the teachings in this document are but the tip of the iceberg in regard to their meaning and the possible depth of knowing.

> Among the initial responses to my questions was this statement: What I have heard is that you are inquiring about our way of life. With our stories, we are going to help you.
>
> It is good how you are asking questions. These other young people who are going to school. They go to those stories that were written by the white people. They go there to know our ways of life. I don't like this. Those stories they wrote, those lives are not theirs. They are only looking at our ways through their own. The person who wrote the books did not have the right to tell our ways. They just see. They never lived the life. The stories we share with you today, we have lived them; therefore, we have the right to tell them.

The convocation had come about by using a tribal framework based on maintaining good relations with the cosmic alliances by participating in ceremony. Traditional protocol was established and maintained throughout the inquiry process. The integrity of protocol is essential for maintaining good relations with the ancestors who guide our processes of knowledge acquisition. They are fundamental to establishing the authenticity of this account. *Kaaahsinnooniksi* validated my process:

> The way you get us together, you will get our advice, we have the rights, we have authority to give you advice.

At the end of the meeting, *Kaaahsinnooniksi* asked me if they had answered my questions. This was my response:

> Respect is one of the responsibilities of being *Niitsitapi*.
> As *Niitsitapi*, our listening is one of the ways we come to know.
> We respect all that is alive, which is everything in the universe; it teaches us our way of life, our way to relate to each other.
> As *Niitsitapi*, in respecting the knowing of life, we cannot take anything for granted.
>
> Secondly, when a person is learning the way of life of the people, they do not take anything for granted; everything in life has meaning. Life is being taught to us in our everyday activities; *Ihtsipaitapiiyo'pa* [Source of Life] puts in our path those teachings that we need for our own life. We learn what is necessary to carry out our responsibilities, even if we don't understand.
>
> And finally, it is important to respect life, every aspect of life. As *Niitsitapi*, we learn through the teachings of the universe.
> And we *Niitsitapi* give – we give gifts, food, material goods. But the most important gift we give is our self through our experiences and stories. As you have shared your lives, your experiences, I have now come to know our ways of knowing. I have taken your experience and have come to know. This is the gift we pass through the generations. It is a gift that I will use for my life.

One of the *Kaaahsinnooniksi* answered:

> If you are going to use it in the future, when you come to something hard or difficult, some imbalance or difficulty, you will

be able to use it; it will be good. If it is too difficult, it means that you did not use what was given to you. If it is hard and difficult, it means that you did not listen to what I told you.

Kaaahsinnoon is saying that the authenticity and responsibilities that are part of the epistemologies and pedagogy of *Siksikaitsitapi* knowing live through the manner in which I live my life. The ancestors' ways of knowing and the teachings of the *Kaaahsinnooniksi* reside in my being. Authenticity is demonstrated through living and applying the teachings daily, thus incorporating the general mission of tribal cultures to maintain balance.

The message of *Kaaahsinnooniksi* began with respect – that I must respect all life, all interactions, and all words spoken. Every aspect of life is sacred in that it is unfolding from the ancestral guides. Knowledge, lessons, teachings, and gifts come from our connections with *Ihtsipaitapiiyo'pa*, which guides, prepares, and teaches throughout our daily lives. The teachings can be subtle or they may be momentous. Life as it occurs must be acknowledged and respected. The reverence for life is one of the ways of connecting with the cosmic intelligence of the universe, *Ihtsipaitapiiyo'pa*.

Each experience can be a source of balance, love, and strength. The actions and thoughts that humans produce and create are potentially for giving love, strength, and dignity to life. Each experience is potentially joyous and loving; it is dependent upon our interrelationships and interpretation of our connections to life. The responsibility that I have as *Siksikaitsitapi* in a cosmic world is to use the gifts given to me by the alliances and to live the teachings of respect and kindness by showing reverence to the simple and profound things in life. *Kitomohpipotokoi* is the term that refers to the responsibilities of *Siksikaitsitapi*; they are the core values of living, and they are the living ways of the natural world and cosmic universe. *Siksikaitsitapi* live in balance with their alliances by fulfilling *Ihpi'po'to'tsspistsi* [those thing we were put here with; implies responsibility for them].

Every aspect of creation, every form of life that exists, has the same basic responsibilities for *Siksikaitsitapi*. Inherent in each living organism are basic values as source of harmony and balance. Each living organism contributes to the ecological balance of our way of life. By maintaining and living *Kiitomohpiipotokoi* [our role], *Siksikaitsitapi* understand the knowledge of nature. *Siksikaitsiyopi* ways of knowing are dependent upon fulfilling *Ihpi'po'to'tsspistsi*; they are the media for communicating with the natural and cosmic worlds originating from *Ihtsipaitapiiyo'pa*.

Reverence for life is expressed through humility. Being humble means knowing my place in the universe. It is by acknowledging the magnitude of the alliances (and guides of *Siksikaitsipoyi* ways of knowing) that I am reminded that it is only through the kindness and generosity of life that I have come to know. *Mokaksin* [wisdom and intelligence] carries the responsibility of living the knowledge and passing it on to the next generation, first and foremost to ensure our survival.

Kaaahsinnooniksi teach by living and modelling the wisdom of the ancestors. By living the wisdom, *Mokaksin*, we come to understand the teachings of *Kaaahsinnooniksi*. Each generation has the responsibility to learn these teachings, and thus they can shape the responsibilities for their children and future generations. This ensures that they learn to survive in an ever-changing environment and pass the teachings on to the next generations. The process of coming to know [*Mokaksin*] proceeds by meditation and prayer, by following the instructions of *Kaaahsinnooniksi*, and by reflecting on the meaning of their instructions. These experiences deepen my connections and my understanding of the teachings and help me to develop a profound respect for life. As my respect for life deepens, my understanding of the knowledge and teachings deepens and becomes incorporated into my daily living habits. The teachings of a cosmic universe continue to unfold. As I mature with respect and kindness, I trust that my understanding will grow because alliances of the ancestors are guiding me.

Indigenous forms of learning are expressed through the spiritual journey – coming home to the heart of the *Niitsitapi*'s knowing, *Niitsi-tapiipaitapiiyssinni*. This is a journey of connecting with *Akaitapiwa* and

Kii Nai'tsistomato'k Ai'stamma'tso'tsspi [embodying or being the knowledge you have been given, making knowledge part of our body]. This process is premised on a reciprocal relationship with the sacred and the ancestors. Subsequently, the ethics of *Siksikaitsitapi* knowing is accepting the responsibility of sharing knowledge and knowing in the manner that maintains the cultural integrity of knowledge as well as the protocol of coming to know. The responsibility is using *Siksikaitsitapi* knowing and knowledge in a manner that respects what I understand to be the concomitant ethics. I will share through my teaching and writing and, more importantly, by who I am.

> White people's laws are different; the way they live their life is
> only to better themselves. The purpose of their lives is to get ahead
> (progress). As *Niitsitapi* we live *Niipaitapiiyssin*; that is the reason
> we are sitting in this room. I am here because I have lived our
> ceremonial way of life. As part of our way of life, I am here for all
> *Niitsitapi*. I am here to assist anyone who wants to live as *Niitsitapi*.
> I help in passing it down to the next generation. If we were
> selfish in the past about our knowledge and advice, and if in the
> past our ancestors had been selfish and they only had used it for
> themselves, then this knowledge would not be here today. We
> would not be sitting here. We would be going to the libraries
> to see how our way of life is. That is how we are taught.

Kainai Kaaahsinnooniksi were part of the conversations that form the core of this book. *Kainai* is one of the *Siksikaitsitapi* tribes. Subsequently, *Niitsi'powahsinni* and references to the ceremonies can be generalized among *Siksikaitsitapi* because these ceremonies are part of the same way of life and society, with minor differences. This book prepares a framework for a *Siksikaitsitapi* studies curriculum. Many of its conclusions will be relevant for other *Niitsitapi*.

The study has raised the expectations of *Kaaahsinnooniksi* that *Niitsitapi* ways will be implemented into the existing educational curriculum.

They have expressed their desire to have the results of the study incorporated into the teaching of young people throughout the school system on the *Siksikaitsitapi* reserves. To a certain extent, this has been accomplished since the University of Lethbridge and Red Crow Community College have jointly offered teacher training courses and have begun negotiations to offer a joint degree program based on a bicultural model. The initiative began with a post-graduate course for *Siksikaitsitapi* teachers. They speak *Siksikaitsipowahsin*, and they can receive a post-graduate diploma from the University of Lethbridge. At the same time, their course of study will assist in the development of an undergraduate education degree program. Moreover, I will fulfill my responsibility by using the knowledge and knowing that has been given to me through the stories of the *Kaaahsinnooniksi* in my own work as educator and scholar.

The guidance and advice shared by *Kaaahsinnooniksi* about the common knowledge of *Siksikaitsitapi* that I share here are meant to be shared with the uninitiated. The personal advice that was specifically given for my own learning as part of the traditional relationship with *Kaaahsinnooniksi* has not been included in this document.

The conversations that form the basis of this book have been conducted in *Siksikaitsipowahsin*. I had to be able to interpret the words of *Siksikaitsitapi* from within the worldview of my specific tribal culture. *Siksikaitsipowahsin* words contain specific relationships to a cosmic universe and maintain the cultural integrity of the tribe. They are used throughout the text as appropriate, and the glossaries at the end of the book are intended to assist the reader. Nonetheless, it is important to remember that the English translations carry only a limited amount of validity for reasons just explained. Any deeper understanding of the knowledge discussed here has *Siksikaitsipowahsin* as a prerequisite.

III. Affirmation of Indigenous Knowledge

8. *Kakyosin* – Traditional Knowledge

Reconstructing *Niitsitapi* ways of knowing begins with sacred knowledge held in the stories and ceremonies that have been handed down through a web of kinship alliances. One of the *Kaaahsinnooniksi* explains how these relationships are learned at an early age:

> We have to respect our Mother and Father. This is what we are all raised with: to respect our relatives. During ceremony, when our relatives are smudging, if we understand, then we understand our way of life. That is where it starts, where prayer [good heart] begins.

Learning *Siksikaitsipoyi* ways of knowing begins with the family, which is literally *Ihtsipaitapiiyo'pa* [the Source of Life] in all domains, especially for the child. The reader is reminded that the *Ihtsipaitapiiyo'pa* is the great mystery that is in everything in the universe. *Ihtsipaitapiiyo'pa* lives in each and every form of creation, as all life forms contribute and participate in giving life. Therefore, learning the ways of knowing originates with the family, because they provide the source of knowledge during early childhood and adolescence.

Knowing is relational and dependent upon relationships that are learned in childhood. *Siksikaitsitapi* ways of knowing are dependent upon relationships, which create and generate knowledge. All life experiences are a source of knowledge. As an example, dreams are a primary source of knowledge for *Siksikaitsitapi*. Often dreams are prophetic,

contain warnings, or reveal knowledge. Such dreams are passed on through the oral traditions among the people and are repeatedly found in stories and ceremonies.

Akaitapiwa prepare and guide us through dreams; sometimes these dreams reveal the future. One of the *Kaaahsinnooniksi* shares her experiences with this form of knowing:

> My dream told me: you are going to be one of the Horns. I saw the buffalo dancing. I heard the song. I said, "this is the song." The way those men are dancing, that is how the buffalo dances. After a while, after a few years, we then transferred. When I was in the Horns, my whole family got to understand the Horn way. As time went on, I had another dream, a baby was calling me. This baby said, "I am from the north; I want you to be my mother." It wasn't long after that that I carried a medicine bundle. I carried the Beaver Bundle.

Dreams like this provide guidance and protection. The individual is shown gifts that can be pursued. If they are accepted, then the individual will be protected. More importantly, dreams reveal knowledge that guides us in our personal responsibilities [*Kiitomohpiipotokoi*] in life.

One of my own experiences in which knowledge was revealed through my dreams occurred in the initial phases of my dissertation. The dream came in the early morning, at dawn. As with most powerful dreams, I awoke immediately after the dream. I have taken up the practice of writing my dreams in a journal so that I don't forget important details. In one dream I clearly heard the voice of *Akaitapiwa*. Their message was: *The knowledge that you are seeking is in the teachings of our people. Come to learn and understand these teachings and share them in your life. Others will be able to use them and apply them to the problems of the day.* The dream revealed the need to generate knowledge from *Siksikaitsipoyi* ways of knowing to combat the problems of the day. I understood that the primary teaching process is life as it unfolds. In each relationship, in each

Blackfoot ceremonial bundle, 1926. Photographer Edward S. Curtis. From "Curtis," *North American Indian*, vol. 18. Glenbow Archives NA–1700–178.

moment in time, in each thought, in each word, and in each action is a teaching, which contributes to the intricate balance of a cosmic universe.

The grandparents provide examples of how daily observances can be used to learn how to maintain good relations and balance, for example:

> This is where it starts. What *Kaaahsinnooniksi* are telling us is meant for a purpose. This is where you begin to understand. For example, you do not walk by or near *Iitawaamatosimmopi* [place for smudge] and you do not disturb [touch] your relatives' possessions. You understand that the teachings of *Kaaahsinnooniksi* are told for a purpose.

Knowing begins with appreciating that life can be understood through the teachings of the relatives, *Kaaahsinnooniksi*, and *Akaitapiwa*. Thus, the identity of *Siksikaitsitapi* is an integral part of where their place is within the cosmos. By knowing one's place in the cosmic universe, we form intricate alliances with the world coming from *Ihtsipaitapiiyo'pa*. From these relationships arises an intricate constitution of *Kiitomohpiipotokoi* that forms the identity of *Siksikaitsitapi*. Through these responsibilities we, as *Niitsitapi*, come to know who we are in the universe; these responsibilities become the source of knowing our place [*Mokaksin*].

Indigenous people have long recognized the consciousness of the natural order, in fact, since the beginning of our time. The fundamental premise of *Niitsitapi* ways of knowing is that all forms of creation possess consciousness. The non-separation of nature and humans is one of the demarcations between Eurocentred and Indigenous philosophy. This demarcation creates completely distinct paradigms of reality, truth, and knowing. For example, a symbol in the Indigenous paradigm is not an abstraction or a representation of reality, but rather a medium for communicating with the cosmic forces of the universe, a spirit, and it is alive with consciousness from *Ihtsipaitapiiyo'pa*. The following story, told by one of the *Kaaahsinnooniksi*, illustrates the power of the cosmic alliances which manifest, in various forms.

My father (*Ninna*) told me this story and my brother also told me the story himself. He began the story:

My brother enlisted in the Second World War. He did not pass
the physical requirements due to a congenital ear defect. However,
he was not discharged but was stationed on the coast. His duties
were assisting in shipping army supplies. Prior to departing for his
duties, one of the *Kaaahsinnooniksi* had made an amulet for his
protection. The young man was instructed to wear it at all times.
However, he took it off for his daily showers. One day while he
was taking a shower, as usual, he put the amulet on the windowsill.
On this particular day, as he reached to pick it up, it was gone. He
asked if anyone had taken it. No one had seen it. He never found
it. After some time had lapsed, he wrote to my old man and he
told him that he had lost the amulet. After some more time, my
old man told *Kaaahsinnoon* that my brother had lost the amulet.
Kaaahsinnoon said, "It is home. It has come home."

The amulet is an example of the absence of separations or categorical
demarcations of the *Siksikaitsipoyi* worldview. Concepts are used for
distinguishing parts of the whole. For example, the amulet possesses
power from *Ihtsipaitapiiyo'pa* that protects the person who wears it.
The entity embodies the relationships of specific protectors. In the world
of *Siksikaitsitapi*, knowledge, science, and religion are not separate.
Reconstructing Indigenous reality involves developing and using
constructs that will distinguish reality, truth, and, subsequently, the
consciousness of *Siksikaitsitapi*. For example, the nature of being, the
nature of knowledge, and the methods of knowing are clearly delineated
in the process of maintaining balance in the world. The interrelationships
of these constructs are the means for understanding the holistic nature of
consciousness and the nature of generating knowledge and truth. These
constructs furthermore reflect the interrelationships of the natural world
and the intricate knowledge that balances ecological and spiritual beings.

The land, animals, and spirits are not separate but an integral part of the *Siksikaitsitapi* world. They, too, are the source of science and knowledge. This same relationship exists with the elements, earth, wind, water, and rock – all are within the consciousness of the universe [*Ihtsipaitapiiyo'pa*] and make up the circle of life. They all have their own roles and responsibilities within the universe. *Siksikaitsitapi* are taught to work with these responsibilities. This is done in part through ceremonies. We call them ceremonies because we are working with the sacred powers of *Ihtsipaitapiiyo'pa* [Source of Life]. Here is an example of how *Siksikaitsitapi* make alliances for sustenance and medicinal purposes:

> The healers will know when they are out walking and they come to some herbs, they will know what they can use them for in healing. We always give thanks; we acknowledge the herbs, berries, and the trees for their gifts. We offer tobacco and pray before we pick the berries.

All knowledge and wisdom comes through the alliances with insects, animals, and plants. Sometimes *Ihtsipaitapiyo'pa* doesn't speak directly to humans; instead, the knowledge is revealed through the natural order, such as animals and stars. As Cajete (1994, 102) comments for *Niitsitapi* in general: "Plants are alive; and you must give them good talk." One of the grandparents shared the alliances of a healer:

> My father was also a healer. X's [referring to another *Kaaahsinnoon* in the room] father was also a healer. Their life is centred on healing people. They never packaged their herbs, and they did not tell the people which herbs they used. They knew when someone was sick, and they went there to doctor them. They would make a brew. They knew the names of the herbs that they used. It is also true that we would be told to use a certain herb for certain ailments. We would try to copy them, but they would work only for those who were given the gift to heal.

I have seen herbs brought to people who have cancer. The white doctors do not know how to mix the herbs. Healing is a gift we get; we will not loose it; it will stick with us.

The healers work with herbs in a holistic manner that recognizes the alliances of herbs and roots; however, an integral component of healing is a gift from *Ihtsipaitapiiyo'pa*, which is the source of healing. As a result, healers have their own ways of diagnosis and knowing whether they can treat ailments and imbalances. If they know that they treat an imbalance, then they will perform a ceremony that is a part of the healing.

One of the grandfathers shares the story of the healing of his father as it was told to him:

> *X* was a healer and he lived at the west end of the reserve. My father had already moved to the northeast end of the reserve. *X* had heard that my father was sick, so he rode down to my father's place. It was in the winter. He told my father: "I know that you did not ask me to come and doctor you." My mother began to gather gifts to give him, but *X* said, "Do not give me anything until I know that I can doctor him."
>
> *Kaaahasinnoon* described the doctoring, and with one of the procedures *X* revealed that he now knew that he could doctor my father. So he proceeded to doctor him.
>
> He then received the gifts that were given to him. My father was healed and made a vow. Soon he was transferred the Long Time Medicine Pipe.

Healers have unique and special powers that have been given to them by the alliances. However, healing is not a given but is dependent upon the relationships of gifts given by the alliances. These relationships are forever premised on the great mysterious force of the universe [*Ihtsipaitapiiyopa*], and the more one understands the dynamics of this tremendous sacred power, the more effective is the work with these alliances. This is one of the reasons that *Kaaahsinnooniksi* are sought as teachers for the younger people.

The nature of the *Siksikaitsitapi* universe is understood as consciousness that manifests in all life forms and is the basis of the principles that underlie conduct, thought, and knowledge. What manifests is *Ihtsipaitapiiyo'pa*, the Source of Life. This understanding of the universe structures reality, the ways of knowing, knowledge, and the truth of a culture. In addition, the theory of the origin of nature, and the methods and limits of knowledge, are also based on this particular understanding of nature. *Siksikaitsipoyi* ways of knowing begin with knowing one's responsibilities among tribal alliances. The next section will explore the ontological responsibilities of *Siksikaitstapi* that are the foundation of our theory of knowledge and its validity.

9. *Kiitomohpiipotoko* – Ontological Responsibilities

The ontological theory of *Siksikaitsitapi* is premised on the experience with the sacred, *Ihtsitaipiiyo'pa*. The individual's experience of the sacred provides the fundamental orientation of what it means to be human among *Niitsitapi*. Therefore, the focus of human development is premised on experiences, which connect the individual to the transformational powers of the universe. (These powers are called "transcendent" in Eurocentred thinking; however, for *Niitsitapi* they are immanent spiritual presences.) This ontological theory contains a complex system of kinship relationships based on which *Niitsitapi* teach their children the meaning of life and the purpose of life. The meaning of life is rooted in the experiences grounded in the sacred relationships of alliances. The understanding of what it means to be a human being is premised on the connections with the sacred and the development of transformational experiences. In essence, the identity of the people and the theory of human development is based on a framework of moral and ethical relationships.

They have been referred to generically as the spirituality of Indigenous people. They are the basis of becoming and being *Niitsitapi*. The tribal identity of *Siksikaitsitapi* begins with having good relations; prayer is the path for good relations among one's alliances; it is also the process of making alliances and acknowledging them. This has been expressed as follows by one of the *Kaaahsinnooniksi*:

> In order to regain our identity and maintain our way of life we need to have good relations. We don't leave out prayer in anything that we do. This is our way. The spirituality, it is just part of the way of life. Being *Siksikaitsitapi* means you have to take care of your mental, your spiritual, your emotional, and your physical. All these things. The spiritual is part of it, especially through prayer [*Aatsimoyihkaani*]. It is a powerful part of it.

One of the essential components of every ceremony is the making of incense by *Aawaatowapsiiks*. It is offered to create and balance an alliance, particularly for communicating with cosmic alliances, e.g., *Naatosi* [the Sun] (Pete Standing Alone, personal communication, December 1998). *Aawaatowapsiiks* and *Kaaahsinnooniksi*, who have been initiated, make incense in the early morning and at dusk in acknowledgment of the rise of *Naatosi*. It is offered for a balanced and harmonious day. *Nii'ta'kaiksa'maikoan* adds that smudge is used to ask for blessings, such as good relations with relatives or that the journey of life be long and full of kindness. Incense carries the words of *Aawaatowapsiiks* to the alliances and its power helps guide and protect their words. The story of *Paiyo* [a.k.a. Scarface, *Ihpowa'ksski*, *Pahtsiipissowaasi* [Mistaken-for-Morning-Star], and *Poiyawa*] describes how the sacred power of incense was given to *Siksikaitsitapi* (N. Blood, personal communication, December 1998). The following is an example of the powerful use of smoke in our tradition:

> If something is so hard and you call upon *Ihtsipaitapiiyo'pa*, then it will happen. Spirit hears us when we call, when we are making

incense. The fragrance goes to *Ihtsipaitapiiyo'pa*. We are listened to, we are loved when we make a vow to the pipe and to *Ookaan*. My brother, he was sick with cancer. The doctors could not heal it. And then we took him to X. And they couldn't take it out. I was looking at my brother. [Pause] He is a big person. [Pause] And then I made a vow to the pipe for him to get better, to get out of the hospital healthy. That is how strongly I believe in my faith. It wasn't long after that that my brother came out of the hospital. I danced with the pipe.

This statement addresses working with the alliances of the Medicine Pipe, incense, and the reciprocity of responsibilities. Children learn the profound powers of smudge at an early age. They learn to respect the cosmic alliances accordingly:

I brought them up with prayer, I taught them to pray and to smudge so that my house is good. I am making smudge because somebody taught me how to smudge. I was given the right to smudge with sweet grass; smudging with sweet grass is good. Smudging restores balance and if things are unbalanced, we smudge. That it how we get our children to respect us.

The transformational experiences are generated and created through the interactions, communications, and participation with the natural and cosmic alliances through ceremonies, such as the use of incense. *Kaaahsinnooniksi* give us the following example:

Certain things in our life are given to us. We *Siksikaitsitapi* have the responsibility to do certain things. That is our way of life. These are very personal (individual) things that cannot be handed down. I think that in some cases those of you who are learning are now trying to understand this part of our way of life.

In the above quotation, *Kaaahsinnoon* is referring to those students of traditional knowledge who are attempting to understand the transformational experiences generated through *Siksikaitsitapi* ways of knowing. By connecting with *Naatosi, Ko'komikisomm, Ksisstsi'ko'm*, etc., and through the use of incense, a ceremony can alter the physical, mental, emotional, and spiritual domains of individuals and the cosmos. This process simply cannot be fully explained, and *Ihtsipaitapiiyo'pa* remains a mysterious power.

Four of the five *Kaaahsinnooniksi* had family and parents who were healers. Three of the four also had been doctored. One of the *Kaaahsinnooniksi*, whose father was one of the most prominent healers in the recent history of *Kainai*, said,

> I cannot explain my father's life. Why did he as an individual get his power to heal? What did he know? I cannot explain my father's life and neither my mother's. All I know is what he did; I have also observed him healing. It is given to us by the *Ihtsipaitapiiyo'pa* [Source of Life]. It was given to him. He could not teach anyone. He could not pass it on.

The experiences of his father's healing power are premised on the ontological theory of *Siksikaitsitapi*. Experiences of the sacred are the basis for the definition of humanity. The understanding of what it is to be human is based on the cosmological origin of *Siksikaitsitapi*. Cosmological beings are allied with such powers as *Naatosi, Ko'komikisomm, Ipissowaasi, Pahtsiipissowaasi, Miyohpo'koiks* [Pleiades], and *Ihkitsikommiksi* [Big Dipper]; they have revealed or given to *Siksikaitsitapi* the natural laws of the universe. They hold and are the original instructions for maintaining life and the balance of the world. These natural laws were given in ceremony, and the creation stories provide a context for the responsibilities that define humanity for *Siksikaitsitapi*. Cosmological beings also provide an orientation to the natural world, a place to come from and a place from which to enter the natural world.

Naatosi and *Napi* reveal the knowledge of the mysterious cosmic force referred to as *Ihtsipaitapiiyo'pa*, which is the source of the transformational powers as experienced and transferred to *Siksikaitsitapi*. Such transformational powers are common among *Siksikaitsitapi*, but an increasing disconnection from the alliances has changed our experience – we experience them to a lesser degree now. The sweat lodge, *Tsisskaan*, is another a source of transformation. It was given to *Paiyo* as one of the numerous ceremonies that embody the transformational powers for *Siksikaitsitapi*. The story of *Paiyo* is also a form of traditional knowledge instructing *Siksikaitsitapi* how to live their lives; it is passed on from one generation to the next. Story and ceremony are the primary ways of learning to be human, to be *Niitsitapi*, "one of the people"; this means having the connections and integrity of *Paiyo* and the ability to participate in a way of life that is transformational. The story of *Paiyo* tells of the blessings that one receives when one is connected to the teachings. *Niitapitapiiyssinni* means to live by the traditional teachings and to participate in the renewal and transformation of the world. One of the *Kaaahsinnooniksi* illustrates *Kiitomohpiipotokoi*, the ontological responsibility of participating in ceremony, and the characteristics required for participation:

> As long as I live, I will continue to do my ceremonial work.
> We share love, kindness, and generosity. We help each other.
> We are helping each other. My friend here is going to open
> his Medicine Pipe bundle. I will always help my friend in his
> ceremonial work, too. The gifts you gave me, I gave them to
> him. You see for yourself, you did not hear about it.

In addition to participating, at an early age, *Kaaahsinnooniksi* learned the ontological responsibility of listening:

My father passed away. I was still very young. I don't remember too much about my father. I grew up with my grandfather. At our home, there were many things that we were told not to do. We were told to be quiet when we had visitors. *Kaaahsinnoon* would say, "Sit down and be still when the visitors come to tell stories."

You can tell if a young person is listening. You can observe what I am talking about.

At times, when *Kaaahasinnoon* had visitors, we were told to leave the room. We were not ready to hear the conversation. When other visitors came, we could stay and listen. It was *Kaaahasinnoon's* way of saying, "listen to what we are talking about because you are ready to understand our talk. You will be able to use it to understand your life as you get older."

Children were often told the legends of *Napi*, which contain the sacred teachings of what it is to be human among *Siksikaitsitapi*. *Napi* stories provide the context for human development, specifically regarding the necessary moral and ethical sanctions to follow in order to be *Siksikaitsitapi*. The origins of *Napi* are not clear (Bullchild 1985, 86). One interpretation (P. Standing Alone, personal communication, October 1997) is that *Napi* has creative powers that are similar to the powers of *Naatosi*. Without the sun, life could not be sustained on the planet. *Naatosi* is literally *Ihtsipaitapiiyo'pa*, which means: we live only because of *Naatosi's* life force (without *Naatosi*, there is no life). *Naatosi* is a manifestation of *Ihtsipaitapiiyopa*. Bullchild also addresses the origins of *Napi*. He states that *Naatosi* gave his spiritual powers to *Napi* and taught him the teachings that were needed in order for his brothers and sisters to survive on Mother Earth and to lead them to more learning from time to time (Bullchild 1985, 86). *Napi* came to live among the people to teach a good way of life. He taught them two very sacred precepts: to hold the sacred ways of *Naatosi* and to be faithful and obedient to the natural laws of balance. These are the precepts that maintain the cultural integrity of *Siksikaitsitapi*. The cultural integrity of most North American tribes as perceived by

Kaaahsinnooniksi is held in the stories of our ancestors and in the teachings contained in these stories. Each culture has its own way of being *Niitsitapi*.

> Now, this way of prayer was given to us. Those who live outside
> our boundaries, they live a different way of life; they were given
> a prayer too.
>   This is what is given to them [their own cosmologies]. We are
> given our forms of ceremonies.

The ceremonies, lands, stories, ritual, language, roles, and responsibilities are the hallmarks of a holistic worldview. They are intertwined and interdependent with each other and form the cultural and ceremonial integrity of *Niitsitapi*.

The stories of *Napi* teach *Siksikaitsitapi* fundamental responsibilities and powers given to them in accordance with the natural laws of the universe. It is the responsibility of *Siksikaitsitapi* to use these powers to strengthen life and not to use them for selfish and foolish reasons. Most importantly, they must not be used for personal vanity. The greatest weakness that can befall the people is for them to think they possess the powers and begin to use their knowledge for their own selfish purposes.

Stories of *Napi*'s exploits impress upon the listener the destructive aspects of humans and the powers of the universe. Through these stories, *Siksikaitsitapi* are taught that human beings can be fraught with deceit, greed, cruelty, cowardice, egocentricity, brutality, and fallaciousness. The trickster *Napi* illustrates not only how the destructive tendencies can become dominant, but how they have consequences in the social world (Harrod 1992, 167). The stories also talk about the ability to transform. The powers of the universe give life, but they also destroy. *Siksikaitsitapi* must learn to balance these powers; through the *Napi* stories, they understand the purpose of their existence and the relationship to their own powers as human beings. One of the *Kaaahsinnooniksi* illustrates the power that ceremonies have for maintaining balance:

I was raised in the residential school. I prayed every day, but it did not mean anything. Prayer is for grave imbalance. If a person is in grave imbalance (trouble/problems), he/she will think of prayer. He/she may be in a grave imbalance in life. It may be a sickness that makes them think of the *Omahkohkana-kaaatsiisinni*, *Maotoki* or *Ookaan* [ceremonial societies]. They go and have their faces painted. We *Siksikaitsitapi* say our life is shown to us. Life was shown to me.

Kaaahasinnon, and all *Kaaahsinnooniksi* who participated in *Kanohsin*, were ceremonial brothers and sisters through their initiation into *Omahkohkana kaaatsiisinni*. They had began the revitalization and renewal of this society:

At one time at *Aakokatssin* there were only nine teepees. There were only a few *Omahkohkanakaaatsiisinni* dancing. The other bundles had been sold. I am one of these people who was very bad in the past. Then I thought that I wanted to get involved in *Omahkohka-nakaaatsiisinni*. I joined *Omahkohkanakaaatsiisinni* with my friend and these people that are sitting here. I was around when *X* was still alive. He was a person who totally lived our way of life. There was nothing that he did not know. He talked about spirits telling a person what to do. An old person would experience this. You would say that he is holy. We continue our prayer. That is what I have to tell you. If you don't live our way of life, then it won't be. That old man said prayer is what keeps the way of life going.

Ookaan transformed the lives of these *Kaaahsinnooniksi*. They are living the knowledge of the alliances. Their understanding of the teachings, which they have developed through their experiences, is the primary knowledge of the ways of the alliances. This is how their lives have been transformed. Today their teachings and guidance can assist others who want to know *Niipaitapiiyssinni* and who want to transform their lives by coming to understand their relationships with the alliances.

Ceremony and prayer are an integral process for connecting with the "good heart," which is a path of kindness and generosity. Respect presupposes kindness, which acknowledges the life-giving nature of all creation. Respect maintains a balance among the powers of *Ihtsipaitapiiyo'pa* [source of life]. Death is inevitable and part of balance.

These teachings are given through stories from *Kaaahsinnooniksi* and *Akaitapiwa*. The first humans were very pitiful; they had no knowledge for survival on earth, so *Napi* provided them with the path and necessary conditions to survive by maintaining their responsibilities for balance. He showed them roots, berries, and animals that they could eat, as well as various plants for healing.

> Whatever these animals tell you to do, you must obey them, as they appear in your sleep. Be guided by them. If anybody wants help, if you are alone ... cry aloud for help, your prayer will be answered. The response may come from the eagles, perhaps by the buffalo, or by the bears. Whatever animal answers your prayer, you must listen to him. (Harrod 1992, 44)

Humans possess senses and abilities different from other animals. Non-human animals create a consciousness that has different powers than human consciousness. As a result, they mediate a number of transformational powers for humans. Animals are a major source of knowledge because their knowledge of the natural world exceeds that of humans.

The deer has been a source of knowledge and guidance for me. In 1985, I went to a conference in Niagara Falls, Ontario. During the conference I participated in a workshop in which the facilitator, through ceremony and meditation, guided the participants to that "place Indians talk about" (Cajete 1994, 42) or the "still quiet place" (Colorado 1988, 54). I refer to this place as the centre of the universe. As I experienced the "still quiet place," a deer walked up to me and gave me love and understanding. The experience was transformational. I learned that the power of love pervades the universe and that dignity and respect arise from mutual understanding. Since that experience I have often seen the deer in times of conflict and despair. On these occasions it has brought love or understanding to the situation and thus transformed an experience of imbalance. I remember one of the difficult times I had at one of the intensive seminars during my dissertation work. I even thought of withdrawing from the doctoral program. I had left the residency and walked into the hills among the redwoods. Suddenly I felt the presence of someone. I stopped to look up the hill I was approaching. A doe stood quietly, a mere ten feet from where I was. As our eyes locked, I felt the quiet, gentle love that was immanent in her presence. I felt a sense of peace come over me; tears began to fill my eyes and soon rolled down my face. At that moment I realized any conflict could be resolved with the understanding that each person has a unique journey, which must be respected with love.

Niitsitapi have always had a relationship with animals. At one level, this interconnecting and interdependent relationship reflects the people's need to consume animals as food. On a different level, *Niitsitapi* are also dependent upon animals for guidance and protection. The animals are helpers because they possess a powerful source of knowledge and wisdom. Their behaviour, if observed carefully, will reveal many secrets of balance and harmony. The natural world knows how to live in harmony. Among the Plains cultures, animals not only possess consciousness, but will and soul. Subsequently, they are often the medium for the transfer of sacred power between *Ihtsipaitapiiyo'pa* and the people. This is why animals are integral partners in the transfers of bundles.

The ontological responsibilities or transformational powers bestowed on the people by *Naatosi* as well as the dark potentials of humanity are characterized in the adventures of *Napi*. The stories teach the characteristics of *Siksikaitsitapi* understanding of psychological health. They are attained by living the laws of the natural order, respecting the powers emanating from *Ihtsipaitapiiyo'pa*, and working with all the powers of the universe. The stories shape the identity of *Siksikaitsitapi* as heroes, tricksters, and creators – an identity founded upon transformational experiences with the sacred. It is described in the distinct narratives that illustrate appropriate forms of relationships for each way of being (Harrod 1992, 64). However, the dark powers of humankind and their consequences are also described in many of the adventures of *Napi*.

The following story, told by a *Kaaahsinnoon*, illustrates the vanity and selfishness of humanity and the effect that these may have on one's life:

> *Napi* went to the women's dance; the women had medicine. The men were all standing in line. The women were choosing which men they wanted to marry. The head woman wanted to marry *Napi*. *Napi* did not want her. The women then went to put on their finest clothes. After they had dressed in their finest clothes, they went back to the men. *Napi* noticed the beauty of the head woman. He wanted to marry her. However, the head woman told the other women, "Do not take Napi for a husband." On their return, *Napi* stood in front of the head woman hoping she would choose him, as he found her extremely attractive. She paid no attention to him. He continued to avail himself to her, but she continued to ignore him. *Napi* was left alone, no one had chosen him for a spouse. Now, this story is found in our language, and when we go to dance, we may often hear a man say, "I was never asked to get up and dance."

The story teaches humility. The adventures of *Napi* also provide the history of the people, showing how the world came to be such as it is, and the characteristics of humans. The roles, responsibilities, and characteristics of the animal world are also included, as are the origins of sacred places and the friends and neighbours of *Siksikaitsitapi*.

The *Napi* legends are the teaching tools for *Ihpi'po'to'tsspistsi*. The stories hold the origins of *Siksikaitsitapi* as well as the means for interpreting and making sense of our world. Coming to know [*Mokaksin*] means experiencing the alliances; they form the ontological ground for *Siksikaitsitapi*. Following the principles expressed in the stories gives rise to an educational philosophy that fundamentally teaches *Siksikaitsitapi* to be good human beings. It means coming to know the characteristics of humanity that produce powerful alliances and create transformational changes in *Kiipaitapiiyssinnooni* [our way of life] and our ancestral connections.

Siksikaitsitapi are dependent upon all of creation for survival. Learning how life is interdependent is therefore a preeminent objective in the educational process. Learning how to connect the power of self with all other forms of life is the essence of human development. *Siksikaitsitapi* talk about interdependence by saying that human beings exist only in relation to their relatives. An individual cannot exist without a network of kinship alliances. Knowing who you are is knowing your relatives – and knowing your relatives is being in your centre. Being in the centre of the universe means knowing one's place in the universe, and that place is at the centre of our tribal, natural, and cosmic alliances. Being centred means knowing the specific interdependent relationships one has with natural and cosmic beings. The process of coming to know [*Mokaksin*] is a life journey that begins with coming to know your own responsibilities [*Kiitomohpiipotokoi*] to your relatives and the alliances. In short, *Mokaksin* is knowing oneself in this way.

The self is central to the process of understanding tribal responsibilities within *Niipaitapiiyssin*, the cosmic order. The "concept for life sake" (Cajete, 1994) is the pursuit of understanding the complex interdependence of all life. This brings one to that "place Indians people talk about." It is the centre of thought, the centre of one's being (Cajete 1994, 45–50). The "place Indians talk about" is the journey of becoming complete and whole; it is a place of experiencing oneness with the universe. Often this place is expressed through the phrase "we are all related."

A good heart means many things. Its benchmark is maintaining one's integrity with the natural laws of the universe. They allow the heart to align with the sacred knowledge of tribal life. *Mokaksin* comes about by experiencing and living the teachings.

The sacred science is concerned with "revealed" knowledge and with the "beginnings of things." It rests in the assumption of a

"common energetic origin to all bodies," an ultimate spiritual
source which alone is able to animate matter, an undefined cosmic
energy. (Ani 1994, 99)

A good heart aligned with *Ihtsipaitapiiyo'pa* enables sacred science,
the effect of undefined cosmic energy that reveals the sacred teachings
through the heart. This science is understood and practiced by
Siksikaitsitapi through the concept of *Pomma'ksinni* [transfers]. It is
the process of initiation into the sacred ceremonies of *Siksikaitsitapi*.
Pomma'ksinni is a process of renewing the power alliances of kinship
relations. The ceremony transfers sacred or medicine power. The powers
of natural and cosmic alliances are transferred by and through those
who are carriers of the bundles and pipes. Their being becomes
connected with the alliances of the particular bundle or pipe. In the
transfer of sacred medicine power, the bundle holders and pipe carriers
are initiated to perform the ceremonies that renew the alliances of
Siksikaitsitapi. As a result *Aawaatowapsiiks* and *Kaaahsinnooniksi* return
to the sacred state of balance and harmony. This is taking the good
red road or having a "good heart." *Kaaahsinnooniksi* have identified
the following responsibilities as essential for a "good heart" or the
"place Indians talk about":

> As *Kaaahsinnooniksi* we should tell the truth. We are asked
> to be *Kaaahsinnooniksi*. *Kaaahsinnooniksi* must be honest,
> speak straight, speak the truth, be kind. We tell what is true.
> If the truth is not told, then the Society may be hurt, or we
> ourselves may be hurt.

Truth is dependent upon the experience of the speaker. *Kaaahsinnooniksi*
teach from their individual experiences, the stories, and the ceremonies.
They teach and pray from their heart, which is the very essence of their
being. The good heart or coming to the quiet place is where the sacred
balance of harmony can be experienced. It is a process of connecting with

Akaitapiwa. Kaaahsinnooniksi have learned that honesty and kindness is the means of coming to the still quiet place of the ancestors.

The transfer of knowledge is not always direct. It requires learning to recognize the interdependent relationships with the natural order. Thus, to be a *Siksikaitsitapi* requires rigor, integrity, and self-discipline. *Niitapitapiiys-sinni* comes from fulfilling ontological responsibilities [*Kiitomohpiipotokoi*], which in turn is rewarded with the transfer of knowledge.

As a result of experiencing the universe as an integral whole, the knower becomes one with the known. In this way one intuitively knows what it is to be the other, because the other is an extension of oneself. Among the sacred sites I have visited are the pyramids of Mexico. One afternoon, an Aztec ceremonialist took a group of us to the Pyramid of Thunder on top of a mountain. The climb was arduous, the rocks were slippery, and it was hot. There were many times during the climb when I thought I would not make it to the top of the mountain. As we sat down and began our prayers, I instantaneously felt aliveness, the universal power from *Ihtsipaitapiiyo'pa*, the sacred medicine power of *Naatosi*. At that moment I knew I was at the centre of the universe. I was one with the sacred medicine power of the universe. I felt the perfection and the intelligence of the universe. This experience transformed my relationship with the universe and altered my way of relating to life and myself. Transformational education is the pursuit of spiritual knowledge through participating in ceremony. It is through experiencing the alliances that I have connected with the spiritual forces from *Ihtsipaitapiiyo'pa* and experienced the transformational powers of the universe.

My cousin, Leonard Bastien, who is one of the *Kaaahsinnooniksi*, told me, "It does not matter if you do not understand what is going on; come anyway." He is referring to ceremony. I interpret this to mean: if you begin seeking the cosmic alliances in the teachings of the ancestors, then the understanding will come through participation. *Kaaahsinnoon* P. Standing Alone (October 1997, personal communication) explains further, "Many of the young men who join the *Omahkohkanakaaatsiisinni* [Big All Comrades] may not understand the purpose of the society, because membership is not based on selection criteria but on the willingness to vow to join the society." Membership is self-selected. He also stated, "Many only understand their roles and responsibilities after they have been initiated or long after initiation." The critical aspect of coming to know is participation.

To summarize, *Siksikaitsitapi* ontological experience of the sacred arises within a complex system of kinship relations. They constitute our ways of knowing and construct the human development and educational practices of *Siksikaitsitapi*. The epistemological function of this elaborate and complex system of relations generates the knowledge; the practices of living this knowledge create *Siksikaitsitapi* transformational powers.

10. *Siksikaitsitapi* Ways of Knowing – Epistemology

Epistemology concerns itself with theories of knowing and provides frameworks for discussing validity issues. It provides cultures with a philosophical and theoretical framework of assumptions for seeking knowledge as well as processes that define truth. Epistemology impacts the informal and formal educational process that is dependent upon such theoretical interpretations and understandings of the nature of the universe, reality, and truth. The educational foundation of a culture originates from its epistemological assumptions, its pivot of reality interpretation and maintenance.

Most Eurocentred epistemologies are premised on rationality and the objectification of knowing. As a result, nature is understood to be made of identifiable qualities that are, at least potentially, completely knowable. Scientific inquiry is the pursuit of discerning the knowable qualities of an objectified universe. The rational goal of objectifying observation is to identify the various discrete parts that are assumed to exist and from which understanding and knowledge are derived. By identifying the component parts of the universe, or understanding how these parts are interconnected, the knower garners the power to control, manipulate, and predict the movements of people and objects (Ani 1994). Reality, as understood in the Eurocentred worldview, consists of physical, observable, quantifiable, reproducible, and controllable phenomena. Scientific rationality and objectivity are considered possible because of the assumption that humans are fundamentally rational beings. The Eurocentred paradigm distinguishes human beings not only as separate from each other, but also as separate from the natural world by virtue of their intellect or ability to reason.

> To think properly about an object, to gain knowledge of (mastery over) an object, we must control it. We can only do this if we are emotionally detached from it. And we gain the emotional distance from the "object" by first and foremost gaining control over ourselves; that is by placing our reason (intellect) in control of our emotions (feelings). (Ani 1994, 37)

Marimba Ani further describes Eurocentred epistemologies as invoking certain ontological foundations that have a cognitive bias. These assumptions are even embedded in the structure of the English language. Language in general is the medium through which structures of power are perpetuated and concepts of "truth," "order," and "reality" become established (Ashcroft et al. 1989, 7).

> Truth is what counts as true within a system of rules for a particular discourse; power is that which annexes, determines and verifies truth. Truth is never outside of power, or deprived of power, the production of truth is a function of power ... and we cannot exercise power except with the production of truth. (Ashcroft et al. 1989, 167)

It is imperative for colonized people to step outside the implicit body of assumptions carried by the English language and to resist a dissociative and objectifying epistemology. If Indigenous epistemologies are to survive, the use of native languages and the appropriate storied philosophies is mandatory. Indigenous epistemologies have to assert their distinctness to ensure that they are not appropriated or undermined by universalistic assumptions and other features of Eurocentred epistemologies, languages, and value systems (Ashcroft et al. 1989, 11).

For *Niitsitapi*, intelligence means participating within the world from which one has acquired the wisdom of nature and the knowledge of experience. This understanding invokes a number of relationships that contrast with the Eurocentred concept of intellect. The objectification of knowledge through the manipulation and control of observation has negated other forms of epistemologies, modes of cognition, worldviews, therefore limiting the ability for people to experience the universe as cosmic (Ani 1994, 37–39).

Niitsitapi epistemologies are premised on a set of assumptions through which knowledge and validity are constituted. All knowledge rests within a cosmic union of human beings who are interconnected with the natural order through the spiritual forces coming from *Ihtsipaitapiiyo'pa*. They constitute the collective consciousness of *Niitsitapi*. It is based on the spirituality of a cosmic order. One of the *Kaaahsinnooniksi* shares his experience with *Siksikaitsitapi* epistemologies:

> I had moved to the Sundance with my parents. *X* [an older person who was a member of *Omahkohkanakaaatsiisinni*] approached me to assist him with his dancing [ceremony]. He said, "Would you assist me when I dance out from *Tatsikiiyakokiiysinni*, the centre tepee. I did not want to do it. I did not feel good about doing it. *Y* [another man, who overheard *X* asking for my assistance], interjected and said, "He is asking for your assistance. Why don't you want to assist him?" I then agreed to help *X* with his dancing. *X* said, "You watch me, when I come out of *A'mii*, *Tatsikiiyakokiiysinni*. I will wave to you." *X* did as he said, and I entered the centre and danced with *Omahkohkanakaaatsiisinni*.

In the morning, I was sleeping and was awakened by the sound that people make when they want to enter a lodge. The sound is a way of announcing their arrival. My mother called to them to enter. Three *Omahkohkanakaaatsiisinni* members had come to visit my father.

Kaaahsinnoon meticulously and elaborately informs the members of *Kana'kaaatsiiks* [society members] about the household arrangements of the lodge, and the proper place for the various occupants (family and visitors). He then proceeds to discuss protocol:

> After the visitors told stories and had tea, my father asked them, "Is there a purpose for your visit?" *X* told my father, "Your son created a grave imbalance yesterday [Note: an uninitiated person dancing with the bundle without proper preparation caused the imbalance]; it is not good. He went to the centre and danced with the bundle." *X* continued, "When it is midday, he will go to the centre lodge. The person who is going to paint his face will be sitting waiting for him." *X* did not say whether I would dance with the bundle again. After they left, my mother told me, "Do as you are told; go to the centre lodge." She gave me offerings [gifts] for *Kaaahsinnoon*, who was going to paint my face.
>
> At midday I went to the centre lodge. *X* was there. He pointed to *Kaaahsinnoon*, who was going to paint my face. Later, I danced with the bundle. This was an imbalance I made. It bothered me. Later, I knew I wanted to join *Omahkohkanakaaatsiisinni*.

In the above narrative, *Kaaahsinnoon* addresses how he was guided by the ancestors and the alliances of *Omahkohkanakaaatsiisinni* in becoming a grandfather. His participation began with an imbalance that could have had severe consequences for himself and his family. However, through their advice and guidance he was protected. Through this experience *Kaaahsinnoon* began to learn the ways of balance and harmony. For example, in his narrative, he addresses the proper movements within the lodge, which exist for the purpose of maintaining balance and harmony among the occupants.

As we have seen earlier, *Pommaksinni* [transfer] is central to *Siksikaitsitapi* epistemology. It is a process of transferring spiritual knowledge through an intricate and complex system of kinship relations. *Siksikaitsitapi* ontology and epistemology are inextricably intertwined. The following epistemological assumptions illustrate these relationships:

- The nature of the universe is interconnectedness.
- It is interconnected through spiritual intelligence or consciousness, *Ihtsipaitapiiyo'pa*.
- It is the nature of the universe to work for balance.
- The universe has sacred power and influence; it works in reciprocal ways among all the interdependent parts.

Siksikaitsitapi epistemology creates a way of being, a way of relating to the world that embodies a system of kinship relationships. They entail responsibilities, which are connecting to a "body" of knowledge which is experienced – knowing is experiential. In this way knowing becomes a part of the knower, *Mokaksin*. Knowledge itself has spirit that is "transferred" in the relationships between the knower and the known. Through these methods and rules of knowing, knowledge and self become and are one. In addition, in coming to know, transformation is achieved by changing the relationship between knower and known. In describing such an experience of *Siksikaitsitapi* epistemology in action, one *Kaaahsinnoon* said:

> There are certain things in our way of life that I understand are given to us. You have to do certain things. That is your life. These are the real personal things that *Siksikaitsitapi* must do. These things cannot be handed down. I think that in some cases those of

you, who are attempting to learn our ways, you are trying
to understand this aspect of our way of life.

It comes directly from *Ihtsipaitapiiyopa* to you. It will be shown
to you in one way, shape, or form. It will be taught to you.

It is given to you, for you to use in a good way.

Kaaahsinnoon refers to one of the most powerful assumptions of Indigenous
epistemologies: it is in the nature of the universe to give in the form of
gifts, blessings, and lessons – all meant to be used in a good way. Many
of the gifts given to us are not immediately understood nor do we see
their value; at times we never do. Many of them will only be understood
after a long period of time as life unfolds. Sometimes it can take nearly a
lifetime before we understand the meaning and purpose of a gift. They
are personal and shape an individual's purpose in life. This is how each
person contributes to the overall balance of life. One example was given
by one of the *Kaaahsinnooniksi* who was given the gift of ceremonial
songs. These songs are a personal gift from *Ihtsipaitapiiyo'pa* and are given
to strengthen and contribute to ceremony. This is very special since many
of the ceremonial songs have been forgotten.

In my own personal life, I have come to understand the power of my
experience in residential school and in the Eurocentred academic system.
I now have come full circle. After being almost completely disconnected
from my own tribal kinship alliances, I began the journey of reclaiming
and reconstructing the ways of knowing. As part of it I have come to
understand the difficulties in letting go (or giving up) the dissociated self.
I have also come to understand the prerequisites for reconnecting with
tribal relationships. I continue to grow in awareness of the mechanisms
used by the state and church to destroy the spiritual connections of *Niitsitapi* ways of knowing. As I deepen my connections with ancestral guides,
my past experiences become a resource for the work of reconstruction.
They are providing insights into what is missing and what I need to do.

Among *Niitsitapi*, the unfolding of universal intelligence is revealed
through careful observation using our Indigenous epistemologies.

Transfer of knowledge is the exchange of medicine power and responsibility. The physical reality is sourced through thoughts, ideas, language, and knowledge unfolding from an undefined cosmic energy, which *Siksikaitsitapi* refer to as *Ihtsipaitapiiyo'pa* [Source of Life]. It is through the relationship or interaction with *Ihtsipaitapiiyo'pa* that the physical order is altered and the knowledge necessary for renewal and balance is learned and lived.

Kaaahsinnooniksi state the epistemological assumptions of *Siksikaitsitapi*:

> The white people, they try to break down everything. Everything is broken down too much. Everything has to have logic. If it doesn't have an explanation, if you cannot explain it, they don't care; they don't believe in it if they cannot explain it.
>
> I refer to the great mystery, to the legends, sacred stories – that is something that they cannot do anything about. *Siksikaitsitapi* have their connections with Ihtsipaitapiiyo'pa. It put us here. We don't try to analyze; why do you think *Ihtsipaitapiiyo'pa* created me in this way. I don't try to analyze my life. I go back to *X* [*Kaaahsinnoon*]; he told me a long time ago, "In the future you will be sitting here [meaning that the speaker will be *Kaaahsinnoon*], listen carefully and observe carefully. This is our way of life."
>
> Our ancestors, it was through their connections that they were instruments. We call them in and honor *Ihtsipaitapiiyo'pa*. These are the stories, some of the things that we pass on. *Akaitapiwa* did not just sit with them. And I just don't sit with them.

Our theory of knowledge is found in the sacred stories that are the living knowledge of the people. The stories explain the nature of reality, the science, and the economic and social organization of *Siksikaitsitapi*. They are the accumulated knowledge of centuries. Each generation of *Kaaahsinnooniksi* is responsible for retelling the stories to the next generation. The knowledge contained in them is living because it is applicable to each generation. Each generation, however, must listen carefully so that they can adapt the lessons and wisdom that apply to the present situation. The ways of knowing, of acquiring knowledge and truth, are dependent upon skills of observation, *Kakyosin*. They include the knowledge that has been accumulated in the retelling of stories over time and by applying knowledge to the present. Knowledge lives in the process of observing, reflecting on connections among observations and applying the experiences of *Akaitapiwa* and interrelationships of alliances to one's personal observations and experiences.

Reconstructing the ways of knowing allows me to integrate my experiences, to know myself, and to know how I am a part of the universe. In my own work, specifically during the process that eventually resulted in this book, I have deepened my understanding of tribal responsibilities in a number of ways. Participation in ceremony has deepened my understanding and purpose of life. It helped me to develop my personal purpose, mission, and responsibility. In ceremony I have asked for the ancestral alliances to guide my inquiries and writing. I have established alliances with *Kaaahsinnooniksi* and allowed their wisdom to guide my process. Their counsel and prayers have helped me to interpret my own experiences and the teachings they have shared. I have also established alliances with *Niitsi'powahsinni*, the language, reconnecting to the breath of life, *Niipaitapiiyssinni*. I recommended speaking the words of *Akaitapiwa*, which allows me to learn, teach, and write about the wisdom of the ancient ways of knowing.

Niitsitapi epistemologies represent knowledge from an ever-present time. It is experienced in the moment, which is infinite and all-encompassing. Following *Niitsitapi* logic means experiencing the whole, the interconnectedness of an indivisible universe. Rationality, on the other hand, denies the spiritual nature of knowledge and sacrifices the wholeness of human beings (Ani 1994, 32). One example of the denial and sacrifice that results from Eurocentred logic is one that my friend, colleague, and ceremonialist, Duane Mistaken Chief shared with me regarding the use of plants and herbs (personal communication, December 1998). He said, "Eurocentred scientists dissect the herb and extract the elements of the herb that they have found to have medicinal properties. However, what

they don't understand is that the plant functions as a whole – other properties of the plant may be important because of their cleansing functions."
It is the nature of the universe to function as an interdependent whole.
This natural law has profound implications for education and the process
of learning.

The following principles encompass the epistemologies of *Niitsitapi*;

- Knowledge, truth, and meaning are revealed to *Niitsitapi*
  through their relationship with the *Ihtsipaitapiiyo'pa*
  [Source of Life] and through a network of interdependent
  kinship relations. Knowledge is holistic, and every aspect
  of nature contains knowledge that can be revealed.
- Knowing, learning, and teaching are reciprocal in nature.
  Niitsitapi learn the nature of existence through the guidance
  of kinship alliances.
- The reciprocal nature of knowing is understood and appreciated
  through the concept of transfer [*Pommaksinni*]. It is premised
  on creating and generating the knowledge necessary for
  maintaining balance.

These principles of coming to know [*Mokaksin*] correlate to the manner
in which the education and human development processes and practices
are traditionally organized among *Niitsitapi*. The primary medium for
seeking to understand life, *Niipaitapiiyssin*, and for coming to know
[*Mokaksin*] *Ihtsipaitapiiyo'pa* [Source of Life] is through kinship relations.
Knowledge is transferred through these relationships. Knowledge exists in
a process of renewing and generating alliances for knowing. (*Pomma'ksin*
and *Aipommotsp* are discussed further in chapter 14 below.)

Ceremonies are the forms through which a common sense of transformation and transcendence is experienced. The meanings associated with
Pomma'ksin are shared by the people (Harrod 1992, 67). As long as these
bundles remain in the community, the people will retain their connection
to the transformational ways of being. They will continue to renew their

responsibilities as instructed in the original *Pomma'ksin* described in the old stories. Song, prayer, dance, and other mimetic movements were given, and they embody the vibrational patterns by which the power of the alliances can be transferred to *Siksikaitsitapi*. For example, in *Pomma'ksin* of sacred power and knowledge of *Niinaimsskahkoyinnimaan* [the Thunder or Leader Pipe], *Ksisstsi'kom* said:

> I am of great power. I live here in the summer, but when winter comes, I go far south. I go south with the birds. Here is my pipe. It is medicine. Take it and keep it. Now, when I come in the spring, you shall fill and light my pipe, and you shall pray to me.... For I bring the rain which makes the berries large and ripe. I bring the rain which makes all things grow, and for this you shall pray to me, you and all the people. (Harrod 1992, 70)

> Whenever you transfer the Pipe to anyone, steal quietly upon them just before daybreak, the time I am on the move, and take him by surprise, just as I do, chanting my song, and making the sound of a bear charging. When you catch a man and offer him the Pipe, he will not dare refuse, but must accept it and smoke it. It is sure death to refuse, because no one dares to turn away from the grizzly bear. The owl is also a prominent figure in the Pipe because he is a bird of the night. When the society are after a new member, they chant Owl songs and pray to Owl for power to enable them to catch him in a deep sleep. In this way, a spell is cast over him and he cannot escape." In order to have the help of Owl, they also use the root that is the Owl's favorite food. (McClintock 1992, 253–54)

The *Niinaimsskaahkoyinnimaan* story lives in the ceremonies and through the lives of *Aawaatowapsiiks* and *Kaaahsinnooniksi*, who renew these alliances to bring peace and prosperity to the people. Each year after *Ksisstsi'kom* [Thunder] is first heard, *Ninaimsskaiksi* know it is their responsibility to hold the annual Medicine Pipe dance. The narrative

Nii'ta'kaiksa'maikoan, Pete Standing Alone, ceremonialist at a sacred site in Southern Alberta.

illustrates the reciprocal responsibilities of prosperity and balance between *Ksisstsi'ko'm* (including all the alliances represented in the bundle) and the people. The protocol requires people to show respect, seek good relations, and maintain alliances with *Ksisstsi'ko'm* each year when *Niinaimsskahkoyinnimaan* are opened, the ceremonial dances are performed, and songs are sung to honour the *Siksikaitsitapi–Ksisstsi'ko'm* alliances for another season.

Each of the *Kaaahsinnooniksi* who participated in the Source of Life had family that had been *Niinaimsskaiksi* or had personally been Medicine Pipe Holders at one time in their lives. Each of them related their own transformational experiences with the alliances of *Niinaimsskaahkoyinnimaan*. The following is an example:

My daughter, who has had previous miscarriages, became pregnant again. She was visiting the doctors in town. I told her while she still carried the unborn child, "Your baby will dance with the Medicine

Pipe this spring." I went to X's house [Medicine Pipe Keeper], and I told him the story.

The child was born premature and in the spring the baby danced with the Medicine Pipe.

Another statement tells about a young child who was often sick and hospitalized:

> After I had brought the Medicine Pipe into my home, I was left with a young boy (a relative). I had been resting while the child was sleeping. I saw an old man smoking the Medicine Pipe. He was healing the boy. The old man smoked four times. I related the story to my spouse. I told her it is not mysterious: He will dance with the Medicine Pipe.

Medicine pipes are used for curative purposes. In contemporary Indigenous societies, many individuals are plagued with alcohol and drug abuse; one third of Aboriginal people die from violent deaths, and incarceration and lack of meaningful work is at an unprecedented level and continues to rise. These conditions are indicative of the need to reconnect with the healing knowledge generated through alliances, such as the Medicine Pipes. Healing means reclaiming and regaining the tribal ways of generating knowledge and restoring the responsibilities to life. Learning the responsibilities of traditional alliances is the path of coming to know one's purpose in life and learning the sacred knowledge that can address adversity experienced by contemporary *Niitsitapi*.

The sacred power of the universe is pervasive and reveals itself through all of creation, including thoughts, objects, speech, and actions. It speaks through rocks and animals, it may take the form of an animal that transforms into a person, or it may begin with a person who transforms into an animal (Harrod 1992, 23). As one aspect of the transcendent or transformational powers of the universe, people migrate regularly into what is described by Harrod as dream worlds. These migrations provide the meaning and knowledge sought and acquired by *Siksikaitsitapi*. In fact, all human beings, according to the Plains cultures, transcend beyond the limits of their embodiment through these migrations. They are normative experiences, which means that they were interpreted as ordinary experience (Harrod 1992, 25).

In summary, *Siksikaitsitapi* epistemology manifests in the practices of *Pomma'ksin* [transfers]. It is a theory of knowledge that purports that all knowing comes from *Ihtsipaitapiiyo'pa* [Source of Life] and manifests simultaneously through a web of kinship alliances. It is through a complex network of relationships that *Siksikaitsitapi* "come to know," *Mokaksin*, and the knowledge that is revealed supports and strengthens the cosmic and natural order. Inherent in knowing is the responsibility of living the knowledge. Living the knowing is a fundamental aspect of identity and the source from which self emerges.

Through *Pomma'ksin*, *Kaaahsinnooniksi* attempt to live with respect and generosity according to the natural laws of a cosmic universe. They teach by performing the ceremonies and strengthen the lives of the people by renewing the alliances through *Pomma'ksin*. Giving and sharing the sacred knowledge in this way reflects the essence of *Niitsitapi* relational and participative epistemologies. This way of knowing is living the knowledge. Teaching and learning traditional knowledge are not separate from living the knowledge. The essence of education is living the knowledge and connecting with the alliances. *Kaaahsinnooniksi* literally give their lives away in sharing knowledge, wisdom, and experience with students. Sharing my own experiences in reconstructing the tribal ways of knowing is also giving my life away. *Kaaahsinnooniksi* who participated in this inquiry gave their lives away in hopes that I can write their words for those who want to learn their tribal responsibilities of giving and strengthening the alliances of tribal knowledge through *Pomma'ksin*. One *Kaaahsinnoon* had the following experience when she transferred her bundle:

> After a while, after a few years, we transferred our bundle. I was sad when we transferred, but I also knew that it was the way you

BLACKFOOT WAYS OF KNOWING

make it live. You give another family the opportunity, so they too will come to know.

The bundle keepers become extremely attached to their alliances. They are the most reverent and precious of kinship alliances. Often their lives have become transformed through the relationships with *Otsisstapiistsi* [bundles]. For *Siksikaitsitapi*, they are also the source of the most profound experiences with the sacred medicine powers of their alliances. In addition, bundles, in essence, are our family. An extremely deep and profound relationship exists with each one. One *Kaaahsinnoon* told me, "we do not leave our bundles home alone, we have someone stay home with them or we bring the bundle to the home of another *Iitsskinnaiyi*, so that they can keep it in their home. This is a practice we do if we cannot keep it in our own home" (D. Weasel Moccasin, personal communication, November 1996). Subsequently, it can become very difficult emotionally to transfer these bundles. However, *Pomma'ksin* is the process of strengthening life among *Siksikaitsitapi*. It strengthens the collective experience of the tribe with the natural and cosmic alliances of pipes and bundles.

11. Knowledge is Coming to Know *Ihtsipaitapiiyo'pa*

In the traditional context, knowledge comes from *Ihtsipaitapiiyo'pa* [Spirit] and knowing means connecting with *Ihtsipaitapiiyo'pa*. Knowledge has spirit. Knowledge is spirit. Knowledge grows through the ability to listen to and to hear the whispers of the wind, the teachings of the rock, the seasonal changes of the weather. By connecting with the knowing of animals and plants, we strengthen our knowledge. As in all relationships, consent must be given and obligations and responsibilities need to be observed (Peat 1994, 65). Ceremonies embody the delicate balance of the cosmic order and thus provide connections to knowing. These relationships are also evident in creation stories and cosmology.

Spirits participate in teaching the ways of knowing. *Kaaahsinnoon* shared the following pertinent story, which describes an alliance with spirit:

At the time we were *Omahkohkanakaaatsiisinni*. Now *X* is dead. He knew our way of life very well. He had gone looking for horses. He became hungry and had seen his grandfather's house. He decided to go there and have something to eat. That was our way in the past. He went to his grandfather's home.

In the past, we would not go in front of the owner of the lodge's bed, unless we were told. We sit on the other side of the lodge. My friend, he sat himself near the door.

The night before, they [his grandfather and grandmother and other *Kaaahsinnooniksi*] had *Kanotsisissin* [All-Smoke Ceremony] from which they had some berry soup left over. Grandmother was serving the berry soup. Grandfather said, "Give some of the soup to your son." She replied, "I am going to serve him." She got up and reached for a dish to pour the soup into. As she placed the soup by his place of seating, he felt someone sit beside him.

The Ghost helper had come into the house and had sat down beside the young man. He was jealous because a place was not set for him. He told grandmother, "How come you serve the soup to him first?" My friend knew the Ghost helper was upset. Grandmother replied, "I will serve you too." She poured his soup and my friend *X* continued to feel the presence beside him. He wondered: how is he going to drink the soup?

Within the blink of an eye the soup was gone.

In the meantime, *X* took his time eating. He did not know if the Ghost helper was younger or older than him. He decided to talk to him. The Ghost helper called him "*Tsi'ki*" [a name which is used to refer to a younger person than the speaker]. *X* knew then that the Ghost helper was older. *X* thought he would ask him some questions. The Ghost helper responded, "Tsi'ki, before you ask me any questions, I will tell you, there are some things that I cannot tell you. And there are things that I could tell you." X asked him, "What is better, here where I am, or where you are?"

Ghost Helper responded, "*Tsi'ki*, I already knew you were going to ask me that question. This is why I told you, there are some things that I cannot tell you. If I told you: it is very good the way that you are living and where I am is very sad, then, maybe in the future, there may be no way out of a sickness. You may get sick and you will remember what I said. You will think it is not good where I am going. You will be frightened; you will not want to lose your body and perhaps you will not be able to help yourself get better. On the other hand, if I say the opposite, then if you get sick, you will want to lose your body. You will not want to keep it. You will find out for yourself when you get here."

The social organization of *Niitsitapi* reflects the influence and teaching role of *Akaitapiwa* [ancestors]. As Goodman (1992) illustrates in his discussion of Lakota star knowledge, the star world and the microcosmic world of the plains are intricately interconnected. The same connections are considered important among *Siksikaitsitapi*. In partial fulfillment of these relationships, we have four major annual ceremonies that correspond to the seasons. The ceremonies are: *Niinaimsskahkoyinnimaan*, the Medicine Pipes, which are opened after the first *Ksisstsi'kom* in spring (Thunder is a potent sky spirit who has given protection to *Siksikaitsitapi* through the Medicine Pipes); *Aakokatssin*, the Sundance, which is held in July or when the Saskatoon berries ripen; *Ksisksstakyomopisstaan*, the Beaver Bundle, held after the ice breaks in the spring; and *Kanotsisissin*, the All-Smoke, held in the winter when the nights are long. These ceremonies are the collective consciousness of *Siksikaitsitapi*, which places them at the centre of their universe. During these ceremonies we acknowledge and give thanks to our alliances for another cycle. We ask for continued protection, prosperity, long life, growth, and strength.

Aakokatssin is currently hosted by the sacred and secretive *Omahko-hkanakaaatsiisinni*. The gathering of those who live by the ways of the smudge come to renew the delicate balance of life and death and ensure the continued survival of the people. This is a renewal of the ancient and ancestral ways of knowing and healing. Each tribal member's collective responsibilities in maintaining the sacred balance of the world are renewed. *Aakokatssin is the place in the universe where we the earth people, strengthen the sacred alliances with which the delicate balance of life is renewed.* In contemporary terms, the translation of *Aakokatssin* has been referred to as the Sundance, but its literal translation means "circle encampment" (Taylor 1989, 153). Standing Alone informs me that *Aakokatssin* also means "moving to the centre" (personal communication, October 1997). The term symbolizes the movement to the centre of the universe where one is in balance. Many other society members and other tribal members have specific responsibilities, but all members of the tribes can participate in various roles and responsibilities. It is an opportunity for all members to collectively renew their alliances and live up to their fundamental responsibility to strengthen the alliances with whom we work interdependently for the survival of life.

A *Kaaahsinnon* told this story about the relationship between ceremonial societies and knowing:

There was the time when *Omahkohkanakaaatsiisinni* were going to transfer. My father was a member of the *Maohksiipssiiks* [Red Belt Society] at the time. He did not want to join *Omahkohkana-kaaatsiisinni*. I think it was because he had problems with his legs. He never said it, but I think that he found it too difficult to join with an impediment. He moved to the mountains when the *Siksikaitsitapi* began to gather for *Aakokatssin*. He moved with his family to attend to the task of cutting timber in the mountains.

He had been up there for many days. One night, he dreamt of X [a member of *Omahkohkanakaaatsiisinni*], who was going to transfer. My father was older than X. In his dream, X was chasing my father. He came to a fence and he crawled under the fence. As he crawled under, he got his leg caught in the fence. So he was caught.

In the morning, after he woke up, he began to pack and moved his family back down from the mountains. He sent a message to *Omahkohkanakaaatsiisinni* to let them know he had surrendered. He would take whatever role and responsibility they would give him.

The narrative speaks of the power from *Ihtsipaitapiiyo'pa* in the transfer of knowledge. This is understood and experienced. Transformation occurs in this transfer of knowledge. Validity of knowledge is demonstrated through the observed transformation of individuals. One dream that altered my life occurred in the early dawn in the fall of 1987. I awoke with a powerful message. The ancestral guides spoke clearly, and their message was that the consumption of alcohol was weakening my connections with *Ihtsipaitapiiyo'pa* by obscuring and confusing my social responsibilities and negatively affecting my physical composition. The moment I awoke, I knew that I could no longer consume alcohol. I did not understand why a message such as this would be given to me because I did not have an issue with the use of alcohol. I was known among my family and friends as a non-drinker, although I did occasionally consume alcohol. While I do not understand why the message was given to me,
I have remained abstinent from alcohol since then.

The spirit of knowledge often speaks through dreams. They are central to the tribal ways of knowing. The general principle of understanding one's responsibilities is through the process of participating in ceremonies. They are participatory and experiential and provide traditional forms of education. In a sense, they function as a university for traditional knowledge.

The ceremony of *Aakokatssin* is central to the survival of our ways of knowing. The following excerpts describe the origins of *Aakokatssin*. The story explains to the reader the relationship between knowing and celestial relatives that are the basis of this knowledge. It is the story of the *Ookaan* of an elderly woman whose child was very sick. She asked *Naatosi* for help. Potvin reports the story in the following way:

Tsiinaki, Rosie Red Crow, ceremonialist teaching me the art of making pemmican, a traditional food among *Siksikaitsitapi*.

One night as the woman was asleep Natos himself appeared to her. He told her if she built a lodge for him and offered sacrifices, her child would recover. When she woke up she told her people about her wonderful dream. With everyone's cooperation, a lodge was constructed, sacrifices were offered, and a festival was held in honor of Natos. As a result, the woman's child regained health. Ever since that day, the great celebration of the Sundance has been held every year. (Potvin 1966, 86)

During the time in which the government and the church prohibited the *Aakokatssin* ceremony, a woman, the wife of Eagle Child, made a vow to have this ceremony, because her husband was very sick. Soon her husband was well; he had recovered from his illness. In the summer then, Mr. and Mrs. Eagle Child moved and set up camp at the place where *Aakokatssin* was to be held. Other *Siksikaitsitapi* began to move and set up camp too. The Indian agent sent word to the Eagle Child family, reminding them of the prohibition and advising them to move back to their homes. It is reported that Eagle Child sent word back, telling him to personally come and speak to him. The Indian agent did not do as he was asked. *Aakokatssin* continued and effectively ended the prohibition against *Aakokatssin* among *Kainai*.

The alliances of the ancestors continue to live through the ceremony of *Aakokatssin*. The following is one of the narratives of *Paiyo*, who is the brother of *Ipissowaasi* [Morning Star]. He had traveled to meet with *Naatosi*. This alliance continues to live through stories and ceremonies. *Paiyo* was given the living knowledge based on which *Siksikaitsitapi* continue to experience this alliance.

Then he told Scarface everything about making the Medicine Lodge, and when he finished, he rubbed a powerful medicine on his face and the scar disappeared. Then he gave him two raven feathers saying ... "They must be worn by the husband of the woman who builds the Medicine Lodge" [Grinnell footnotes:

the word "sun" is translated as "having sun power" or "something sacred"] (Grinnell 1962, 101).

Their relationship with the cosmic world is manifested in every aspect of *Niipaitapiiyssin*. The story of *Paiyo* and the knowledge that has been given by *Naatosi* are the instructions given to *Siksikaitsitapi* for acquiring knowledge and alliances from which our sacred science is gleaned. The ways of coming to know [*Kakyosin/Mokaksin*] are in the stories, the ceremonies, and the language of the people. Knowing is an interdependent relationship with the cosmic order. *Kaaahsinnoon* explains coming to know:

> I am still learning about our way of life. I am learning by listening to the stories. They are true stories. When I was young, I sat in many bundle openings. I worked. *Kaaahsinnooniksi* often told stories. After they told their story, they may ask, "How did you come to know?" The story maybe a little different, but it would be the same. They knew the way we were raised, the way we live. You heard what we said, use the stories in the way you heard them.

Being true to the traditions, *Kaaahsinnoon*'s advice is to listen to the stories that they have given me, and to take and apply them to my life. I need to use them in a manner that will benefit the people; this includes sharing them.

This knowledge is a living knowing. It is illustrated through the heart of *Siksikaitsitapi* epistemologies and pedagogy, *Pomma'ksin* [transfers]. In this way the initiated take care of the bundles and pipes that are the connections of alliances, the partners of *Siksikaitsitapi* in maintaining the delicate balance of life. This includes an all-encompassing responsibility to teach and pass on the knowledge to the next generation of initiates. These alliances are the source of *Siksikaitsitapi* identity, of their knowing and knowledge of balancing and maintaining good relations in life. These responsibilities must be passed on to ensure the survival of all. *Pommaksi-*

istsi are the ceremonies which transfer knowledge and maintain the tribal integrity of *Siksikaitsitapi* ontology and epistemology.

12. *Kakyosin/Mokaksin* – Indigenous Learning

Traditional learning is an interactive process that involves a network of relationships known among *Siksikaitsitapi* as "alliances." Traditional learning is premised on a "knowing" that is generated through a participatory and experiential process. This chapter and the subsequent chapters discuss the dynamic and intricate relationships of traditional learning through language, experience, and *Pommaksin*. These modes of learning are founded upon experiencing the knowledge of the alliances through these processes. They are the basis for learning the sacred knowledge of protocol, which forms the path of the sacred science of *Niitsitapi*.

Pedagogy is the Western term for the "art and science of teaching." It usually presents an organized method of teaching and a rational way of explaining its functions and practices. Pedagogical practices complement the epistemology of a culture. The cultural methods of teaching reflect conceptions of the natural world and cultural reality.

Central assumptions within Eurocentred pedagogy are linear rationality (the idea that there is a logical sequence of thought which advances from a single cause to a definite conclusion) and objectification (the philosophical doctrine that stresses the external, independent existence of what is perceived or known). The same assumptions are part and parcel of the process of colonization during which participatory *Siksikaitsitapi* pedagogy becomes replaced with an objectifying and predominantly rationalizing approach to teaching. Education under conditions of colonization denies the epistemologies of Indigenous cultures, which emphasize interrelationships.

Dossey (1985) argues that the relationship between culture and pedagogy manifests itself in a society's approach to teaching and learning.

For example, methods of teaching that are based on a Cartesian approach maintain the separation of body and soul, allowing the dissection and formal analysis of the various parts of phenomena. They are based on the notion that the universe has machine-like characteristics. This made it culturally acceptable, for example, to dissect human bodies, since it was believed that no harm would come to the soul (as the soul and body are seen as separate). The dispiritualization of a cosmic universe (in which the European peoples lived in earlier times) has become part of the pedagogical foundation of Eurocentred cultures. The secularization and desacralization of the universe is extended to human beings and to the entire process of learning.

Eurocentred methods of teaching are dependent upon a system of logic that is often insufficient for understanding complex phenomena – it is counter to the systemic logic of Indigenous perspectives. Various critiques, including those by postmodern philosophers, have shown the limitations of merely rationalistic approaches. It is no longer possible or legitimate to ascribe machine-like qualities to the basic functioning of the universe. Philosophers and physicists, such as Bohm, Capra, and Peat, see the universe as an indivisible dynamic whole whose parts are essentially interrelated and can only be understood as patterns of cosmic processes (Capra 1982, 77–78).

Traditional learning begins by identifying who we are in the context of tribal relationships. It is the life journey of understanding *Niipaitapiiyssin*. It is made up of the tribe's cosmogony containing the basis of its philosophical precepts. Subsequently, learning is an individual process, but it occurs in the context of the tribe's way of life. Children learn through participating in and experiencing their intimate and interdependent kinship relations.

> My grandparents raised me, there were a lot of people in my
> family. They taught me to respect everything, even the rocks.
> *Ihtsipaitapiiyo'pa* put the rocks there, so they are there for a reason.
> The trees, the water, all that you see is there for a purpose and we're

supposed to respect it. In the past, rocks were heated to make fire, which maintained warmth all night.

Children also learn their cosmic relationships through the stories that they are taught within the oral tradition. Language, *Niitsi'powahsinni*, brings stories to life and conveys to the child the world of *Akaitapiwa*. The child experiences the stories in a language that embodies the connections with a cosmic universe. The stories hold the alliances and *Ihtsipaitapiiyo'pa* moves through the words as they live in our breath. *Kaaahsinnooniksi* state that today the children are only learning the words, but not the connections. Even when they speak *Niitsi'powahsinni*, it may carry the imprint of thinking in English.

> One *Kaaahsinnoon* shared a story that had been told to him:
> My great grandmother would tell my father the stories. Great
> grandmother would tell the stories in secret. There was not
> much written then.

Another *Kaaahsinnoon* said:

> There are some things that we do not talk about. We talk around it.
> The person must reflect on what is said. There is only one way we
> can talk about certain things.

Nowadays, many children do not experience the relationships and the deep knowledge that language holds. Most importantly, they are not experiencing the alliances of a cosmic world.

> When they come, they will see the value of the language, because it
> is a spiritual language and it is all because of ceremony. [It is good]
> if people are really interested or inquisitive. Just to be curious, just
> to [want to] know what is in the bundles [is good]. I often offer:
> "Come and get painted, you will see them open up." So, to me the

ceremony makes more sense because I have experienced it, because it is my lived experience.

The language carries our breath to the ancestors. A good example is found in the importance of names. The people who give names also have specific responsibilities. The tribal names among *Siksikaitsitapi* have many purposes and functions. We have a ceremony for giving a child or infant a name. Names are a connection to the cosmos. As we call the ancestors, each person must identify himself or herself by name. When sharing with one of my relatives the significance of names in relation to our connections with the ancestors and the support they provide in our daily living, she related the following story:

> When I was a child, my grandmother, who was at one time a keeper of the *Missamaahkoyinnimaan* [Long-time-medicine-pipe], took me to Aakokatssin and had my face painted. Also at that time, she gave me my tribal name. My grandmother died and no one seemed to call me by my name, but I never forgot it. It is strange that I would remember my name mostly in times of crisis and grave challenges in my life. I would call my name and remember who I am. Somehow I would find the courage and strength to overcome my challenges." (Josie Smith, personal communication, October 1986).

This story inspired me to recover and reclaim my own tribal language. I began to pray for my connection with *Ihtsipaitapiiyo'pa* by way of my native language, and a year later, in July 1997, my friend Pete Standing Alone and I initiated a language immersion camp. We had invited *Kaaahsinnooniksi* to participate. We had also secured the services of the tribal administration video recorder to tape the conversations. I was extremely pleased throughout the proceedings because I wanted the words of the people captured on tape so I could revisit the messages of the *Kaaahsinnooniksi*. I felt the spirit of *Niitsi'powahsinni* throughout these conversations and was elated. The words seemed to infuse my very being with energy, love, and connections. After each day I felt whole and at peace. Throughout the process I wanted to take notes to remember and preserve the sacred words of my language, but I didn't because I was confident that the conversations were being preserved on videotape. A few weeks after the camp, I asked to review the tapes. I was told then that the first day's tapes were blank and the quality of the second day's tapes were was so poor that they had to be thrown into the trash. I was extremely disappointed. Then I remembered that I had prayed to connect with the spirit of the language. This had happened. I also remembered that I had experienced traditional learning immersed in language and the words of *Kaaahsinnooniksi*. This allowed me to re-connect more deeply with *Niitsi'powahsinni* and the source it comes from, *Ihtsipaitapiiyo'pa*. I don't remember much of what was said during my time at the camp. I could barely speak in sentences. Yet, what was important was that I was immersed in the spirit of language.

I have since spoken publicly in my own language on numerous occasions. In the fall of 1998 I gave a speech at the inauguration of newly elected trustees of the school board in my home community. I apologized to the elders for the mistakes that I would make in pronunciation but expressed my sincere desire and effort to engage in the thought structure and decision-making processes that are held in the language. I felt the elders' overwhelming support as I spoke in my broken tribal language. The feedback I received was good.

Traditional learning is an experiential and integrative process that uses all faculties necessary for learning. The people are dependent upon each other for strengthening and preserving the *Siksikaitsitapi* way of life. Children and students can learn this through traditional learning. One *Kaaahsinnoon* explains that this means listening to the stories, reflecting and observing the cosmic world, and participating in ceremonies. Here he describes learning through the transfer ceremony:

We got transferred; we lived the life, the way of life given to
Siksikaitsitapi for us to use. *Niipaitapiiyssin* is passed on; it is
passed down to each child.

I still go to *Kaaahsinnooniksi* for guidance. I am still learning
our ways. My grandfather too, he gave me advice.
If we were selfish about our ways, the teachings, and our advice,
if we only used it for ourselves to better our lives, then this way of
teaching and learning our way of life would not be here today.

Kaaahsinnooniksi are living up to their responsibilities by sharing
experiences that live through their words. These words touch my heart.
I feel their love and kindness. I am aware of my own responsibilities to
share and live this way of learning. They speak their wisdom in hopes that
I will understand and begin to live accordingly.

In our previous research, *Kaaahsinnooniksi* addressed the critical nature
of learning the responsibilities of *Siksikaitsitapi* relationships as part of the
general education process. They said:

> Children who are not raised with the ways of *Siksikaitsitapi* do
> not understand their role or responsibilities as *Siksikaitsitapi*. It is
> important to know these things because they structure the thinking
> of the *Siksikaitsitapi* and shape our behaviour. It is through the
> language and the knowing of our relations and our responsibilities
> that we know who we are. For example, many of the uninitiated do
> not know how to assist or contribute to the *Ookaan*. It has come
> to a place and time where we *Siksikaitsitapi* are afraid of our own
> ways, our prayer; we scare each other with it. Many of our people
> do not know.

The children of those who have been colonized by Christianity have
become afraid of their own kinship alliances because they did not
learn about them by participating in ceremony. This fear is reflected at
various levels of society and can be observed most obviously in acting

out through spousal, child, and elder abuse in Indigenous communities. *Kaaahsinnooniksi* cautioned the educators that families are alienated from each other as a consequence of fear. Since language embodies the connections, relationships, and responsibilities of *Siksikaitsitapi* alliances, children must be taught orally, and the search for the understanding of life must be maintained at the relational level (as opposed to developing a curriculum focused exclusively on cognitive understanding).

> *Kaaahsinnoon* offered guidance about traditional pedagogy to me: The Eurocentred way is easy to follow – in fact, it is a lot easier to follow than our ways of learning. We have to follow our protocol, our Indian way of life.

He then gave an example:

> Maybe with some of the stories we told you, you could begin by reflecting upon them with your heart, and perhaps keeping the questions you have asked us in mind. You will begin to find your answers in the stories.
> Your ingenuity and reflection will put into place an understanding for you [of the questions that you have asked us].

The traditional *Siksikaitsitapi* pedagogical method teaches children to listen, and they are encouraged to meditate and reflect on what they see and hear. This requires self-discipline and a conscientious effort to understand how to apply the stories to one's life. The stories are holistic and encompass all aspects of life.

One *Kaaahsinnoon* said:

> Through language there is the opportunity for children to learn their responsibilities and to come to know who they are.

Traditional instruction begins with *Siksikaitsitapi* ontological theory (see chapter 9 above), which addresses the origins of the people. What does it mean to be *Siksikaitstapi*, to be *Niitsitapi*? What is the ultimate substance of the universe? Answers to these questions are provided by our *Siksikaitsitapi* theory of being and reality, which addresses the origins of their relationship to a cosmic world. It is a framework from which the individual, from early on, begins to learn the responsibilities of family and tribe or community. Children are taught through language and through the care they receive from family and community.

Kaaahsinnoon shared the following child-rearing practices during *Kanohsin*:

> A woman would put her child on her back. The child would be with the mother while she did her work. I would be cooking and my child would be on my back. Or I would take a long piece of rope and make a swing. I would sing to the child. [She sings a lullaby.]

The song is a story about a small child. It warns the children that if they sneak out at night, they may be eaten by a man. The story continues by stating that the man eats blood clots and sings. She finishes her statement by saying:

> This is how we sing to our children as we work.

Infants begin learning the stories through lullabies even before they can speak. The songs establish very powerful connections with the ancestors. I had a profound experience with one of the sacred songs at *Aakokatssin*. As the dancers were coming out of the lodge, I was carried to a time where I could see *Akaitapiiksi*, the previous keepers of the bundles. It seemed like I was immersed and absorbed into the cosmic world of the ancestors. The feelings associated with these connections were the kindness, generosity, and acceptance of the cosmic alliances. I was filled with feelings of joy, humility, thankfulness, wholeness, and acceptance.

This, I knew, was truly a gift. I now understand that when I go to get my face painted for protection and guidance, I connect with all those who are my ancestors and who also were previous keepers of the bundle. Each year, as *Aakokatssin* begins to draw to completion, I have feelings of loss and sadness as I see *Iitsskinnaiyiiks*, *Maotokiiks*, and others, who came with the sacred bundles, return to their homes. The power of their song, their dances, their presence is tremendously overwhelming, and their absence is correspondingly sorrowful. After *Aakokatssin* I wondered how someone could compose a song that would be so ingenious that it would produce this kind of effect on me. It is a song that truly exists for all time.

Traditional learning prepares children to survive in their world. Among *Siksikaitsitapi* survival has various meanings. In fact, most prayers are finished with the term "*Kaamotaani*" [surviving of all perils], the intentions for long life. It is also used when someone has successfully overcome grave challenges and imbalances. *Kaamotaani* can be translated literally as "survival" and is also used to mean "to be complete with a specific challenge in life, being receptive to the challenges and obstacles of life." Implicit in the term is an understanding of the process of coming to know the connections of alliances that will enhance and nurture these intentions. As one of the *Kaaahsinnooniksi* noted:

Education is teaching children the ways to survive as a people.

13. *Niitsi'powahsinni* – Language

Language reflects the philosophical system of a people. *Siksikaitsipowahsin*, an agglutinating language, evokes and describes the relational perspective of *Siksikaitsitapi*. *Niitsi'powahsinni* is a mirror of the sacred world of the *Niitsitapi*. *Nipaitapiiyssinni* is the *Niitsitapi*'s life; it is the world of the sacred – a world that is called into being by the people's words. Language holds the knowledge, the content, and the relationships that constitute the sacred way of life, the "good heart" of the people.

In the following quote, one out of the group of *Kaaahsinnooniksi* clearly states that *Niitsitapi* ways of teaching [*Niipaitapiiysin*] are based in language. Oral tradition is the mode and the grandparents are the medium for this form of learning:

> I told her we would call those old people, *Iipommowaiksi* – those who have been transferred [initiated ceremonialists], those who pray the Indian way. It goes with it. It is a part of the language. They go together. Our speaking, our talk will be on the good path of our Indian prayer, our way of life – if we do not lose our language. If we lose our language, then it is no longer in the same way as our way of life.

Kaaahasinnoon is stating that *Siksikaitsipowahsin* [the Blackfoot language] and *Aatsimoyihkaani* [the good heart] are one and the same. If *Niitsitapi* lose their language, then the way of life, the good heart and prayer, the connections to the cosmic world of alliances, and, subsequently, the good path will be altered. Kremer (1994) describes this process of separation as "dissociative schismogenesis," (as discussed in Chapter 5 above) a form of dissociation that is culturally based and normative for Eurocentred cultures. It is the separation of heart and mind and the separation of human beings from their natural world. This separation is also the disengagement from *Siksikaitsipoyi* sources of knowing.

English is a colonial language that continues to have a significant impact on the consciousness of *Niitsitapi* and their experiential relationship with natural phenomena. Eurocentred concepts are often abstract distinctions contextualized within the philosophical orientation of the colonizer. They reframe the holistic concepts of *Niitsitapi*. For example, English concepts such as "person" or "individual" do not evoke the experiential connections to the sacred that the *Siksikaitsipowahsin* equivalents do. Rather, the relationships correspond to the worldview of the colonizer in which meaning is organized in a linear sequential format of subject, verb, and object relationships. On the other hand, *Siksikaitsipowahsin* involves the spiritual connections with *Ihtisitpaitapiiyo'pa*.

The separation and disassociation of Eurocentred consciousness from the natural world changes the reality of *Niitsitapi* by altering the cognitive and psychological aspects of their relationships. English fundamentally nullifies these relationships through the assumption that *Siksikaitsipowahsin* is directly translatable. It disallows awareness of the relational complexities that are thinned into abstractions in translation.

Our language expresses the natural alliances of *Niitsitapi*. The process of conceiving reality is shaped by the fundamental question of humankind's relationship to self and nature. Language distinguishes humanity from the rest of creation. Human consciousness has, as part of its distinguishing ability, concepts to determine what it means to be human. Through this process, it identifies itself as human. Language is critical in this process of developing the consciousness that becomes the essence of human creativity. This creativity is expressed by distinguishing "humankind" as concept, by giving it distinguishing characteristics that become the essential elements for experiencing and interpreting the world. This creative process develops the characteristics of what it means to be human. Thus the self is rooted in a specific worldview and constructed through a language using specific cultural constructs.

Language reflects the meaning and purpose that humans ascribe to their existence. Language contains the assumptions and relationships of people. In other words, language links the self to the universe.

European consciousness distinguishes reality categorically into separate entities and objects. Human consciousness is conceived as an abstract entity distinct from the rest of the natural world, including other human beings. Reality becomes linear, and objects affect or impact each other in this fashion. The mental constructs generating and maintaining reality result in an objectified world, created and recreated through abstractions that are easily manipulated and controlled in their separateness. The manifestation of such constructs in a given culture creates specific abstracting relationships among people, together with a distancing perception of the world. In the case of the English language, its concepts facilitate the perception of natural phenomena as a world that can be manipulated. Youngblood-Henderson (1992) states from a tribal perspective that Algonquin-speaking people define themselves linguistically as do most other *Niitsitapi*. Using the English language to translate *Siksikaitsipowahsin* means altering the relationship of *Siksikaitsitapi* and their connections within a world of cosmic alliances. *Niitsitapi* cultures engage in direct connections with the spiritual beings of the natural world. These connections are concrete and cannot be dismissed as mere ideas; they are a way of being.

Siksikaitsitapi pedagogy is embodied in the use of our language, *Niipaitapiiyssin*, meaning "to teach the way of life." It carries the sacred knowledge expressed in *Niitsi'powahsinni* which transmits the context for making meaning out of the human existence of *Niitsitapi*. The word refers to a verb-based language reflecting the view that human existence is transformational. *Niipaitapiiyssin* is a facet of an interactional and relational world. In this transformational world, *Niitsitapi* learn experientially the ways of striving for balance within their world. The experiences we have as we live are perceived as learning opportunities and challenges for living in harmony with ourselves and within a cosmic universe. Striving for balance is the way of life of *Niitsitapi*. Language constantly informs speakers and listeners about rules of conduct to follow and responsibilities to fulfill in order to maintain balance. This experiential learning process is interpreted through the *Niitsitapi* paradigm of connecting and maintaining balance with the alliances. For example, the concepts *Inna'kotsiiysin* [respect] and *Isspommotsisinni* [giving and sharing] provide rules of conduct. These basic values are acknowledged in daily living and are part of recreating and validating the natural order of balance. These rules of conduct or values express the unity of an organic universe and are the manifestation of a balancing way of being with oneself and with others.

Language describes the relationships that create the identity of *Siksikaitsitapi*. It is in these relationships of responsibility that we become human beings in the *Siksikaitsitapi* way. These ways, values, roles, and responsibilities of *Siksikaitsitapi* are held in a sacred way within the language.

Language carries our ways of knowing, and through *Saitamsin* [the breath of speaking], life among *Siksikaitsitapi* is informed and expressed. Language orients us as we learn and understand where we are and what our relative level of maturity is. In addition, language carries the responsibilities of the people because they cause things to happen (Cajete 1994). It is this aspect of the language that is essential for *Siksikaitsitapi* pedagogy. It is instrumental in creating the reality of *Siksikaitsitapi* by altering the order and structure of relationships toward balance. This aspect of the language transmits the transformational consciousness of *Siksikaitsitapi*.

When I was a child, my grandmother often reprimanded me for saying things that were inappropriate. She taught me that word and thought give birth to events. Although I did not understand the significance of what she was telling me, I realized that I had to be careful with what I said. The power of words is demonstrated through prayer and the power of breath in song. Every aspect of life has breath and therefore influence and impact; breath is the manifestation of what comes from *Ihtsipaitapiiyo'pa* (Source of Life). Cajete (1994) states that the inner forms of mountains have language, they have words, songs. For example, in the Diné tradition thoughts are the result of winds (*Niłchi*) acting on individuals and their "winds standing within" (Cajete 1994, 53). The cardinal directions are the sacred winds who have influence on life forms; they, too, have responsibilities in the cosmic world. Each direction holds knowledge for the people. For this reason they are respected and acknowledged for their gifts in all ceremonies. The breath of life is the power that takes pity on the people. *Siksikaitsitapi* understand it as the power from and through which Thunder, buffalo, berries, and others give people the knowledge necessary for living. It works through words, songs, and ritual. Prayerful words and the relationships among them give a visual image of the constant movement of energy. Any and all movement of breath has influence. It is life's source.

Language connects the people to the experience of the dynamic motion of life. *Kaaahsinnooniksi* use praying with sacred songs [*Naatoyinnaiysin*] to connect with cosmic forces and to balance the structure and order of the universe. Prayer is central to the ability of co-creation and transformation of reality; it is a way of aligning with the universal energies as co-creators of reality. One fundamental responsibility while praying is speaking from the source of a good heart – your heart must be in a state of all that is good in order to be able to maintain and perform the responsibilities of balance and harmony.

Niitsi'powahsinni, speaking our indigenous language, is a spiritual process that originates in an organic holistic world. An example of the organic nature of *Siksikaitsitapi* language is the root "*aato*," which can be found in a number of concepts that form an intricate and complex web of relationships. This group of letters or sounds is found in the words for sun, sacred, prayer, and power. The sun is referred to as *Naatosi*, meaning "sacred power." *Naatosi* is found as a particle in such words as *Aawaa-toyinnaiyi* [to sing powerful sacred songs] and *Aato'si* [to have (healing) powers]. The interrelationship of these words reflects the intricate nature of cosmic relationships. They originate from *Ihtsipaitapiiyo'pa*. Sacred Power is the spirit or force that links these relationships. It is the life force, and this is the name that *Siksikaitsitapi* use when addressing the source of all. It connects them to an organic and indivisible whole. *Ihtsipaitapiiyo'pa* links the concepts of sun, sacred, prayer, and power. This illustrates that the connections between sacred power and the manifestation of natural alliances and responsibilities are the sacred knowledge in language and the source to draw on to express the meaning of the everyday relations of *Sik-sikaitsitapi*. Language has the capacity to articulate sacred knowledge based on experience and is the medium for transmission from one generation to the next. Language provides words for understanding the nature and structure of the natural and cosmic worlds of *Siksikaitsitapi*. Nothing in reality can be taken for granted nor can it be assumed to exist without power or influence. People who have great influence are described as *Aato'si*, as having sacred power. The concepts reflect the interchangeabil-ity and transformational world of *Siksikaitsitapi*. Each of the concepts puts "self" in a particular place of the universe and provides the context for meaning to unfold. Sacred power places the people in the centre of the universe. The relationship that *Siksikaitsitapi* have with sacred power is central to their identity.

I will use *Aatsimoyihkaani*, the concept of prayer, as example to illustrate the dynamic power and knowledge held in language. I want to attempt to convey its holistic nature, but in so doing I also want to illustrate the difficulty in using English to convey the meaning, knowledge, and experience held in *Siksikaitsitapi* language. The example illustrates two major functions of language: the complex web of kinship relations in one all-inclusive organic universe and the prerequisite protocol.

Aatsimoyihkaani requires a good heart, which builds the connection to a sacred and harmonious state within a cosmic universe. It is made up of *Ihtsipaitapiiyo'pa*, the great mystery of the universe. Through *Ihtsipaitapiiyo'pa*, the universe is organic and indivisible. *Siksikaitsitapi* participate in this all-inclusive universe through their ancestors, *Paiyo*, *Ksisksstaki*, and *Kisstsi'ko'm*, as well as the people of plants, animals, water, etc. The word teaches *Siksikaitsitapi* about their kinship alliances in a cosmic universe.

Niitssksinnipi Omahtanistaissihpi means, "how we know how things (the universe) are the way they are." The nature of the universe has consciousness, and through it all life is connected to *Ihtsipaitapiiyo'pa*. In effect, universal consciousness of life is *Ihtsipaitapiiyo'pa*, and through it our relationships as *Siksikaitsitapi* are strengthened, and alliances are established and renewed. By connecting to *Ihtsipaitapiiyo'pa*, *Siksikaitstapi* learn the natural laws of the universe. They contain the traditional knowledge of responsibilities.

"*Natoa'pi*" can be translated as "sacred science," the knowledge contained in ceremonies. It means knowing the responsibilities of working with *Ihtsipaitapiiyo'pa*. *Pomma'ksin* [transfers] are the essence of renewing the responsibilities for living and strengthening, renewing, and maintaining the cosmic order. This word teaches *Siksikaitsitapi* that all knowing and knowledge is for survival and that we can ensure our survival through ceremony.

Ksahkomma Ikatsimapsiwa, Aawatsimihkasatawa means, "The Earth is sacred, our relationship is sacred." In this relationship, like all of our relationships, we see behaviour that maintains harmony with the earth. (We make amends to it for everything we do to it and take from it). We give tobacco; the giving of tobacco is renewing the state of balance. When we take from the natural world, then it potentially upsets the harmony and sacredness of our relationship, for example, when we kill animals. When taking their life we attempt to continue our good relations by offering tobacco to their spirits; we put it in the ground or on their dead body, i.e., *Aawaatsimihkasatai.* The act of offering tobacco is an act to return relationships to the previous balanced state. *Aatsimihkasin,* from which *"Aawatsimihkasatawa"* is derived, means "sacred way behaviour, actions, acting." Through sacred actions we maintain the state of sacredness that was threatened by taking life. The relationship to land, resources, and technology is based on the connections with sacred alliances. For example, knowing the roles and responsibilities of interacting with herbs, roots, plants, berries, and animals is essential. The buffalo rock and Saskatoon berries are examples. Both play a role in ceremonies depicting their relationship to survival and balance of life.

Niitaoni'pi ki'tao'ohsinnooni means "how we recognize our land by its geographical features," geography. The relationship of *Siksikaitsitapi* to sacred places such as *Ninnaistako* (Chief Mountain), *Katoiyiisiks* (Sweet Grass Hills), and other presences (such as the sacred four directions, plants, rocks, rain, and thunder) are lived examples. *Niitaoni'pi ki'tao'ahsinnooni* teaches *Siksikaitsitapi* the behaviour or rules of conduct with these alliances. This is the ecological knowledge of the natural world; life is maintained through specific responsibilities assumed for the sake of cosmic balance.

Inahkotait sinik a' topi means "that which has been passed on through the generations through stories," history. The stories and legends of the ancestors include narratives of the lives and stories of

Oonistaahsiiso'kasimiwa (Calf Shirt), *Naatosinnipiwa* (Comes Down the Sun), *Mi'kyaisto* (Red Crow), winter counts, migration, and war exploits. These stories connect *Siksikatsitapi* to the history of holistic relationships. They reflect the transformational relationships with *Ihtsipaitapiiyo'pa* and teach fundamental principles and responsibilities.

Niitsikso'kowammootsi'opi means "how we are related to each other," social structure. The societies, clans, and family relationships are examples of the normative structure of the *Siksikaitsitapi* world. Each of the age grade societies teaches each person *Kiitomohpipotokoi* [ontological responsibilities]. These responsibilities are the manifestation of knowledge, skills, values, and roles of holistic living. As tribal members mature, responsibilities grow accordingly, and subsequently their own understanding of these responsibilities (*Kiitomohpipotokoi*) deepens. These ways of *Siksikaitsitapi* being emulate our understanding of *Ihtsipaitapiiyo'pa*. They are the ways of *Niitsikso'kowammootsi'opi* [social organization]. The meaning of our relationship to others emulates our understanding of the cosmic order. Relationships that form the social structure of *Siksikaitsitapi* are directed by this understanding of our ontological responsibilities. Human existence complements the cosmic order by being responsible for balance, for good relations with all relatives, for maintaining their natural alliances, and, finally, by having strong connections with spiritual guides as partners in building knowledge. It is understood that the alliances and guides are partners with *Niitsitapi* in the continuing creation of reality.

The following ontological responsibilities are examples of the values imbuing and forming our social structure. The words are who we are as *Siksikaitsitapi*, our existence means manifesting these values.

They include *Kimmapiiyipitsinni* [compassion], *Isspomotsisinni* [sharing and support], *Ainnakowa* [respect], and *Isskanaitapsstsi* [relationship]. These responsibilities are the source of our collective and tribal identity. They form the stages and processes for human development among *Siksikaitsitapi* and subsequently delineate distinctions and integrity among tribal societies.

Kimmotsiisinni and *Kimmapiiyipitsinni* relate to being kind, compassionate, and generous. These values are premised on the observation and understanding that the universe is fundamentally compassionate and generous. This orientation of the universe is the heart of the *Niitsitapi* way of life. The oral traditions and ceremonial alliances are contextualized based on this premise. Many of the stories of the initial transfers of *Siksikaitsitapi* ceremony begin by recounting the compassion and kindness of these alliances. Thunder, Beaver, and others were given to the tribe for survival. Compassion transcends any conflict and misunderstanding, because it negates judgment.

Isspomotsisinni [sharing and support] denotes the gift of contributing to the existence or activity of others. It is through this way of being of service to others that we strengthen relations – thus the cosmic alliances of the universe are strengthened. Each person relates to the collectivity or wholeness of the tribe through this way of being. It is by way of this responsibility that tribes comprehend the reciprocal and indivisible nature of the universe. People have a gift, which, as it is put in service of the tribe, is their contribution to the collective. Individuals may be gifted with song, medicines, creativity, and insight. These and other gifts are pieces to strengthen the circle.

Ainakowa [respect] is attempting to preserve the natural or sacred state of the universe. Tribal protocol and customs are the manifestations of this mission. Respect is contextual, and as tribal members mature they understand that intuition is the best indicator of how to be respectful. This way of being is constantly mindful of the interrelatedness and interdependence of our relationships. For example, by learning to respect the natural world, one becomes knowledgeable about the inherent properties of plants and their contribution to the survival of the tribe. This means learning how to maintain harmony with particular medicines. This same example can be extended to all relationships that make up our collective identity.

Isskanaitapstsi [relatedness, relationship] means that life is purposeful and all-inclusive. This responsibility is premised on understanding the natural order and the mysteries of the universe. The wisdom in traditional knowledge and custom manifests the understanding of the sacred nature of relationships and relatedness. Often personal experiences are reflected against the stories of *Kaaahsinnooniksi* and other ancestral stories. The appropriate form of relationship is clearly delineated, for example, in the stories of *Napi*, as well as the consequences of undermining them. The pedagogical practices for becoming *Niitsitapi* are based on personal inquiry, reflection on stories, and advice from *Kaaahsinnooniksi*. Without these, there is neither wisdom nor the opportunity to fulfill one's responsibilities. The life experiences of *Akaitapiiks* [ancestors] and *Kaaahsinnooniksi* are the means of fulfilling and extending the wisdom of a cosmic universe to the next generation.

Responsibilities, such as respect (i.e., following protocol), are what help us to connect with and become a conduit for the manifestation of the spiritual forces. When we embody these responsibilities, we align ourselves with the spiritual forces around us and manifest the spiritual nature of life and humanity. This means we are spiritually authentic. And, conversely, authentic presence manifests life force in our conduct and fulfillment of responsibilities. If claims to spiritual authenticity don't manifest in relationships, these claims are seen as untrue, invalid, and inauthentic. Authenticity arises from the maintainance of good relations with tribal kinship and cosmic alliances. They implement the mission of Indigenous cultures to strive for harmony and balance.[3] Once understood, good relations guide to ways of being that allow *Siksikaitsitapi* to connect to *Ihtsipaitapiiyopa* and thus to their true identity. The values that support these responsibilities include: consensus decision-making; a fluid structure for leadership; integrity of word; giving and sharing; being humble, honest, patient, and kind; listening attentively; and being of service to others. These are the ways to strengthen prayer, and they constitute the source of tribal strength. Human existence and, subsequently, the identity of *Siksikaitsitapi* are directed toward giving of oneself for the survival of our relations and fulfilling our responsibilities within the alliances we are a part of.

---

3. For example, see the story by Narcisse Blood in chapter 2.

The notion of prayer has its root in a good heart. It is at the core of *Siksikaitsitapi* identity. For example, there are many sacred songs and rituals for the initiated that provide connections with the sacred and the powerful. The grave responsibilities associated with having access to such great power are learned through specific rules of conduct and protocol during initiation. Knowing and maintaining the proper conduct necessary for balance protects the initiated. The good heart is a process arrived at by following the rules of conduct as expressed in *Niitsi'powahsinni*. The language used in ceremony connects people to a universe of ancestors who are part of the spiritual alliances.

Language determines the nature of human beings by forming part of the normative structure of the culture by identifying values, roles, responsibilities, and rules of conduct among people and in their relationship to creation. It expresses a matrix of relationships that is, in essence, the connection to *Ihtsipaitapiiyo'pa*.

The way of life, on the other hand, is *Niipaitapiiyssin* or the constant motion of breath. I visualize this as the movement of *Ihtsipaitapiiyo'pa* permeating creation. Sacred power is the source that generates the distinctions that allow our perceptions of reality. The words "*Ihtsipaitapiiy'pa*" and "*Niitpaitapiiyssin*" identify the meaning and purpose of life. They construct the context in which language carries identity, knowledge, relationships, and the meaning of relationships for life itself.

Traditional learning is grounded in the importance of direct knowledge gained through experience. Experience is the teacher of life and cannot be exchanged or inherited. *Kaaahsinnooniksi* are the teachers because they have experienced the life of *Siksikaitsitapi*. They said:

> It is good to sit here in this way. The subjects that we are talking about are not things that we have heard; these are the things that have occurred. We have experienced these things you have asked us. This is why it is good that you come to ask us these things that you want to know.

Primary knowledge comes through the integration of self with the roles and responsibilities of *Siksikaitsitapi* tribal alliances. Learning these responsibilities occurs in the context of a good heart, i.e., the moral responsibility of maintaining balance. *Ao'tsisstapitakyo'p*, knowing, the completed act of cognition, means active participation in the world and the integration of experience through reflective meditation. Knowing is the ability to make reference to past experiences and to contextualize them in a system of meaning that makes sense of present experiences. Decision-making is a process of assessing meanings rooted in the moral and ethical responsibilities of *Siksikaitsitapi*. They comprise knowing the inherent patterns of relatedness in an interdependent ecological world.

Dissociated from the pedagogical foundation based in experience, *Siksikaitsitapi* are not able to perpetuate the values of human development and education that are essential for our survival as a people. In other words, survival of *Siksikaitsitapi* is dependent upon knowing how to participate in life together with cosmic relatives. This knowledge comes from experience and participation, the ways of learning the basic responsibilities of being *Niitsitapi*.

The continued integration of experience, reflection, and meditation leads to an understanding of the connections within the holistic patterns of life. This translates into kinship relations as part of an organic reality. Experience alters the knower and the known; in experience the known and knower can become one. Learning through experience and reflection involves listening for connections and meanings in the words heard. By listening carefully, we respect the breath of life as it flows through the words and through our lungs. The wisdom in the breath of life is understood in the singing of songs that connect us to the ancestors. In loving the child for the gift of life, we come to know the delicate balance of life and death. Speaking with resource creativity and kindness strengthens the alliances. Giving strength through words to others allows individuals to achieve what they ordinarily could not do. *Siksikaitsitapi* learning is dependent upon the oral tradition and *Niitsi'powahsinni* [language]. Oral tradition is the medium through which tribal people enter into relationships with the *Ihtsipaitapiiyopa*. It represents the life and spirit of learning. Storytelling has three aspects: (*i*) the teller, who enriches the story and brings to the story understanding based in experience; (*ii*) the listener who is experiencing the story and through it a connection to the ancestors; and (*iii*) the relationship between the teller and the listener(s) of the story. In this way, the stories are alive and people are engaged in the experience of the relationships. The function of language is its embodiment of the transformational consciousness of *Siksikaitsitapi*. The words hold the sacred vibrations that alter the cosmic world by creating distinctions that are experienced through the alliances of the cosmos. Speaking is connecting to all of creation, and through language one touches, relates, connects, and participates with the powerful force of the universe. The mysterious force or *Ihtsipaitapiiyo'pa* moves through language. It touches, connects, and lives through words as it makes life move.

14. *Aipommotsspistsi* – Transfers

Traditional learning is experiential. This forum for learning is centrally exemplified in the *Siksikaitsitapi* practice of *Aipommotsspistsi* – the practice of ceremonial transfers. They bring *Siksikaitsitapi* ontology, epistemology, and pedagogy together through methods of transmitting sacred responsibilities and knowledge from generation to generation. They are the initiations into sacred responsibilities and knowledge that are passed down through each generation to ensure the renewal of cosmic alliances. These medicine bundles have been transferred to *Siksikaitsitapi* with the original instructions for coming to know, *Akaotsisstapitakiop*, so that "we have come to understand (not merely know) it." During the original *Aipommotsp* of the medicine bundles, the initiates were given instructions of how to conduct the ceremonies. In essence, the transfer ceremony is working with *Ihtsipaitapiiyo'pa*, the Source of Life, from which knowledge is revealed or transferred. As such, the transfers are the processes of renewing the original responsibilities as taught to the *Siksikaitsitapi* in the original transfer.

One of *Kaaahsinnooniksi* said:

> Traditions, as they have been taught to us through our ancestors and through the ceremonies, are the most accurate at this time; as opposed to other forms of knowledge, such as reports from ethnologists and other academic or published materials.... Tribal identity is learned through experience. Conversely, students and non-Native people who want to learn of our ways often will use the literature; they do realize that the literature is fraught with inaccuracies and false information. The language and the experience of our relationships has been our way of teaching and learning.

Aipommotsspistsi are a medium of becoming one with the universe. They are the connections to all time as well as the ancestors and ancients since time immemorial. They ensure the continuance of *Siksikaitsitapi*. As one ceremonialist said,

> "Our life is transferred to us." Transfer is the way knowledge is passed on, it is the way to maintain balance among all our relations. The ceremony maintains the connection with *Ihtsipaitapiiyo'pa*, the Source of Life.
>
> It is our responsibility, in the *Siksikaitsitapi* way, to give back what we have been transferred. It is not the way of the people to sit with or keep that which has been given to you. For example, those who have received an education return and give it back to the people. The *Siksikaitsitapi* way, our way, the *Niitsitapi's* way, is to help, to assist, and then Ihtsipaitapiiyo'pa will help us. We have to try hard and work hard. It is good, *Ihtsipaitapiiyo'pa* will help. We need not worry.

The *Siksikaitsitapi* way is premised on giving and sharing knowledge and, through prayer, it assists and helps the group to survive. It gives strength and supports life.

The basic ontological responsibility, *Kiitomohpiipotokoi* or role, of giving and sharing is embedded in the fundamental philosophical premises of *Siksikaitsitapi* education. Sharing and giving are ways of being that connect to and perpetuate *Ihtsipaitapiiyo'pa*. Actions of sharing and giving are consistent with the natural order of the universe and help to maintain it in balance. According to *Siksikaitsitapi*, a fundamental aspect of the cosmic universe is reciprocity, which is experienced in *Aipommotsspistsi*, the practice of ceremonial transfers. As a *Siksikaitsitapi* word, "*Aipommotspsi*" means "we are transferred; it was given, or passed on." The word depicts reciprocal responsibilities or an exchange of responsibilities among participants. The natural law of reciprocity is extended by *Siksikaitsitapi* to their daily customs and activities.

The ceremonies are for connecting, renewing, and maintaining good relations with the alliances to ensure that life returns to a sacred and peaceful way. The ethical and moral behaviour identified through customs, language, values, and roles are often referred to as protocol or ritual. Protocols and rituals encapsulate the responsibilities and behaviour [*Kiitomohpiipotokoi*] that are the means for returning to a state of balance or ensuring good relations. A few daily examples are: give food and a drink to visitors; do not walk in front of ceremonial people or *Kaaahsin-nooniksi*, always walk behind the person; greet and acknowledge every one with some gesture; and, finally, always move in a sunwise direction if you are moving in a circle. Tribal protocol acknowledges the sacred state or the good relations of food, the energy of individuals, and the movement of life.

One of *Kaaahsinnooniksi* shared the following story to illustrate the importance of the following protocol:

My brother was looking for horses. He had been riding a sorrel thoroughbred. This horse was given to him. It was a very handsome horse. My brother rode to X's house. This was where X was wintering [X is Niinaimsskaiks, a medicine pipe holder]. My brother was a Medicine pipe child. [His father was a Niinaimsskaiksi also].

Brother went to ask X whether he had seen the horses. He rides over to X's house, and in his hurry, he jumped off his horse and ran inside the lodge with the reins of his horse remaining in his hands. X knew the protocol, but I think he did not want to follow it, perhaps it was because it was a good horse.

After my brother had received a reply from X, he returned to his horse and rode away. As he was riding west, my brother met Y and another person. Y had been driving a team with a double sled, traveling east. My brother decided to approach him to ask him if he had seen the horses. Dusk was fast approaching. My brother rides over to Y, who was getting firewood.

Kaaahsinnoon explains,

On the snow-covered earth sleds make a clear sheer flat surface. This smooth surface can be very slippery. As my brother was approaching Y's sled, his horse slid on the smooth surface made by Y's sled. The horse fell and hit his head. The fall was fatal.

Another *Kaaahsinnoon* adds,

These are the things for which we cannot give you an answer. I ask: why is it that you cannot enter the lodge [home] of a *Niinaimsskaiks* with a cigarette? Why is it, if I have given you something to eat when you come to visit me, that you have to tell four stories, if you want to take the food out of the home. This is our way of life. These are the things that are taught to us.

Through generations of *Aipommotsspistsi*, *Kaaahsinnooniksi* have been taught the rigorous discipline of the sacred science of participating in ceremonies. The knowledge inherent in their ceremonial protocols transcends the classical Eurocentred conceptions of reality and nature. However, more recent experiments in quantum mechanics have revealed that reality is the manifestation of a "set of relationships" which, upon interacting with an observing system, change knowledge and physical reality discontinuously (Zarkov 1979, 54–79). This particular scientific view is consistent with *Siksikaitsitapi* understanding. *Ahkoyinnimaan*, the Medicine Pipe, can be said to be a web of kinship relationships which, through active participation of *Siksikaitsitapi*, alters and transforms reality. Included in this web of relationships are relationships with non-human animals, who also have roles and responsibilities in the transformation of life. Through participation, *Siksikaitsitapi* become a conscious part of an interactive system; they are transformed in the process of participating. This aspect of traditional learning is referred to as *Aipommotsp*. Once the transfer has occurred, the initiated becomes transformed [*Aipommotsp*] because the transfer has become a part of the living body. The alliances collectively strengthen life for the sake of life, for the survival of humankind, and the universe. In the legend of *Ksisstsi'ko̓m* [Thunder], this knowledge is given to the people as *Aipommotsp*, the transfer of the Medicine pipe [*Ahkoyinnimaan*]. The relevant alliances that are active here are illustrated in the following excerpt:

> A long time ago, Thunder struck down a man. While he lay on the ground, the Thunder Chief appeared to him in a vision, showing him a pipe and saying, "I have chosen you that I might give you this Pipe. Make another just like it. Gather together also a medicine bundle, containing the skins of the animals and birds which go with it. Whenever your people are sick, or dying, a vow must be made and a ceremony given with a feast. The sick will be restored to health." The Grizzly Bear afterwards appeared to the man and said to him, "I give you my skin to wrap around the sacred bundle, because it is larger than the skins of other animals. The owl possesses knowledge of the night. The Medicine Pipe is wrapped

with raw hide and decorated with feathers and the winter skins of the weasels. Many animal and bird skins are gathered for the sacred bundle, wrapped in a large grizzly bear skin. In the spring, when the first Thunder is heard, the Pipe is brought out and held up." (McClintock 1992, 253–54)

Niitsitapi education is distinct from the Eurocentred educational system. It is governed by the natural law of balance and harmony. *Aipommotsspistsi* are the means of maintaining the reciprocity and generosity required in order to maintain balance among *Siksikaitsitapi*. They maintain the natural order that insures the gifts of life; reciprocity is essential for the survival of all life. *Aipommotsspistsi* are the embodiment of this way of life. Transfers form the fabric of *Siksikaitsitapi* culture and the social organization of our people.

McClintock (1992) gives the following example which illustrates the behavioural manifestation of cultural and societal principles: Lone Chief, *Nitainawa*, gave forty horses, an enormous pile of clothing, blankets, and provisions during his initiation. Gifts given to the previous *Niinaims-skaiksi* [keepers of the pipe] included: a saddle, horse, bridle, whip, and lariat for the man; the woman or wife received a buckskin dress, beaded moccasins, and leggings, a robe with red paint worn only for ceremonials. *Kaaahsinnoon, Niita'kaiksa'maikoan*, P. Standing Alone (personal communication, October 1997) states that during *Pomma'ksin*, gifts are given because generosity is an inherent characteristic of the universe; it is the responsibility of *Siksikaitsitapi* to live up to the natural laws of the universe. *Naatowapo'kos* [keepers of bundles] traditionally give *Naatosi* [Sun] offerings that were always their very best possessions. This is to reflect the enormous gifts given by *Naatosi*, gifts that come from *Ihtsipaitapiiyo'pa*, the Source of Life. No price can be put on health, longevity, and an abundance of berries and game. Generosity has been demonstrated as part of the natural order, and therefore *Siksikaitsitapi* organize themselves to mirror these relationships among themselves and through their alliances.

The bundles are the embodiment of the sacred medicine of *Ihtsipai-tapiiyo'pa*. Grave respect is therefore given to them; I was once told by one of the *Naatowapo'kosiks* that one could not be angry in their presence. Particular personal attitudes and specific conduct are strictly adhered to by the keepers and those who interact with them. Grinnell (1962) reports that the daily care of these bundles included taking them outside during the day and suspending them above the owner's seat inside the lodge at night. Once inside the lodge, no one was allowed to pass between the pipe stem and the fireplace. No one except the man or wife could move or open the bundle.

This required conduct is also demonstrated in ceremonies. The highest respect and integrity are asked of those who participate. For example, in *Naamaahkaan*, *Kaaahsinnooniksi* tell four stories of exceptional feats. I am told by *Niita'kaiksa'maikoan* (P. Standing Alone) that this individual must not tell a lie. The honesty and integrity of the individual during the ceremony must be paramount, otherwise she or he may suffer grave consequences. When I asked, "what types of consequences," he replied, "Perhaps the individual's good health." He added, "One cannot lie to *Naatosi*" (personal communication, October 1997).

The following components summarize the principles of *Siksikaitsitapi* educational processes and content:

- knowledge of tribal and cosmic responsibilities;
- experiential knowledge of tribal alliances;
- embodiment of knowledge and skills acquired for the well-being of a cosmic universe;
- transfer of knowledge and skills to the next generation.

The traditional educational system of *Aipommotsspistsi* develops and reinforces the identity of *Siksikaitsitapi*, their place in the universe, and the skills and knowledge they need in order to function in their society.

15. *Kaaahasinnooniksi* – Grandparents

Kaaahasinnooniksi are the teachers; they have been initiated and have experienced *Aipommotsspistsi*. The transfer is the initiation into a *Kana'kaaatsiiks* [sacred society] and/or the initiation as one of the *Naatowa'pokos* or *Niinaimsskaiksi* [bundle or pipe keepers]. The initiated are the ceremonialists who later become *Kaaahsinnooniksi* and perform *Aipommotsspist*, the rites, songs, and dances of ceremony. The transfer embodies the original instruction given by *Ihtsipaitapiiyo'pa* [Source of Life], *Naatosi* [Sun], *Ksisstsi'ko'm* [Thunder], *Ksisskstaki* [Beaver], etc. Each ceremony offers secrets and sacred knowledge that helps maintain balance within the partnership of these alliances. This is the sacred science of *Siksikaitsitapi*.

Those who teach and perform the ceremonies and transfers are *Kaaahsinnooniksi*. They have lived the life of ceremony and are the embodied knowledge of the sacred. Their experiences with the alliances of *Siksikaitsitapi* are the source of their teachings. Their initiation is the precondition for participation in ceremonial practices.

Kaaahsinnooniksi have cautioned regarding issues of Pan-Indianism. Pan-Indianism is largely an urban phenomenon and is quite different from the maintenance of the integrity of tribal knowledge. It is a conglomerate of various intertribal customs that may include religion and reform. Its aim is to promote traditional values and to facilitate Indian involvement among the professions and businesses (Frideres 1974, 115). As *Kaaahsinnoon* said, Pan-Indianism "creates confusion among the young people who are searching for their tribal identity; tribal identity is the connection with the ancestors in the broadest sense of the word and connects us to all time."

The ceremonialists and *Kaaahsinnooniksi* show tremendous responsibility and discipline in keeping that connection with the ancestors. The essential responsibility of *Iipommowaiksi* or *Niinaimsskaiksi* [bundle or pipe keepers] is to maintain balance. Wolf (1991, 55) describes the responsibilities of the ceremonialists and his own experiences of initiation:

The whole is composed of parts that are connected just as dew drops of water are held by a spider's web. One drop vibrates in the breeze and the whole web responds. Every drop feels the breeze. But what was the web that connected us together? I felt that it had something to do with consciousness, but I wasn't sure. I also suspected that this vibration could heal.

Kaaahsinnooniksi addressed the responsibilities for healing and balance:

> Our way of life is responsibility, the responsibility to teach the people the way of life. The teachings are kindness, respect for relatives, listening to those who talk to you and who give advice and teachings.

The consciousness of the initiated is constituted by such responsibilities as respect, integrity, humility, and kindness. Kindness and generosity are the forces of the universe, they are the forces through which *Ihtsipaitapiiyo'pa* functions. To give with love is the natural order of the universe. *Kiitomohpiipotokoi* [responsibilities] enable the initiate to maintain balance and identify what constitutes the identity of *Siksikaitsitapi*.

Siksikaitsitapi have always attempted to align themselves with the sacred power and intelligence of the universe through the development of their particular identity and social order, through sacrifices and offerings. Aligning with the sacred power of the universe is dependent upon the acknowledgment of the abundance of gifts bestowed on *Siksikaitsitapi* throughout the cycles of time. *Aipommotsspists* honour the animals and the plants who sustain *Siksikaitsitapi* and who are their teachers of natural laws. For example, the rituals, songs, and practices of ceremony map out the proper thought and behaviour required; at the same time, they delineate the proper and necessary behaviour for all their other relationships.

Indigenous epistemology is coming to know your heart, the "good heart" of *Siksikaitsitapi*. *Ikiniioiskitsipahpahsinni* being of good heart] is the source of connecting to the lifelines of a cosmic universe, it is the basis of *Siksikaitsitapi* ways of coming to know. Coming to know means *Ikiniioiskitsipahpahsin*, and it necessitates the maintenance of connections with the alliances of the macrocosmic and microcosmic worlds.

The principles and protocol held in *Aipommotsspistsi* govern the knowledge and determine its validity. *Kaaahsinnooniksi*, having experienced the ceremonial responsibilities of transferring within tribal protocol and understanding the rules and the validity of coming to know, share this knowledge. The science of *Siksikaitsitapi* is taught by *Kaaahsinnooniksi*.

> It is up to us to make sure that we teach properly. It is good when someone tells me they are getting involved [becoming initiated]. I encourage them.

As one of the *Kaaahsinnooniksi* explained:

> Those of us sitting here have experienced our way of life. The things we have given you are things that you could use in your life. And you could make good use of it in the future. There are no other persons or people that we could turn to. We have reached that place in our ways. The ancestors and grandparents have taught us in the past. It can be seen, it has all been seen, those things we are telling you [our teachings can be observed and are observed through our experiences]. It is all included in the teachings that we are sharing with you.
>
> It is in the stories that we have told you. Those are the things that are there. These are the teachings that have maintained and ensured our survival.

In summary, the pedagogy of the *Siksikaitsitapi* embodies the following practices:

* Experiential learning centres on individual *responsibility*. Each person in becoming *Siksikaitsitapi* is learning to understand

his or her place in a set of relationships and responsibilities from which he or she can participate in a cosmic universe (i.e., social and society initiations are the foundations of the developmental phases of being *Siksikaitsitapi*). Learning and understanding is dependent upon the maturity and volition of the individual and occurs from the inner centre of the person and thus is primarily an individual responsibility.

- Understanding the way of life and the responsibility to life are connected.

Siksikaitsitapi learn through their relationships and connections to family, environment, geography, animals, etc. Within these relationships they experience the knowledge and understanding of responsibilities for maintaining the balance of their world.

- Understanding is demonstrated and embodied through the attitudes and behaviour of the individual. Learning means *integrating* the wisdom and knowledge experienced into who you are, into tribal identity.
- To summarize: Learning occurs experientially in direct interaction and through participation with *Ihtsipaitapiiyo'pa*. It is an integrative and transformative approach to holistic knowing. Learning occurs by understanding one's own nature (personality and purpose in life) and one's relationship to life.

Traditional learning means coming to know the basic ontological responsibilities of giving and sharing by listening, observing, experiencing, and reflecting. *Kaaahsinnooniksi* who have come to know within the various aspects of self as well as the social and natural world, and who have learned their responsibilities from the ancestors, become teachers. *Kaaahsinnooniksi* embody and carry the knowledge to each new generation. This method of knowing and of generating knowledge is the essence of *Siksikaitsitapi* survival as a people and the basis for the survival of the rest of the living world.

IV. Conclusion: Renewal of Ancestral Responsibilities as Antidote to Genocide

16. Deconstructing the Colonized Mind

The process of decolonization refers to deconstructing colonial interpretations and analyses and includes solutions to problems that are imposed upon tribal peoples through the processes of colonialism. Decolonization can occur simultaneously with the process of reconstructing tribal relationships because it displaces colonial thought and behaviour while reconnecting with the alliances of a cosmic universe.

Reconstructing our tribal alliances gives a clear understanding of the dynamics of the colonial mind and the subtle but pervasive and insidious alteration of the reality of the colonized through changes in consciousness and, subsequently, their reality. Fanon (1963, 43) describes this in the following manner:

In the colonial context the settler only ends his work of breaking the Native when the latter admits loudly and intelligently the supremacy of the white man's values.

And Adams (1995, 37) comments:

In the process of colonialism, Native populations gradually accepted the belief of European bourgeois ideology which over time became part of the Aboriginals' own system of beliefs and values. The importance of this colonial ideological process is that it became and still is one of the major tactics used to control and oppress Aboriginal people.

Tribal peoples' reality is altered by the interpretation of their experiences through the framework of colonized ideology. Tribal people have internalized Euro-Canadian beliefs and values through this process, and, as a result, interpret their own experiences from an alien and alienating value and belief system. Colonial consciousness is internalized through the systemic support of literature, the media, health services, the school system, etc. Indigenous peoples' experiences are primarily interpreted in terms of victimization. This supports the advances of colonialism by focusing on the powerlessness of Indigenous peoples. This idea is further legitimized by the notion that tribal cultures are primitive and irrelevant, thus enhancing the hegemonic power of the colonizer's ideological control.

Blackfoot Indian camp on the prairies, Alberta, 1874. Photographer Royal Engineers. Glenbow Archives NA-249-78.

Duran and Duran (1995, 7) propose an alternative:

As we move into the next millennium, we should not be
tolerant of the neo-colonialism that runs unchecked through
our knowledge-generating systems. We must ensure that the
dissemination of thought through journals, media, and other
avenues have "gatekeepers" who understand the effects of
colonialism and are committed to fighting any perceived act of
hegemony on our communities. Post-colonial thinkers should be
placed in the positions that act as gatekeepers in order to insure
that western European thought be kept in its appropriate place.

Key to the task of "gatekeeper" are tribal people who participate in their
own ceremonies. They need to know where they stand as Indigenous

individuals in terms of their self-understanding so that they have sufficient discrimination to assume such responsibility. Ceremony is the process during which postcolonial thinkers can renew their ancestral alliances and deepen the understanding of their own responsibility so that they are able to generate knowledge that will strengthen and renew the connections to the alliances of a cosmic world. Furthermore, participation in tribal ceremonies protects and guides the process necessary for decolonization and reconstruction.

The concepts "victim" and "victimization" are born from a colonial interpretation of tribal peoples' experiences. They are characteristic of a particular type of psychology used for ideological control; the use of these terms facilitates the consciousness of powerlessness or victimry. The idea of victimization can be found in much of the social science literature (Frideres, in Bolaria 1991; Davis & Zannis 1973; Boldt 1993).

> The person-blame approach enables the authorities to control deviants under the guise of being helpful. Another social control function of the person-blame approach is that it allows deviant individuals and groups to be controlled in a publicly acceptable manner. Deviants – whether they are criminals or social protesters – are incarcerated in social institutions and administered a wide variety of therapies. In the end, a person-blame approach requires the individual to change, not the structure of society that is causing the problem. (Bolaria 1991, 129)

The general figure of thought is that Indigenous peoples have lost control over their lives and that this loss manifests in self-hate, as evidenced in self-destructive behaviour patterns such as violence and alcohol abuse. This interpretation popularizes the belief that tribal peoples are primitive and self-destructive. Victimization, it is argued, leads to a level of despair tantamount to self-hatred (Duran & Duran 1995, 28–29).

Research has demonstrated that grim reality of internalized hatred resulting in suicide…. Native American people have been dying in great numbers due to suicide. Another way in which the internalized self-hatred is manifested symptomatically is through the deaths of massive numbers by alcoholism. (Duran & Duran 1995, 29)

In essence, the interpretation and characterization of tribal peoples has been based on the notion that they are less than fully human and thus less capable. Evidence for these ideas can be found from the earliest colonial times onward, e.g., in the declaration of the Pope in 1512, where he stated that the Aboriginal people of the new world were, indeed, human (Brizinski 1993, 25). The shocking need to affirm the humanity of Indigenous peoples becomes obvious when we remember the annihilation of the Beothuk of Newfoundland as an example of the level of hate found in the earlier history of the Americas. The conscious as well as unconscious conspiracy to systematically destroy Indigenous peoples and cultures has been active for five hundred years (Duran & Duran 1995, 28). The literature, through its focus on the victimization process and by using the notion of self-hate as a rationale for the deterioration and destruction of Aboriginal communities, is, in final analysis, blaming the victim instead of looking at the hate-filled acts of genocide. The powerful ideological control that results from blaming the victim alters the consciousness of Indigenous peoples and leads them to internalize the powerlessness generated by these concepts. Thus they remain locked in vicious circles of victimization.

The idea of powerlessness is persuasive with governmental bureaucracies that develop policies accordingly. They manifest, for example, in the over-representation of Aboriginal people in compulsory programs within the child welfare and justice systems. The caretaker function of state institutions reinforces the powerlessness of Aboriginal people and communicates the obsolete nature of their own culture as dependency increases. In fact, anything that tribal peoples possess, such as their heritage, their color, and any other characteristics of their ways of life, is perceived to be inferior. Ideological control is premised on assumptions of inferiority of tribal peoples and their culture; they become stigmatized with "unnatural passions," addictions, unemployment, and suicides. In essence, they are perceived as being not quite human. The powerlessness of tribal people is continually reconstructed and recreated. Stigmatization and racism become the justification for cultural genocide implemented through paternalistic policies. These racist assumptions are the basis for the fundamental ideological and structural relationship between the state and tribal peoples. Indigenous inferiority remains the overall premise underlying the relationships between the two groups. It manifests in analysis and theory-building when approaching the "problem," meaning *the consequence of genocide*. Alternate postcolonial theories would focus on independence, self-affirmation, and sovereignty, i.e., the value of Indigenous knowledge in maintaining or re-creating self-sustaining and self-sufficient sociocultural systems.

Many social theories interpret the social and political problems of Indigenous peoples within a framework of blame. This relieves pressure for state institutions to address fundamental assumptions underlying their theories, legislation, and practices and rules of conduct. Moreover, this framework legitimizes social control exercised by state institutions and is perceived by the dominant society as acceptable, perhaps even humanitarian (Bolaria 1991, 128–30).

Tribal people must begin to reconstruct their tribal paradigms based in their own cosmologies. This is a move outside the framework of blame, victimization, and victimry as well as mere opposition to colonization. Without the development of a paradigm grounded in their own knowledge and science, tribal people will remain the hostages of a colonial consciousness that inherently ascribes to them deficiencies in character and abilities. Duran and Duran (1995, 6) propose the following framework:

> A post-colonial paradigm would accept knowledge from differing cosmologies as valid in their own right, without their having to adhere to a separate cultural body for legitimacy. Frantz Fanon

felt that the third world should not define itself in the terms of European values. Instead, Fanon thought that everything needs to be reformed and thought anew, and that if colonized peoples aren't willing to do this we should leave the destiny of our communities to the European mind-set.

Any hope that the Eurocentred paradigm can address issues of inferiority is either illusory or an emulation of that paradigm. Rather, the cognitive process of imperialism must be deconstructed by examining the underlying conceptual assumptions used in the analysis of the dynamics of ideological and psychological control, particularly as represented in Eurocentred psychology.

The construct "victim," for example, forms the basis for many Eurocentred psychological theories and is a tool for analysis. However, this framework supports a world of imperialism, one of power and control. Once the traditional alliances have been destroyed, the major interpretation available to tribal people is the interpretation of the colonialists; notions of victimization take the place of ceremonial balancing and the exchange of gifts and offerings. The new framework supports the overall objective of imperialism: cultural genocide. One does not know the loss and disruption of one's culture from an Indigenous perspective unless one has consciously experienced the phenomenon as holocaust. Diseases that destroyed two thirds of *Niitsitapi* population (Brizinski 1993, 94) and the whisky trade, which almost caused the complete extinction of *Niitsitapi*, are two experiences that are a part of this holocaust. It is estimated that poverty caused by the whisky trade directly or indirectly killed more Indians than the entire regular army did in ten years (York 1990, 190). Although Eurocentred thinkers have experienced their own forms of colonialism, their experiences are not analogous to the North American Indian experience. Furthermore, tribal people rarely had the opportunity to share these experiences in a forum that affirms their validity. Rather, the experiences of tribal people continue to be interpreted by Eurocentred thinkers who did not actually experience the phenomenon but are interpreting tribal experiences from their own Eurocentred perspective, commonly pathologizing the effects of genocide as well as distancing and isolating them as "culturally other." In addition, they advance the notion that the Eurocentred analysis of tribal people has universal application, thus legitimizing the overall interpretation of deficiency. The following quote illustrates such "analysis of deficiency":

> The effects of genocide are quickly personalized and pathologized
> by our profession via the diagnosing and labeling tools designed
> for this purpose. If the labeling and diagnosing process is to have
> any historical truth, it should incorporate a diagnostic category that
> reflects the effects of genocide. Such a diagnosis would be "acute
> and/or chronic reaction to colonialism." In this sense, diagnostic
> policy imposes a structure of normality based in part on the belief
> in the moral legitimacy and universality of state institutions.
> (Duran & Duran 1995, 6)

Effects of genocide are clinically classified as pathological, therefore requiring control and alteration in the form of clinical treatment. The concept of "personalization" is part of "blaming the victim," while pathologizing supports the idea of the need to alter and adjust the victim to European-style norms. The theory of deficiency can be readily illustrated by the recent theory of the "residential school syndrome."

The "residential school syndrome" is a term coined by psychologists who have noticed a set of symptoms comparable to the grief cycle characteristic of a person losing a close relative among those who have shared the residential school experience (York 1990, 37). They focus on symptoms of anger and denial among Indigenous people, rather than on the dominant society's own inability to formulate theories that analyze the insidious process of colonialism and the genocidal consequences of social science theories. "Syndrome," according to Webster's dictionary, is defined as "symptoms occurring together and characterizing a specific condition, or any set of characteristics regarded as identifying a certain

The "isms" of European ideology combine into one idea system that cloaks the sentiments of European cultural imperialism in a syntactical maze of universalistic terminology and logic. Each component of the system is dependent upon a conception of the cultural other as the embodiment of the negation of value; for each provide the ideological function of supporting the European self-image as the universal "agent of change," the "doer," the personification of intelligence and the "inheritor of the earth." (Ani 1994, 478)

The notion that the objectified self is the universal nature of humanity provides the licence for Europeans, through colonialism, to alter the natural order and process of Indigenous cultures and people. This has been referred to as the "white man's burden" (Ani 1994, 478). In the following equation, Ani (1994, 478–79) identifies the collective behaviour of Europeans towards the "cultural other":

European +	European =	Cultural Other	Cultural Other
Ideology	*Self-Image*	*Image as*	*Must be*
Christianity	Religious, moral, cultural being	Heathen, non-religious, immoral	Saved
Idea of Progress	Progressive, modern, cultural being	Backward	Developed, advanced
Evolutionism	Civilized cultural being	Primitive	Civilized
Scientism	Scientist, knower	Object	Studied, known, controlled
White Supremacy	White racial being, pure, human	Black, dirty, non-human	Avoided, pitied, enslaved, destroyed

The European collective behaviour toward the "cultural other" is based on ideas of superiority and power. From the interrelationship of these ideas originates the notion that existing conditions of the cultural other need to be changed. The self-image of tribal persons requires alteration because it is not acceptable to the European self-image. The modes of alterations are commonly described as "solving," "advancing," "developing," "analyzing," and "study." None of these terms indicates an identification with the cultural other. These concepts embroil Indigenous people in a power relationship that is intended to dehumanize and despiritualize Indigenous cultures and peoples.

Power and superiority fundamentally govern relationships within the Eurocentred worldview. As a consequence, theories and research become primarily reactionary responses, often supporting the existing power relationships inherent in such a hierarchical worldview. The solutions proposed from such a hierarchical perspective become part of the relationships of the colonized. The solutions proposed for the colonized are subsequently based on the constructs of power, domination, and control. They support the thought structures embedded in colonial consciousness. Therefore the theoretical analysis of colonialism itself is hegemonic unless done outside the cognitive system that gave rise to colonialism (i.e., cultural affirmation and the recovery of Indigenous roots).

An example of this hegemonic process of analysis is the following analysis by Clignet (1971). He describes the psychological characteristics of the colonized mind in the following manner: When real opportunities are presented to the colonized and these opportunities are authentic, meaning that they are not for the purposes of control and domination, then the colonized does not recognize them as opportunities. Clignet adds that the consciousness of the oppressed has no way of distinguishing real from inauthentic and manipulative opportunities. He identifies this as the reciprocal nature of the relationship between the colonized and the colonizer. On the side of the colonized, this is primarily a reactionary response and is described as one of the mechanisms that maintain the colonized order. Furthermore, it is the structural basis for the interaction between the two groups. According to this model, any action by the colonized is seen as having no effect on the power relationship between the two. The analysis presented by Clignet is based on the assumed powerlessness and futility of actions by oppressed people.

Deconstructed colonial thought as well as self and social structure can only arise from within an Indigenous paradigm. It begins with the Indigenous concept of humanity and the Native interpretive assumptions about relationships and behaviour. The use of the European self-image and concept of power automatically victimizes tribal people, since they continually reconstruct powerlessness, victimization, deficiency, or inferiority as characteristics of tribal people. A postcolonial paradigm must not only deconstruct the inherent assumption of the Eurocentred ideological process, but begin by reaffirming and reconstructing tribal concepts, the fundamentals of Indigenous theories and ontological assumptions. The use of tribal ontologies begins the process of reconstruction of self and the identification of one's place in a cosmic universe as a basis for Indigenous ways of knowing. For *Siksikaitsitapi*, the beginning point is the awareness of their alliances that are at the heart of the culture. They shape tribal identities. Through these relationships, *Niitsitapi* identity can manifest and express itself outside the colonial paradigm, neither colonial nor postcolonial, but wholly and self-sufficiently engaged in its own discourse.

17. Eurocentred and *Niitsitapi* Identity

Self is that part of one's identity that provides the source for decision-making in life. It creates meaning out of experiences and provides motivation for behaviour. These processes are the internalization of social beliefs and values. However, when choice is removed and we are forced to look outside of our own culture for direction and motivation, it easily leads to cultural paralysis resulting in genocide. This process severed tribal people from who they were and continues to promote a Eurocentred human development perspective based on looking outside of one's self, outside of one's tribal culture, and outside of one's relationships with a cosmic universe. The dissociated self and its dissociation from the natural order are the result of conceptual abstraction in an objectified, separate world. This view of reality is fundamentally contradictory to a world premised on interconnectedness and interdependency of relationships.

The interconnections of relationships in a cosmic world are the basis of life, reality, and truth; they give rise to the responsibilities of *Niitsitapi* people. In addition to knowing how these alliances are formed, and knowing the concomitant specific tribal responsibilities, these alliances correspond to the mission to maintain balance and harmony. Without the celebration and affirmation of interweaving relationships through the alliances, the means of cultural reproduction are severed. The creation of Indigenous knowledge in response to existing problems of genocide and colonialism is thus severely limited. This results in obstacles that make it difficult to break the cycles of dependence and to adapt to and survive in the contemporary world.

In order to begin to heal the genocidal effects of assimilative theories, policies, and practices, research must address the heart of Indigenous tribal paradigms. Inquiries must be meaningful to Indigenous peoples, premised on tribal ways of knowing, and generate ideas and practices that facilitate the resurgence of their own ways of knowing. Thus they can generate knowledge and research practices that not only address the core of genocide, but, more importantly, connect tribal people to the alliances of "knowing" and "heart." The alliances of knowing constitute the spirit of knowledge, and the heart of knowing is knowledge that will strengthen alliances within a cosmic universe. The process of inquiry must be grounded in the concrete relationships of Indigenous populations. If the purpose of research is to find solutions to Indigenous problems, the definitions of problems as well as their solutions must be grounded in the paradigm and methodologies of Indigenous cultures. The inquiry process and the knowledge must come from meaning generated by those people who will benefit personally by having their own lives enriched. This will strengthen the community. Tribal people must identify and define their own problems and work through their own processes of seeking solutions.

The continuation of research outside of one's culture and the attempt to develop research questions based on experiences within the Eurocentred paradigm continue to create dependency among tribal peoples. Such problem identification on behalf of Indigenous peoples is alienating as its definitions are based on an alien paradigm. Solutions defined by Euro-Canadians will not solve the cultural difficulties that have been created by assimilationist advances. Rather, such practices continue to perpetuate dependency, and they subsequently result in the death of a people. Dependency is perpetuated by denying Indigenous people their own ways of knowing and self-definitions, thereby denying them the ability to solve their own problems as defined by themselves. In order to stop these practices, inquiry must be grounded in Indigenous ways of knowing.

A fundamental demarcation of dependency is the willingness to have some external force or entity define one's identity and the world in which one lives. This type of dependency translates into the absence of tribal identities grounded in the cultural integrity of the people and their ceremonial ways. The result is an absence of tribal ways of renewing and generating knowledge.

Absence of tribal knowledge to address fundamental survival issues only legitimizes the belief that the group rendered dependent is incapable and incompetent. As a consequence, their perceived incompetence requires a benevolent external force as caretaker to generate knowledge. This benevolent caretaker and the policy of paternalism represent the mystification of practices of cultural genocide. The natural alliances of tribal people that are constituted through ceremonial protocols and practices, based on Indigenous knowing, are destroyed in this process. What is central to dependency is not the inability of those rendered dependent to make decisions, nor is it that they are incapable of finding solutions to the challenges of their lives. Rather, it is the denial or destruction of their Indigenous opportunities and resources to make sense of life and to create meaning from experiences and circumstances that have become central in the creation of dependency. Making meaning out of one's experiences is a basic human function designed for the survival of a people and individuals. If the ancestrally given process is destroyed, people become dependent upon an external interpretation of experiences for direction, motivation, and purpose for their existence. For tribal people, this external source is Eurocentred imperialism and its interpretations of who Indigenous peoples are.

The alteration of a people's identity is the most clinical and insidious effect of imperialism and genocide. The prohibition for Indigenous people to access a self that is contextualized in relationships generated from within their own tribal ways of life is genocide. Genocide is the more or less violently enforced inability to make sense of one's existence. It results in debilitation, paralysis, and, finally, death. This process of paralysis can be seen in the experiences of small children in residential school who wet their pants while reading in front of the class. In such circumstances, the perception created by the educational system is that there is no other choice but to endure the residential school system. A colonized mind is one without awareness of choice. Choice is the awareness of different options or the awareness of creating or seeking options or possible solutions to problems as part of our internal self-process. This requires knowledge of one's self. The ability to create is both a function and a process of identity. Identity naturally has a context from which to seek and create options and opportunities. However, when the ancestral context of self is forcefully denied, denigrated, and removed, a dissociative identity founded upon the experiences of colonialism is located outside of the connected self and outside of the tribal context. It is severed from the natural sources of creativity, motivation, and strength. This is genocide.

The literature on colonization and oppression has addressed some of the psychological effects of cultural genocide (Adams 1995; Davis & Zannis 1973; Duran & Duran 1995; Fanon 1963; Frideres 1974; Indian Association of Alberta 1987). This research and analysis has largely been developed from the Eurocentred perspective on human beings. They have addressed the interpersonal and intrapersonal aspects of colonialism using, for example, the concept of the "dissociative self" (Kremer 1994). Eurocentred concepts have been applied to Indigenous peoples. As a result of this narrow and limiting perspective, the literature has failed to provide a forum within which Indigenous peoples can examine the process of colonialism on their own terms, using their own definitions and perspectives of what it means to be human.

The failure of the literature to address the Indigenous perspective of humanity is an essential element of racism. The voice of the colonized has been denied a forum and an opportunity in the Eurocentric discourse to express the experiences of cultural genocide based on Indigenous terms. Instead, their experiences are contextualized and authored through Euro-centred interpretations in the science and research journals. Eurocentred theoretical orientations and research methodologies used to study Aborigi-nal peoples support and legitimize colonial interpretations.

The destruction of tribal identities and connections denies Indigenous knowledge and the science from which it originates. Rather than address-ing the issue of Indigenous knowledge and the production of knowledge, uncritical Eurocentric theories of oppression are founded on the analysis of power. A hierarchical paradigm leads to the development of theories of deficiency. They create and perpetuate concepts of pathologies and syndromes isolating tribal individuals and groups by linking them to a discriminatory context of hierarchical relationships, with Indigenous people inevitably at the low end of the hierarchy. The imposed order of colonialism is a particular set of hierarchical relationships defined and interpreted by deficiency theories. Indigenous people are thus held hostage in a paradigm that is embedded in power relations defined by materialism, wealth, and aggression. Science and economic power be-come the weapons of cultural imperialism and genocide. Science is the discipline used to legitimize the reality created by the Eurocentred world through concepts of hierarchical power and through the accumulation of economic resources. Eurocentred science legitimizes this reality, using its particular discriminatory hierarchical concepts for analysis, while imply-ing their universal validity. Aboriginal people are now almost inevitably defined as deficient. The studies then identify the need for development or assimilation. The focus is primarily on the inability of Indigenous peoples to adapt to the Eurocentred paradigm.

The psychological syndromes defined by these theories ascribe various forms of debilitations and abnormalities to Indigenous peoples. These deficiencies become areas of study for science, medicine, law, and educa-tion. Although the literature may address the violence of inequality, these studies and observations provide few alternatives for any systemic changes for Indigenous people, who occupy the bottom of the hierarchical and materialistic paradigm. In fact, this type of literature on oppression has popularized victimization and has become part of the continuing legacy of cultural genocide. A meaningful, non-colonial alternative to these interpretations is the people's own interpretation from within an identity constituted by tribal responsibilities.

Traditionally, rites of passage provide initiations into tribal responsibilities; they distinguish the phases of human development by marking transitions from one stage of life to another. In traditional Indigenous cultures, these transitions are made visible in ceremonies, such as puberty rites, vision quests, war successes, and marriages, as well as in initiations into social and sacred societies. During the process of colonization, these traditional forms of demarcation and their corresponding ceremonies have been neglected, forgotten, and abandoned. They embody the necessary knowledge, experience, and skill to fulfill specific responsibilities in accordance with human development. The individual learned the appropriate age grade and gender roles of tribal customs and thus the required roles and responsibilities necessary to participate in tribal society. Rites of passage mark the experiences that take individuals to deeper levels of understanding our relationships to responsibilities, thereby deepening the relationship with cosmic alliances. Many of these experiences are an integral part of an individual's developmental process while others are perceived to be uniquely personal transformations. Rites of passages are also designed as demarcations for individuals to successfully prepare for the obstacles and responsibilities as they enter into the next stage of life. It means incorporating the knowledge and skills necessary for a person to become a good *Niitsitapi*. However, through the process of colonization, we have become disconnected from our ancestors, the stories of origin, the ceremonies, the language, the land, and, subsequently, from who we are (exactly the process European peoples went through in the development of their dissociative or empty or masterful, well-bounded selves; cf. Cushman 1995; Kremer 2000). As a result of this disconnection, rites of passages have been neglected and abandoned. Because of this disassociation, I was not aware of the tribal responsibilities that are the basis of my identity as *Siksikaitsitapi*. I did not know what made a good *Siksikaitsitapi*. Later, as I became aware of the concept of tribal responsibilities, I did not have the context to understand my relationship to them. I did not have the concrete relationships through which to connect with these responsibilities. Only once I became involved in ceremonies did I finally begin to understand my own responsibilities.

A personal example of understanding these responsibilities occurred in 1996 when I had an experience that I would call a rite of passage. Prior to this, I had not realized that I attributed my connections with the ancestors to the medium of ceremony. It seemed that I was able to connect with them only through ceremony. These powerful experiences usually occurred in the company of ceremonial people, rituals, or at sacred places. However, during my dissertation work, experience showed me that it is the relationship with the ancestors itself that is central. Of course, I had been taught this by traditional people, but I had not understood the teaching to mean that it is I who invites the ancestors, and that it is I who acknowledges and nurtures the relationship. I realized that my relationship with the ancestors is not outside of myself; rather, *I am the source of this relationship*. This understanding took me to a deeper level of responsibility as an Indigenous person. Part of this responsibility means trusting the process of life, trusting *Ihtsipaitapiiyo'pa*, the Great Mystery and Source of Life. It means allowing others the dignity of their journey and path. It means trusting myself and giving myself permission to be responsible for my own journey as I understand it. At that time, I began to experience life from a place of ceremony and had to acknowledge that ceremony does not only occur in special events and places. Ceremony is my life. My life is ceremony. I am not separate from ceremony at any time in my breathing moments. In ceremony I connect with *Ihtsipaitapiiyo'pa*, which places me in my own centre and in the centre of the universe.

My journey continues and remains on the path of understanding my tribal responsibilities through experiential knowing of my relationship with the alliances. Knowing my tribal alliances occurs only in experience, which forms the essence of our *Siksikaitsitapi* reality.

18. Reflections and Implications

The doctoral work on which this book is based has been a spiritual journey during which I connected with my ancestors and all my human and non-human relatives with whom I share the responsibilities for renewal and balance. Throughout my life I have been primarily a student of the Eurocentred worldview. Until recently the knowledge system in which I operated was the paradigm of colonialism. I had attempted to integrate the knowledge that I had gained through my education with what I had understood to be my own cultural values; however, this turned out to be insufficient because it did not produce the changes that I envisioned as possible from within an Indigenous worldview. My dissertation research provided the opportunity to begin exploring the idea of producing knowledge within an Indigenous paradigm. This became the mechanism that enabled me to begin the journey of connecting with my *Siksikaitsitapi* ways of knowing. I realize in retrospect that my dissertation work was only the beginning of "coming to know." The journey has continued since.

Indigenous science is the metaphor that attracted me to the Traditional Knowledge Program, a program at the time available at the California Institute of Integral Studies. The term "Indigenous science" has been coined by Dr. Pamela (Apela) Colorado. She believes that this term bridges the two worlds – Aboriginal and European, objective and subjective, mind and matter, spiritual and physical orders of reality.

> Until the present, we have had to stretch Eurocentred science so
> far that knowledge about Native culture seemed unreal. Research
> has been perceived and presented as mono-cultural, thus not

accepted by the Native community. All peoples have some way
of coming to knowledge. (Colorado 1988, 49)

Initially the term "Indigenous science" did not have much meaning for
me; I did not understand how Indigenous people could have a science.
Science was a concept that was derived from a mechanical view of the
world. Research implied for me the continuing sterile and unrelenting
effects of genocide. At the time, I did not understand nor was I aware that
Indigenous people had their own ways of knowing, their own protocols for
affirming authenticity and validity of observations and experiences. Simply
put, I did not have a relationship with the sacred. More importantly, I did
not have any awareness that *Niitsitapi* have their own ways of knowing.
For many years, I remained ambivalent toward the term "Indigenous
science." However, as an educator I needed to understand the term in
hope that it would lead me to the ways of knowing of my own people.
I had an intuitive understanding that the term was at the heart of our
traditional knowledge. Thus it became the topic of my dissertation
research and a central term for my subsequent work.

As I began my program, I was advised to begin a mentor relationship
with grandparents of our tribal communities. I quickly learned that I was
connecting to traditional teachers who embody the wisdom of the alliances. At the time, I did not understand the reasons that they were seen as
"grandparents." I approached the grandparent for the Horn Society in the
traditional manner for guidance and mentorship. One of the first questions I asked *Niita'kaiksa'maikoan* was, "What are the *Siksikaitsitapi* ways
of knowing?" His response was:

I cannot give you a response, I have not thought of such a question.
I will tell you this though: if what you are asking is in our ways we
will be able to come up with it. We will go to those who follow the
Aatsimoyihkaan [good heart], the grandparents and ceremonialists,
and collectively and collaboratively we will come up with a response
to your question. And I will say one more thing: what we come up

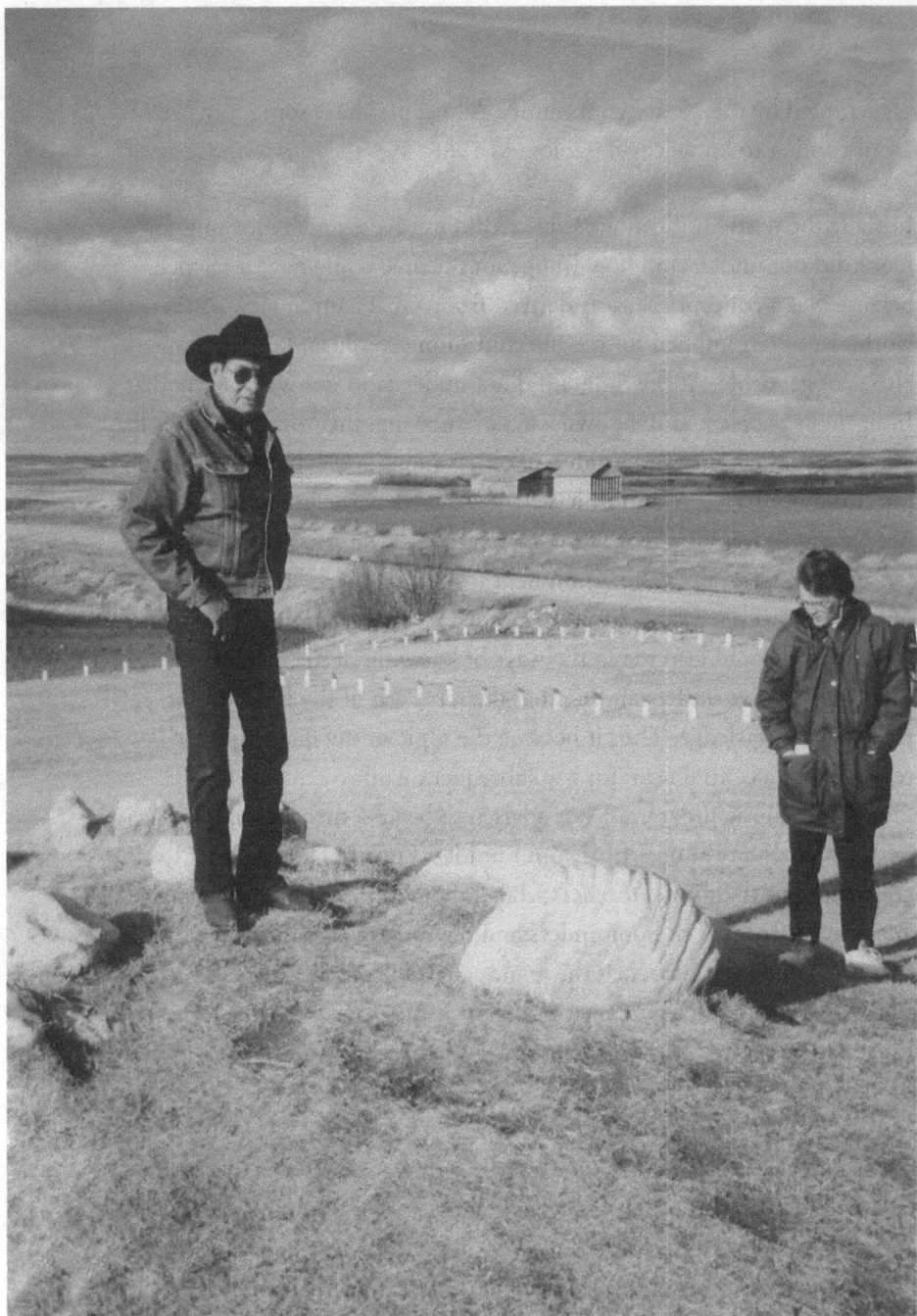

Nii'ta'kaiksa'maikoan, Pete Standing Alone, and friend Alice Charland at the sacred site of the Buffalo
Rib Stone in Alberta.

with will be valid for us. The people who we will go to are the people who have lived our ways and have lived up to their responsibilities through the transfers we were instructed in by *Naatosi, Napi,* and *Ihtsipaitapiiyo'pa.* (P. Standing Alone, personal communication, September 1994).

At the time, I was not aware that he had given me two central pieces of the process: 1) participating in ceremony, and 2) seeking the guidance of grandparents and ancestors. Both are key aspects of traditional epistemologies. These pieces formed the nuclei of my process of connecting with the alliances (including the spirit of knowing and language).

Ways of knowing are like a pebble thrown into a pond: Once I began my journey of inquiry, I began making connections. These connections eventually all converged in one place – my place or *being* in the universe. My being is dependent upon my participation; my existence is determined by my participation. I am an interdependent being. I am the pebble and my participation in the universe has a ripple effect outward. At the same time, my existence is determined in an inward move by my participation. Until I became aware of my relationships, I was not aware of the *being* of *Siksikaitsitapi.* Consequently, I had no access to *Siksikaitsitapi* ways of knowing. During my inquiries, I began a process of connecting, renewing, and strengthening the network of kinship relations that constitute both *Siksikaitsitapi* identity and its collective inquiry process.

The process of knowing began to unfold as my mentor and I journeyed through many discussions, participated in ceremonies, visited with other grandparents and ceremonialists, and prayed at sacred sites. Insights and momentous connections with ancestors became the milestones of my inquiry process, affirming its validity. Connections with the ancestors were the most transformational experiences of the whole process. One of these momentous connections was with the spirit of language. In July 1996, we organized a language immersion camp. The official objectives of the camp were: first, to create the awareness of the importance of language in the work place, and, second, to provide an environment where participants would experience the language, the guidance of grandparents, and the relationship with the land. My personal objective was to remember the language that I had forgotten. On the second evening of the immersion camp, while I was driving home, a doe and her fawn walked across the road. I had been thinking of the day's events and experiences. Suddenly, in the presence of deer, I connected with the spirit in language, the power of breath, and life. Language is our connection with ancestors, the alliances, our responsibilities with the world of *Siksikaitsitapi*. Overwhelmed with this experiential insight, I could not stop talking about my newfound alliance and the implications of this knowing for the education of our children, its ramifications for strengthening, renewing, and reconstructing tribal culture and identity.

After this experience of being a part of the *Siksikaitsitapi* whole, I could begin to encounter the ancestors. I began to trust the process. I came to accept that I did not have control over the universe, but, through prayer and meditation, I could let the ancestors guide my process. I began to trust the universal intelligence. I was able to participate more authentically and to deepen my understanding of the immanence of a cosmic world. As my dissertation process progressed, I relinquished my own agenda for what the process should look like and relied more and more deeply on the guidance of our ancestors.

Although the process involved ceremony, I also gained important insights from hours spent walking in the woods, often late in the evening or as the sun was rising. During these walks, I visited with trees and animals who were very timid and would let me catch only glimpses of them. Late one summer evening, I was fortunate to see the beavers dancing for *Naatosi* just before dusk. In cold sub-zero weather, I saw whitetail deer as they scurried through the trees for protection. On warm sunny days, I could barely see the eagles as they soared high above the clouds seeing life below. In the spring, I sent frightened ducks scampering into the trees, interrupting them as they took their young for swimming lessons. On one occasion, I met up with a coyote on the trail. I immediately became afraid; however, coyote took one look at me and calmly walked across the frozen river as if to say, "We have finally made our alliance." It did not take long before the woods and the inhabitants became family and a place of nurturing, support, and knowing. I had insights, wisdom, and developed knowledge of nature and of the cycles of the season. I noticed the behaviour of the animals who intuitively follow the wisdom of nature. For example, as fall approaches, the trees and plants turn beautiful bright crimson colors, and the smell of the dying leaves has a wonderful fragrance. Nature thus taught me that in death there is beauty and in death there is life. Without death, there would be no life. It is one and the same. Nature is transformational and creative. The constant movement and change of nature is one of the natural laws of Indigenous science.

Traditional tribal wisdom understands the transformational nature of a cosmic universe. There is simply no separation between the subjective and objective, good and bad, sadness and joy, death and life. The convergence of nature is seen in the electron that is both wave and particle. Existence is perceived through a consciousness that is simultaneously part of a multi-level reality from which meaning and connection to all others emerges unceasingly. The holistic nature of tribal consciousness provides a framework for learning – learning that occurs when one participates with the nature of life as lived knowledge. Experiences that deepen one's relationship to the cosmic universe are ultimately beyond human conception and cannot be manipulated or contrived. Knowledge within this realm of participation is not limited by human control or imagination. Knowing is premised on an existence and a reality that are an interaction of past, present, and future. Each interaction in life is an unfolding of meaning that is endless.

The consciousness of *Niitsitapi* is a source for the planet's survival. It occurs through connections with the Source of Life and is understood as balancing. The idea of balance within interdependent relationships has recently been expressed in physics. Scholars have compared Indigenous and quantum physics concepts of reality (Peat 1994; Sharpe 1993; Wolf 1991; Zukav 1979). The most notable comparison is with Bell's Theorem that informs us

I am standing between two beaver pelts. I remember a time when we lived on the land.

that there is no such thing as "separate parts." All the "parts" of the universe are connected in an intimate and immediate way previously claimed by mystics and other scientifically objectionable people. (Zukav 1979, 257)

Furthermore,

we seem to be a part of a basic oneness with the universe, not only concerning the origins of our constituent elements, the chemicals that compromise our bodies, but also in regard to the physical laws that govern us. (Dossey 1985, 79)

Tribal life is premised on the interdependence and interconnection of the universe. This basic natural law permeates ancient tribal wisdom and can be found in the stories, ceremonies, and social organization of *Niitsitapi*. The number four is an example of this: ceremonies include the four elements of the universe, the four directions, and certain rituals are performed four times and often require four songs. The number four is the relationship within which *Niitsitapi* connect with the deeper levels of consciousness and experience the immanent nature of life while renewing their responsibilities of balance.

Living in awareness and being mindful of life is the entrance to becoming *Siksikaitsitapi*. I often found myself reflecting on events that occurred. I developed a habit of constantly being aware of the sounds and movements of life; at the same time, I became increasingly cognizant of my own thoughts and movements. It is through this awareness that I began to understand the process of finding peace and the security of silence. I felt spirits, guides, and ancestors as they came through and around me. But first I had to give up attachments to my beliefs and assumptions about how my life should be while developing my trust in the process of life and universal intelligence. As this process deepened, it seemed to seep into every aspect of my life: into my thoughts, behaviour,

intentions, and the words I spoke. I became aware of my listening and
my emotions, both of which brought me to connect with a knowing that
permeates the universe. Seeing and sensing the beauty, power, and delicate balance of life was another dimension of knowing. I heard the early-
morning and late-night calls of the owl, and the deer seemed to come
visit when I needed to be in a loving and understanding space. These experiences became more pronounced and deliberate, more satisfying and
engaging. Over time, I became aware that the ancient tribal knowledge
that I was seeking was present for all time. *Niita'kaiksa'maikoan* had said,

> Our traditions, our way of life is not lost. It is us, the people, who are
> lost. (P. Standing Alone, personal communication, November 1996).

And the words of one *Kaaahsinnoon* during the dissertation convocation
now had a much deeper meaning:

> These children are really lost. They do not know who they are or
> who their relatives are. Some of them have come back home and
> we don't know who they are. They have been away since they were
> babies. Some were raised far away. It is only when they come back
> that they know who they are and where they come from.

I had a deep connection with the meaning of these words; they seem
to be part of my being. They are me and my experiences. I was raised
far away from my tribal relations and therefore did not know who
I was. My understanding continues to deepen as I experience the world
as *Siksikaitsitapi*.

Our knowledge and knowing process are not lost, nor are they irrelevant
for a highly industrialized and technological society. They are a way that
can begin to generate renewal and balance on a planet that the human
species is destroying. They are a way of being that can produce knowledge
to reunite and strengthen our interdependence as a community of kinship
alliances. The healing power of tribal wisdom, Indigenous ways of know-

ing, and our ability as human beings to renew and strengthen the alliances of a cosmic universe can reverse the path of destruction on which we find ourselves. One *Kaaahsinnoon* said,

> The creator said: we have one more chance to be Indian.

Another said,

> It is time to teach our children our way of life. *Aatsimoyihkaan*, prayer, is the most powerful way. This is how it will happen. If something is difficult, then you call upon Ihtsipaitapiiyo'pa.

Knowing is in the good heart. It means knowing who we are and knowing the Source of Life, the energy that is in constant motion; this we refer to as our way of life, *Niipaitapiiyssinni*. It is the source of *Niitsitapi* ways of knowing. I am only at the beginning point of understanding the relationships that constitute the identity of *Siksikaitsitapi*. My understanding deepens each time I participate in ceremony. Being *Niitsitapi* means living life with the sacred; now "knowing" comes through living up to the reponsibilities of maintaining and renewing the sacred balance of our natural alliances.

The educational institutions who have a mandate to provide culturally based curricula, together with grandparents and societies, are faced with the unprecedented challenge of reconstructing *Niitsitapi* responsibilities of knowing – Indigenous science. This task of recovering our identity and responsibilities is novel in the history of *Niitsitapi*. The challenge for us is to commit to the development and implementation of disciplines, theories, skills, and practices that are founded upon Indigenous epistemologies and pedagogy. This challenge will no doubt make significant and transformational changes among tribal people by altering their consciousness from colonialism to a renewed and contemporary tribalism.

Tribal consciousness is interdependent with cosmic relationships. It is of the same transformational and creative nature as the universe. The nature of a cosmic universe can be seen as ecological balance and ecological knowledge which must, once again, be acknowledged and regenerated through Indigenous ways of knowing. *Niitsitapi* ways of knowing are required for the reconstruction of an ecological world.

The need to implement traditional *Niitsitapi* epistemologies and pedagogy creates unprecedented challenges for the representation of lived knowledge within existing tribal institutions. Such knowledge can be found in the ways of life among *Niitsitapi*. The transformational and creative forces of tribal wisdom are embodied in the songs, stories, rituals, and languages of our cultures. The challenge is to reconstruct our responsibilities by living as *Niitsitapi* and by establishing and maintaining the necessary relationships with stories, language, songs, etc., so that our children can begin to understand how this knowledge can be applied to daily circumstances. *Niitsitapi* educational curricula must incorporate experiential learning, e.g., by visiting and listening to the grandparents, by observing and listening to the ecological changes and patterns of our environment, and by using Aboriginal languages as instruments of curriculum development and means of making connections with alliances.

Tribal educational institutions will impact our communities in a transformational manner by implementing *Niitsitapi* epistemologies and pedagogy. These ways of knowing represent our ethical and moral responsibilities that can produce knowledge that renews and restores balance. This process is the beginning of self-determination. Those who practice *Niitsitapi* ways of knowing will be able to generate knowledge that reunites tribal people with alliances of a cosmic order. Through this process of knowing, we will, once again, experience the collective approach to knowledge that maintains balance among the people and our relatives in the rest of the universe. The knowledge generated by *Niitsitapi* epistemologies will reunite us with our own meaning and purpose of existence. These ways of knowing could possibly transform colonial processes and create meanings and experiences that transform victims to free and self-determining communal people. In consequence, we will no longer perceive and relate to the universe individualistically but as co-creators and participants of the cosmic unfolding of universal intelligence that is observed in the unity and diversity among Indigenous cultures. Unity and diversity are the strength of the natural world. Tribal peoples around the globe maintain and strengthen the natural world through their ceremonies.

The goal of *Niitsitapi* has always been to maintain the balance of life, including our own personal life. In fact, the ontological responsibilities contextualize the experiences of *Niitsitapi* as sacred and regenerative. The sacredness of life and the relationships that are derived from this context charge tribal people with the planetary responsibility of sustainable environment. This tremendous obligation can be achieved through the application of Indigenous science. The opportunity of generating this knowledge would place tribal people in positions of fulfilling their basic ontological responsibilities. The transformational forum of *Niitsitapi* ways of knowing is premised on our ways of being, these ways of being are with a world and a universe, which are predicated on relationships that form the basis of their sacred science. Transformations occur by way of the consciousness of human beings and not through scientific technologies, whether Indigenous or Eurocentred; they occur in the context of sacred responsibilities to cosmic alliances. These sacred alliances constitute *Niitsitapi* ways of knowing. Tribal educational institutions that incorporate *Niitsitapi* ways of knowing will alter the existing conditions of dependency among Indigenous peoples and foster a consciousness of tribal responsibilities and, consequently, self-determination.

Afterword: Remembering Ancestral Conversations

by Jürgen W. Kremer

Why should a person who is not *Siksikaitsitapi* or *Niitsitapi* read this book? Why should a social worker, educator, psychologist, or health professional from a different cultural background or tradition be immersed in *Siksikaitsitapi* ways of knowing? Why did I as a White, Euro-American and German person become involved with this text, and how did I approach it as colleague, consultant, editor?

Attempting to answer these questions leads to the heart of one of our significant contemporary challenges – healing the wounds that have arisen as a consequence of colonial history and a set of European ideologies that have had a devastating impact on Indigenous peoples. In a system of victimization, both victimizer and victim carry wounds. Decolonization is not just a challenge for Indigenous peoples, but just as much for peoples who have consciously or unconsciously participated in a supremacist and racist system. Dr. Betty Bastien's book speaks powerfully about the importance of the remembrance of traditional ways for future survival, cultural integrity, and renewal. In fact, she has translated *Siksikaitsitapi* epistemology to a degree unequalled in the literature. This is the unique achievement of this book. Tribal renewal is a way out of victimry. This raises the question: What are "White people" to do? How are they to decolonize? How are they to engage with Indigenous peoples if the occasion or the request arises?

At the heart of any answers to these questions lies the challenge to establish egalitarian and respectful exchanges among cultures, whether in the arena of natural science knowledge, healing expertise, psychology, or any other. This means to establish legislation, social services, and educational systems that are not based on implicit or explicit supremacist notions.

The first step in this process may be to recognize that not all cultural differences are of the same order. The cross-cultural differences between indigenous and Eurocentred peoples as qualitative, rather than quantitative. Another way of saying this is: Cross-cultural differences between Eurocentred peoples are of the same order, and cross-cultural differences between *Niitsitapi* peoples are of the same order, but the differences between these two groups are of a different order or quality. This may be one of the most important messages of this book. Dr. Bastien identifies these very distinctions in her discussions of differences in self-construction. If we read her message carefully we cannot fail to notice the blinders that the Eurocentred paradigm provides to its initiands and the qualitatively different ontology, epistemology, and pedagogy that results from a qualitatively different way of being. Of course, the Eurocentred social sciences have in many places come to the point where nineteenth-century evolutionism has been abandoned and where the claim that industrial societies are more evolved than the varieties of indigenous societies has been jettisoned. Yet, how did we of European ancestry come to the place where we would make claims of supremacy that, in retrospect, are as pernicious as ludicrous? People of European descent or people who have entered the Eurocentred process of consciousness have split themselves off from an ongoing interaction with place, ancestry, animals, plants, spirit(s), community, story, ceremony, cycles of life, and cycles of the seasons and ages. This dissociation has created a conceptualization of social evolution in which a major shift has occurred from prehistory to history, from oral traditions to writing civilizations, from the immanent presence of spirit(s) to the transcendence of god(s). We engage in acts of imperialism – however subtle they may be – as long as we don't understand our own shamanic and indigenous roots, our ancestral alliances and nurturing conversations with our relations. We can only be part of an egalitarian knowledge exchange and dialogue if we know who we are as indigenous people. If I know who I am as an indigenous or cultural person (however fragmented that understanding may be), then I *may* be able to relate to Indigenous peoples as an equal partner in dialogue, rather than arrive as an outsider intent on finding "Truth" (the implicit assumption of the Eurocentred paradigm is that this "Truth" then ultimately *should* also become the tribe's "Truth" as evolution continues, and the tribe investigated advances on the evolutionary ladder, thus presumably incorporating the "Truth" of advanced civilizations as self-identified by their elites).

Dialog partners have the historic task of healing the history of projective identification in relation to indigenous peoples. The Eurocentred, well-bounded ego frequently cannot see how colonial past and present are part of the deep structure of such encounters, how they are present whether talked about or left unspoken or unconscious. Dr. Bastien discusses the potentially pernicious and deadly impact of such self-construction in her discussion of the ongoing history of genocide. It is this masterful ego which is likely to project from its personality make-up whatever it has dissociated from into its own past or onto indigenous peoples. In fact, projective identification may be the most apt clinical term to point to the psycho-emotional process Eurocentred cultures are engaged in with contemporary Indigenous peoples (this term also acknowledges that history is carried and handed down specifically in the process of socialization within each individual). Projective identification means that other people are made to feel the highly conflicted and split-off material dominant cultures unconsciously inject into them – so that they feel and experience it as if it is their own. Indigenous peoples may feel the Eurocentred dissociation from prehistory, ancestry, nature, etc., as self-hatred ("primitives"), the internalized destructive notions of supremacy. Of course, self-hatred as an effect of internalized colonization warrants a much longer statement than I can offer here. Notably, in individual psychotherapy, projective identification is known to be a pathological process oftentimes quite resistant to change because of its strongly self-reinforcing nature; this would seem to imply that we can assume strong resistance to healing of the history of colonialism in the relationship between Indigenous and Eurocentred cultures. I would think that the retraction of these projections is the first order of business for members of dominant societies; for this we need a different metaphor than "regression in the service of the ego," which is appropriate for individual psychotherapy. I suggest that the integration of history and prehistory qua connection with indigenous roots (recovering indigenous mind) is an appropriate terminology. The reintegration of cultural shadow material presupposes the possibility of an ego – the indigenous ego in communal conversation, if you wish – which would be differently constructed than our contemporary ego can easily imagine. This means, fundamentally, to realize that there are no Indians. *Siksikaitsitapi* are *Niitsitapi*, not Indians. The word *Indian* is not only a mistaken identification, but also a continuing signifier for the supremacist discourse of whiteness. As Gerald Vizenor and many others have pointed out, *Indians* were invented by the latecomers who could not see Indigenous peoples for who they were and are. Socialized as a white man in Germany, it was *Indians* I had been trained to perceive. My idealizations of Native American people were initially fed by the romanticism the German writer Karl May[4] infused in me as a child.

My answer to the question "how should White people decolonize?" or "how should we engage with *Niitsitapi*?" is this: We need to engage in and recover what might be called a nurturing conversation, in other words: seek that deep still place "that Indians know about." Such quality of inquiry and conversation means that I make myself present to the current moment and to what went before, to present and past; it means to be present to the cycle of seasons, the celestial movements, the weather, the land, the past of the land, the plants and animals, and to fellow human beings; it means seeking a place in community, whether natural or intentional, where story, ceremony, cultural history, and individual history matter; it means the struggle to align rational, emotional, somatic, and spiritual senses, understandings, and meanings; it means remembering the stories of languages, the history each word carries; it means looking at

---

4 Prolific German author Karl May (1842–1912) wrote many novels about the wild west, with legendary tales about a noble Indian named Winnetou and his German blood-brother, Old Shatterhand. They have sold over 100 million copies and have been translated into over thirty languages.

shadow material as well as acknowledging and healing denials and splits (internal and external). It means not just thinking about rights, but also obligations. It means discovering spirits in symbols and using metaphors to create the possibility of spiritual presence. And then there is the creative play of chance, vision, and insight, the movement of tricksters. Visionary narratives of this kind are boundaried by the land lived on, by the seasons, by the movement of animals, now seemingly chance, now predictable. Tradition, when alive, is mirror and inspiration, it challenges and is challenged as old vision rubs against new. This is something quite different from an asphyxiating traditionalism. Tradition is never singular as it is kept alive through different individuals experiencing it and caring for it, except in the minds of some mythologists or anthropologists; living tradition is always an agonistic play of contending interpretations cared for as lived knowledge and embodied by different individuals, cared for with the intent of being true to its heart and spirit. More than anything, the practice I am trying to point to seems to mean listening and inner quieting, rather than speaking. Entering such nurturing conversation means for White people the beginning of decolonization. For Indigenous peoples, the remembrance of their alliances means self-affirmation and the healing from colonial history.

Engaging in inquiry and conversation of the quality just described means recovering connections to my own indigenous roots, the times and places where such nurturing conversations or balancing ways may have occurred. However, the proposition that a German connect with indigenous roots is a difficult one. I have been exhorted to do so by Native American friends and colleagues on numerous occasions. The only way I could conceive of doing so was by painstakingly tracking the various historical changes and distortions of what might be called the layer of an Indigenous paradigm analogous to the *wina·má·bakěya'* or *Siksikaitsitapi* paradigm (the Pomo and Blackfoot people of the dominant discourse). I do not regard this dimly visible layer as ideal; not at all; however, I do think it mandatory that we give it greater presence in the awareness of the

Eurocentred mind and that there are important paradigmatic matters we can learn from it.

The beautiful surprise for me was, once I had worked my way through embarrassment, shame, and various forms of resistance, that I began to discover powerful images that describe a worldview very different from, yet related to, the *Siksikaitsitapi* cultural practices described in this book. They seem to have similar qualities. The central image of my ancestral tradition is the tree of life, and outside of Koblenz on the river Rhine a circle with a pole in the centre has been unearthed by archaeologists – it bears an apparent resemblance to the outline of a sundance arbor. At the root of this tree sit three women who reach into the well of memory to lift fertile riches, *auður* (the white clay, *aurr*) to dabble the dales with. One of the women is called *Urðr*, memory, the second *Skuld*, the woman of obligation, the keeper of the moon cycles and scorer of runes, and the third is called *Verðandi*, becoming or unfolding. In this ancient Norse or Germanic worldview, one could not take a step forward into the future without taking a step backward into memory – moving forward in balance meant remembering, reaching into the well of memory. On top of the tree stands *Heimdallur*, guardian and shaman; he watches at the beginning of what is the rainbow bridge during daytime and the Milky Way at night (*bilrost*). From here people may travel to the realms of the ancestors. The first humans of my tradition were created by three men and three women from two trees. This gives a brief idea of the old Vanir way of conceiving of balancing. With it comes a notion of healing that is very different from modern medical notions, but akin to *Siksikaitsitapi* notions. "To heal" is etymologically connected with the German *heilen*, and the Indo-European root **kailo-*, referring to a state and process of wholeness ("whole" also being related to this root). But "to heal" is also connected to "holy" (as is *heilen* to *heilig*), which gives an ancient root to the reemergent holistic and transpersonal perspectives on healing. Lincoln (1986, 118) concludes his analysis of "healing" in the Indo-European context by stating "that it is not just a damaged body that one restores to wholeness and health, but the very universe itself.... The full extent of such knowledge is now revealed in all its grandeur: the healer must understand and be prepared to manipulate nothing less than the full structure of the cosmos."

For me there is no presumption at all that indigenous roots help us remember some ideal paradise from which retro-romantic minds can concoct yet another utopian system. What I believe matters is the difference in paradigm between modernist thought and Indigenous paradigms. Here, it seems, the modern mind can learn something urgently needed for the future. Not dealing with the presence of Indigenous European roots and the history of distortions empowers romantic and nostalgic projections onto Native American and other tribal peoples. The "ecological Indian" and similar notions are birthed out of the perverse dynamic of idealization and an unconscious yearning to be Indian or some other Native, on the one hand, and racism and Indian-hating, on the other. That we were all tribal at some point in history is trivial, what is not trivial is the lack of integration of tribal pasts and the resulting racist and genocidal machinations.

What is at times seen as the classical shamanic initiation can be described as a process in which the initiand is entirely picked apart, down to each single bone, before being put back together. It seems to me that the contemporary shamanic initiation for people out of their indigenous minds not only requires something of that sort, but also the prior dark night experience of our collective situation, past and present. Unless we allow ourselves to be picked apart by the monstrosities we have created in history, we may not be able to re-create ourselves as human beings capable of a nurturing conversation without significant splits (while holding those splits that seem inevitable for the moment in compassionate awareness). This I consider the healing of history and the washing of words. The spirits that lurk in the shadows are just as real as the spirit helpers that a practitioner may wish to acquire. For me these issues became obvious as I was looking at the historical relationship between European and Indigenous peoples and as I was trying to understand what equitable knowledge exchange and a cross-cultural nurturing conversation might mean – I could not conceive of it without becoming present to the violent events of colonization, Christianization, genocide, and internalized colonization.

And with it I had to acknowledge the state of consciousness, the normative dissociation, that enabled such global violence. This type of split seems to be the psychological ingredient necessary for the scale of violence we are faced with. Painful awareness of historical shadow material started a slow healing process in myself.

Undergoing the dismemberment by the demons of history is the recovery of the nurturing conversation. Occasional laughter at our follies, hypocrisies, and ludicrous grandiosities may be a useful additive to compassion and empathy in the struggle for more encompassing truthfulness. This may enable us not only to imagine how we might right historical wrongs, but also how we might use the powerful technology, the abundant resources, and the wealth of information in our hands for the benefit of individuals and communities. The initiation by way of the remembrance of indigenous roots entails the death of the self that we grew up to be and the rebirth of this self enlarged and changed by spiritual presences. Historically, people of Eurocentred mind generally have forced Native peoples to die as sovereign people engaged in their own and unique visionary nurturing conversation in the place they inhabited and, if they survived physically, forced them to be reborn as people of Eurocentred mind. The residential schools all over the American continent were the most obvious illustration of this genocidal violence; there, the educational structure was designed to kill the Indian so that a person of European mind might live. Presently the challenge for people of White mind seems to be to die as the dissociated selves they have become and to be reborn as selves that can exercise not just their rationality but other neglected aspects of self-experience. Thus they may re-awaken their potential to become present in the way of Indigenous peoples. This would increase the capacity to honour the multiple truths humans can create.

At one point in my struggle to recover the connection with my roots, I identified myself as "Teuton" or "Myrging." I was standing in a circle of Native Americans who were affirming their presence amidst the projections and denials the dominant culture had foisted upon them. From the Native perspective, such affirmation of ancestry seemed entirely natural.

But from a German perspective, this identification may look anywhere from silly to nonsensical or ludicrous. I don't think it was any of this. The labels "Teuton" and "Myrging" are as problematic as the label "German," albeit for different reasons. "Teuton" provokes a connection with a memory not only of an unsavory part of German history, but also those parts of my ancestral history that are denied the presence that can heal the Karl May projections onto Native Americans – projections of the desire for the mythic, the wild and natural, and communal connection.

So, here I stand on the place of my settlement, in California, on *Wina·má·bbakĕya'* land, listening, listening to my ancestors. It is a place where the people are absent to my German and American mind, yet present to the stories the Vanir people, the pre-Indo-European people of the north, told. My presence arises from lineages that emerged from Lithuania and the Alsace, from border crossings that constitute my ancestral lines and from my own border crossings inside and outside. The Old Norse image of memory with the three women by the well spreading the white fluid of memory and destiny across the lands, with the guardian of the ages standing on top of the tree, has sexual connotations in the deepest sense of creativity. Reaching into memory to tell as complete a story as possible is creative and healing, re-generative. It celebrates the lifeforce we carry and the imaginative possibilities of our visionary presence boundaried by the cycles of the seasons and the flight of the raven. The observation of the black-feathered bird is as important as its mythic counterpart Raven. The presence to *Indian* warriors, *mission* bells, *digger* pines in the California flora means the double presence to scarlet red and brownish purple flowering plants and grayish-green pine trees as well as presence to the history of genocide (the murder of *Digger Indians*) with its creation of a tribal absence.

It is from within this process of reconnecting with my ancestral indigenous roots that I had the privilege of becoming part of Dr. Betty Bastien's process of retraditionalization. I am grateful for the deepening understanding not only of *Siksikaitsitapi* decolonization, but also of my own ongoing immersion in the worldview of my ancestors. The glossaries developed with the help of Duane Mistaken Chief provided invaluable insight into *Niitsitapi* thinking and being. So, why should social workers, educators, psychologists, and health professionals read this book? The answer is simple: Just as Dr. Bastien can function as a guardian and gatekeeper of *Siksikaitsitapi* ways of knowing, so we need guardians and gatekeepers on the other side, as it were – people of European mind and heritage need to work to prevent the enforcement of Eurocentred ways of knowing onto *Niitsitapi* and ensure egalitarian frameworks for knowledge exchange (whether in the form of legislation, government regulations, educational curricula, the delivery of health services or any of the other arenas where *Niitsitapi* and non-*Niitsitapi* people interface). This means White people taking responsibility for decolonization.

The tragedy of the modernist Western mind is the prevalent conviction that closure, Truth, and certainty are possible and desirable goals. Viewed from a distance, this appears to be not only a loss of wonder, presence, and comedy, but an altogether ludicrous folly in view of the historical realities human beings have engaged with. If we people of European mind and ancestry remember our own indigenous roots and confront historical shadow material, then all of us may be able to re-contextualize what indeed may be knowledge advances generated within that tradition of thought by making it part of a nurturing conversation or grounding it in a cosmic universe of alliances. Once dissociated knowledge has become associated again in this fashion, we may be well on the way to overcome the unbearable stories of genocide and the violence of ecocide. Dr. Bastien has done a service not only to her own people and other *Niitsitapi*, but also to people outside of her culture by posing this very challenge of decolonization and providing tremendous inspiration.

Glossaries

by Duane Mistaken Chief, with Jürgen W. Kremer

Siksikaitsipowahsin–English

A'ksistoowapsiwa – An ambitious person.

A'mii, Tatsikiiyakokiiysinni – That centre tepee, or: over at the centre tepee.

A'tso – A particle of *Matsisski*, meaning brave, courageous, daring; *A'tso* does not stand alone at any time; it is combined in the following manner: *Kana'tsomita* [Brave Dogs], *A'tsapssi* [went crazy], *A'tsapssi* [brave or crazy].

Aaahsiks – Former bundle holders, beginning with two generations back. (*Naaahs* [my grandparent], *Kaaahs* [your grandparent], *Kaaahsinnooniksi* [our grandparents], *Oomaaahsowaiksi* [their grandparents], *Aawaaahsskataiks* [those we use as grandparents in ceremony]). "Grandparents" is *aaahsiks*. These are former bundle holders who transferred their bundles to the people who are now the present *Naatowa'po'n* [holy father] and *Natowa'po'ksist* [holy mother]. They are the grandparents in this family structure. They are two generations from the present bundle holders and include succeeding generations of bundle holders. These are the elders of the societies. *Aaahs* means more than just grandparents; in this context, it means "those that you approach and seek advice from," *Aawaaahsskataiks*. See also entry "grandparents" in English–*Siksikaitsipowahsin* glossary.

Aaak Atowapsiyawa – Literally "they are going to be of the sacred nature." They are going to take part in the sacred.

Aaapan – Blood.

Aahkaikinniiyoisskitsipahpyo's – "That we should be of the soft heart."

Aahsaitapiiyssin – Literally "Good living." This is a request for the granting of a good life.

Aahsapsi – "Of the good."

Aahsitapi – "[Of the] good person." The assumption is that a good person is a generous and kind person.

Aakainaimmawa – Authority, literally "we would accord respect to like a leader or chief." Other contexts require different words: If a person is an authority in all aspects of ceremonies, one would say *Iiksoksksinnim Naatowapi*, "that [person] really knows the sacred," "he is an authority on the sacred." If a person has knowledge of many different things, such as, life, the sacred, etc., then one could use *Iikokakiwa*, "he is knowledgeable, intelligent and wise." If one refers to a person that is an authority on the subject of the sacred, one would qualify it by saying *Iikokaksksstsim Naatowapi*, "he is knowledgeable about the sacred." The most important person in any given situation is *O'to'tamsiwa*, "the most important person." This term is translated in the Blackfoot dictionary as "authority." This is an oversimplification, as the following examples show: *Iiko'to'tamapiwa*, "prayer is the most important;" *O'to'tamaaahs*, "the main elder [grandfather] or most important elder [grandfather];" *Niitap O'to'tamapiwa Isskinnimatstohksinni*, "education is very important." Authority cannot be simply translated to *O'to'tamsiwa*. You could precede it by saying *Iito'to'tamsiwa* and add on whatever he is the *O'to'tamsiwa* in. *Siksikaitsitapi* culture frowns upon those who consider themselves as the authority; they are expected to be humble. A person is considered an authority by proving himself/herself knowledgeable and humble, and exhibits humility.

Aakainawa – Many Chiefs (*Kainai*).

Aako'ka'tssin – Sundance; literally "circle encampment."

Aakomimihtaan – Love, or the object of a person's love.

Aamato'simmaan – Incense, smudge.

Aamsskaapipiikani – South Peigan now located in Montana
(a.k.a. Blackfeet)
and the *Aapatohsipikani* or *Skinnii Pikani* (a.k.a. North Peigan) are
located in Canada.

Aanoo itapaitapiiyopi – "Here, here we are living [physically]"; "reality."

Aaotoomakiiiks – "Those that [walk] first." Leaders.

Aapaa – Weasel in white winter phase.

Aapaitsitapi – "White pelt weasel real people;" mistranslated as "blood"
(*Aaapan* is "blood").

Aapatohsipiikani – North Peigan (or *Skinnii Pikani*), presently
in Canada.

Aato – Comes from *Naatoyii*, which some scholars have said is that power
that is in the universe. The same power as the sun. *Naatosi* means
"a thing is of that power." Found in central words, such as "Sun"
[*Naatosi*], "sacred, prayer," and "power."

Aato'si – Powerful; a reflection of the sun's power (*Naatosi* = Sun). To have
sacred power, i.e., healing powers.

Aatooopissin – Sitting holy; sitting meditatively in ceremony.

Aatosin – Sacred medicine powers.

Aatsimapi – Holy or sacred.

Aatsimihkasin – Sacred way, behaviour, actions, acting.
(*Aawatsimihkasatawa* is derived from *Aatsimihkasin*).

Aatsimoyihkaan – Literally "Sacred way of speaking." When one prays,
one should be of good heart. If one's heart is bad as a result of anger,
sadness, or anything perceived as bad, it is not a good heart. Prayer
should always be done with a good heart as its source. *Ikinniiyoiss
kitsipahpahsinni* means "having a gentle or soft heart;" softness is
related to gentleness and peace, *ikinnapi*, meaning "gentle peaceful
ways." *Niitsitapi* strive to live their lives in the way of *ikinnapi*, peace,
gentleness, and caring "softness." Depending on context, being of
good heart can be translated as *Akaikinniiyoisskitsipahpyo'p*, "we are
being of the soft heart." The essence of good heart would be *Ikinniioih
kitsipahpahsin*, "soft, heart, of it (essence)."

Aatsimoyihkaani – Literally "sacred way of speaking." (See *Aatsimoyihkaan*.) *Aatsimoyihkaani* with the "i" is the same as *Aatsimoyihkaan* without the "i." The "i" is added in speaking usually in a third-person context.

Aawaaahsskataiksi – Those elders who are approached for everything from advice to conducting ceremonies. Ceremonial parents. They necessarily have to have acquired transfers of bundles and other sacred items and have now transferred them to others. In some cases, they have to be four generations previous to the present bundle holders.

Aawaatooopi – The person who sits holy in ceremony, i.e., the person sitting next to the "conductor" of the All-Smoke Ceremony (*Kano'tsiisissinni*) who represents the person or persons that vowed to have the *Kano'tsiisissin*.

Aawaatowapsi – "The person is having a sacred ceremony."

Aawaatowapsiiks – Ceremonialist. This term refers to those that have the right to and take part in sacred activities and ceremonies. This term is distinct from *Aopaatoom*, the conductor of a ceremony, "the one that sits." Context, e.g., *Aopaatoom*, ceremonies, would clarify. *Aopaatoom* is usually an elder or grandparent. He or she sits at the head of the circle of the ceremony, the west centre.

Aawaatoyinnaiyi – To sing sacred songs or when a bundle is called on to protect your house, it is said to be *Aawaatoyinnaiyi*.

Aawaatsimihkaasatai – We can think of it as a return to balance for taking – as in asking for forgiveness from the animals we kill and thereby returning to the sacred balance in our relationship with them.

Ahkooomohsin – Vow.

Ahkoyinnimaan – Pipe.

Ainnakowawa – To respect (related to: *Iinniiyim*).

Aipommotsp – We are transferred; it was given or passed on (pl.: *Aipommotsspists*).

Aipommotsspistsi – Those things that we have transferred to us.

Ais saak otsistapitsihk niipaitapiiyssinni – Seeking to understand life.

Aisiimohki – Person is giving guidance and cautioning (*Siimohkssin* = guidance).

Aisiimoki (*aisksinnima'tsoki*) – (Person is giving) guidance; teachings, discipline.

Aisksinnima'tstohki – Teacher.

Aissksinihp – We know it to be like that.

Aissksinnimatsoki – [Subject] is teaching us.

Aistammatsstohksin – Teachings.

Aistommatoominniki – "When you have made it part of your body," "embodying your knowledge." This quality of coming to know your heart designates "indigenous epistemology." When one has come to the point where one lives one's knowledge, one begins to understand. It is through living it that one gains a greater understanding. Also refers to "when a person begins to really know anything," e.g., ceremonies; it is only when *Aistotsis*, "when [the person] actually participates," that he or she knows what they are all about.

Aistommatop – Variation of previous Aistommatoominniki. Aistommatoominniki is used in a context such as telling aperson, "When you have come to embody it, " as opposed to discussing the concept, i.e., "at the point that you come to embody it..." lit. "at the instant you have to embody the knowledge."

Aistotsis – "When [the person] actually participates."

Akaaotsistapi'takyop – To be cognizant and to discern tribal connections; sacred science; knowing as experiential knowing.

Akaikinniioyihkitsipahpyo'p – "We are being of the soft heart."

Akaitapiiks – Ancestors; the old people.

Akaitapiwa – Ancestor; lit. "the old [days] people or people of the past." Plural: *Akaitapiiks*.

Akaotsistapi'takyo'p – Coming to know; the definition of this word is "we have come to understand [not merely know] it." Cf. *Issksinihp*. To be cognizant and to discern the tribal connections; it refers to our sacred science and thus to the way to connect with our relations once again experientially through our ways of knowing; sacred science; knowing as experiential knowing.

Aksistowapsiwa – An ambitious person.

A'mii Tatsikiiyakokiiysinni – The centre tepee over there. ref. to the centre tepee.

A'nn, Aitamatsitsipssatsiiyop – That is it; we will talk again.

Annai – "That is."

Annai maotokowa – Buffalo pound, "that is the Maotokowa," meaning "buffalo pound" or "corral." *Annai* means "that is." (Otherwise, the buffalo pound is commonly called, *Piskaan*.) Within the context of the Maotokiiks origin story *Maotokiiks* comes from *Maotokowa*, i.e., the pound from which a buffalo cow gave instructions for the society. This interpretation is debatable. The *Maotokiiks* [members] know the stories better, yet the account used here comes from a good, although controversial, source. In the end, it is probably the *Maotokiiks* or one of its members that should be the authority on the matter. (See Buffalo Women's Society.) "Corral" is *Miistsipiskaan* – "wooden corral." However, when talking about the buffalo pound, it is called *Piskaan*. *Maotokowa* also means a "washout" or "gully," natural formations often used as buffalo pounds.

Annai Niitsi – "That is how it is."

Ao'kaawa – Lady sponsoring the *Ookaan*.

Ao'kaiksi – Collective term for: those that undertake the ceremony of the *Ookaan*.

Ao'maopo'si, Kii annik poohsapoohtsi – "When we settled [in one place] and toward [today]."

Ao'ohpoiskinahki – "When [person] has had face painted."

Ao'ta'sao'si – Era of the horse; the start of the horse era and any point thereafter prior to "modern" days.

Ao'tsistapitakyo'p – The moment or the occasion you come to know.

Ao'tsistapitakyoki – Transformational consciousness.

Aohkannaistokawa – "Two of everything;" polar opposites such as: male and female; good and bad, etc. No specific term for balance.

Aohpoiskinna – "[Person] is getting face painted."

Aopaatoom – Conductor of ceremony, "the one who sits."

Aotsistapitsihk Maanistsihp – Literally "when we understand how it is," "how the universe is with its natural laws," or "how the order of all things is." Consciousness of the natural order. Cf. *Maksinniiks* story under entry "align" for an illustration. In it, the man was shown what the "order of things"

was for the *Makoiyiiks*; therefore, he was able to emulate them to achieve the same things.

Apaipikssi – Protection to get help, and others.

Api – White.

A'pi'pikssiwa – A person who is seeking help for self or others. Lit. running around in fear of something [and seeking deliverance from danger hardship etc.]. The act is *A'pi'pikssin*.

Ihkitsikommiksi – The seven stars. "Big Dipper."

I'kitstaan – Offering; offering to the sun or other entities.

I'ta'kiwa – "Has spirit."

Ihpipo'to'tsp – What we were put here with.

Ihpi'po'to'tsspistsi – What we were put here with as our responsibilities for our survival.

Ihpowa'ksski – One of Scarface's names.

Ihtiasskinnootsp – So that we are recognized [by the spirits and *Ihtsipaitapiiyo'pa*].

Ihtsipaitapiiyo'pa – Sacred power, spirit or force that links concepts; life force; term used when addressing the sacred power and the cosmic universe; Source of Life; sun as manifestation of the Source of Life; great mystery; together with *Niitpaitapiiyssin* identifies the meaning and purpose of life. *Ihtsipaitapiiyo'pa* is that which causes or allows us to live. The term "natural law" does not have a direct *Siksikaitsitapiwahsin* equivalent; however, it is through *Ihtsipaitapiiyopa* that all "natural laws" are governed. It is *Ihtsipaitapiiyopa* that orchestrates the universe. Its laws govern the universe and including human life.

BLACKFOOT WAYS OF KNOWING

Ihtsipaitapiiyo'pi – The reason why we are caused to be up and living, why we live through the Source of Life.

Iikawa – "He or she was given a share." Often used in relation to giving someone a share of the food, money, etc.

Iiko'to'tamapiwa – It is of the utmost importance, i.e., *Iiko'to'tamapiwa Aatsimoyihkaan* = "Prayer is of the upmost importance."

Iikokakiwa – "He is knowledgeable, intelligent and wise."

Iiksissksta'kyomopistaiksi – Those that have beaver bundles.

Iiksoksskinnim Naatowapi – "That [person] really knows the sacred," "he is an authority on the sacred."

Iimitaa – "Dog" or "horse."

Iinii – Specific buffalo; sg., *Iiniiks* pl., and *Iiiniiwa* coll.

Iiniiwa – Buffalo (when referring to the buffalo; sg. and pl.); *Iinii* (specific buffalo; sg. and pl.); *Iinii* (buffalo, collective form).

Iinni'yimm – grateful; synonymous with *innakowa* – Respect.

Iipommowa – Person, who has been transferred (initiated ceremonialist). Pl.: *Iipommowaiksi*.

Iipommowai – A person or persons having received something in transfers – transferred.

Iipommowaiksi – same as *Iipommowai*.

Iitawaamatosimmopi – Altar, place of smudge; literally, "Where we odorize or scent." It is an altar on the ground (in the old days and today in tepees) or in a wooden box where it is usually made from white clay in various shapes. Or it can be just a cleared or scraped area of ground. Altars vary just as the material used as incense varies from ceremony to ceremony or personal "powers" dictate. On this altar is where the sweetgrass or other material is burned by placing a hot coal on it and then sprinkling the smudge material (i.e., sweetgrass).

Iitotasimahpi Iimitaiks – Dog days. Literally "[the time] when we used dogs as burden animals."

Iitsskinnayiiks – the Horn Society, Horn Society members; also: *Omahkohkana-kaaatsiisinni* = "Big All Comrades" (possibly meaning the "Ultimate All Comrades," because, the Horn Society would be at the top if societies were arranged in a hierarchy. Other age grade societies ultimately led up to the Horn Society). Some of the societies were made up of older individuals, which also explains the "*Omahk*" in the word, which means, "old," as in *Omahkinnaa*, which means "old man." It could mean an amalgamation of several societies to form one large one that would then become an *Omahkohkanakaaatsiisinn*. See English–*Siksikaitsipowahsin* glossary.

Iiyaohkiimiiksi – Beaver bundle holder, "the ones that have water." Or *Ksisskstakyomopisstawa*, "(specifically) the one that has a beaver bundle." The two terms are interchangeable. *Ksisskstakyomopissta iksi*, "(collectively) the ones that have beaver bundles." Bundle is *Mopistaan*. *Ksisskstaki* means "Beaver. "*Ksisskstakyo*, "[of] Beaver [type]." *Ksisskstakyomopisstaan* means "the bundle is of the Beaver type." Beaver and thunder bundles were opened according to certain natural occurrences, i.e., the thunder pipe bundle is opened when thunder is first heard. The beaver bundle holders have the songs for the *Ookaan* and perform other duties as well in relation to the sundance. Their presence is desired and the *Niinaimisskaiks* were said to dictate the camp movement. Unless there was an *Ookaan*, the beaver people were not involved to any great extent. Similarly, the *Niinaimsskaiks* were not always involved to any great extent if they were not opening their bundle at the Sundance. (However, they do have ties to other, less easily noticed, activities).

Iiyiikitapi – "[Person] is brave."

Iiyiikitapiiyssin – "Bravery."

Ikimmapiiyipitsi (Ikimm) – A person exhibits the traits of caring, kindness, pity, compassion. Particle, "*Ikimm*" refers to the caring, kindness, pity, compassion.

Ikimmata'pssi (Ikimmat) – A person who needs caring, kindness, pity, compassion. (The person is in need. Analogous to "down and out.") The particle "*Ikimmat*" refers to caring, kindness, pity, compassion. The particle "*Atapsi*" means "is of the state."

Ikimmatapsi – A person who is deserving of pity; they are pitiful.

Ikinnapi – "Gentle peaceful ways."

Ikinniiyoisskitsipahpahsinni – "Having a gentle or soft heart;" softness is related to gentleness and peace.

Inna'kotsiisin – Respect (dialect. variant).

Inna'kotsiiysin – Respect (dialect. variant).

Innahkotaitsinnika'to'pi – History; "that which has been passed on through the generations through stories."

Inni'yimm – Feelings of gratitiude and appreciation towards a person.

Innakowa – Respect.

Ipissowaasi – Thinly scalloped meat hung to dry; morning star; based on Bullchild (1985), 344–45. This is Morning Star's name. *Ipissowaasi*, however, does not mean "morning star," as is commonly assumed. "Morning star" would be "*Ksiskani'kanna'soiyi*," literally "morning sparkling."

Isskanaitapsstsi – Relationship. Every action affects everything; interrelated.

Issksinihp – "We know it [to be like that]," i.e., the completed act of cognition.

Issksiniip – (Variation of *Issksinihp*) Knowing. Knowing is active participation in the world and integration of experience through reflective meditation. Knowing is the ability to make reference to past experiences, contextualizing them in a system of meanings to make sense of present experiences and formulate the basis for decision-making.

Issksinnima'tsstohksinni – Pedagogy, education in all forms.

Isspomihtaan – Sharing. *Isspomihtaan* means "helping." You share to help people. If you give something to someone, you would "*Noohtsspommowawa* / I helped [that person] with [the item]." The older word, which we hear rarely is *Iikawa*; most people would not understand it when it is spoken, especially if they read it.

Isspommotsisinni – Giving, support, and sharing.

Isstaokakitsotsp – Skills of observation that gives us knowledge through awareness.

Isstatsimihkasatawa – We give tobacco to the earth when we take from it. To give tobacco, or anything for that matter, is part of returning things to a harmonious and balanced state. When we offend someone or have had a falling out, for instance, then we might give them a gift or speak to them to set things right again. That is *Aatsimihkasin*. It is literally "sacred way behaviour/actions." With intent to return to the sacred.

Isstonnatapsiwa – A person of dangerous nature.

Itaisapsiitamiwa – Person is breathing into [subject].

Kaaahs – Your grandparent (ceremonial or otherwise). Your mother- or father-in-law.

Kaaahsinnoon – Grandfather, sg.

Kaaahsinnoona – Same as *Kaaahsinnoon*. Usually used in referring to *Kaaahsinnoon*.

Kaaahsinnooniksi – Collective term for "our grandparents." The term is understood properly in context. When the "common" *Niitsitapi* (Real People), *Niitsipoyi* (Real people language speakers – specifically Blackfoot, in this case) say "*Kaaahsinnooniksi*," it is understood that they are referring to grandfathers and grandmothers in the family structure sense. When members of the various societies or individual bundle and pipe holders say "*Kaaahsinnooniksi*," they more than likely mean previous society members, bundle holders, pipe holders, etc. These ceremonial people use it for previous "bundle/ pipe holders" who were holders two generations (transfers) before them. The set-up is the same as in a family structure. The present members are the *Naatowa'po'kos* [holy children] of the previous holders of the bundles. The previous holders are *Naatowa'po'n* [holy father] and *Naatowa'po'ksist* [holy mother] of the present holders. All former holders beyond two generations are *Aaahsiks* (*Naaahs* [my grandparents], *Kaaahs* [your grandparents], *Kaaahsinnooniksi* [our grandparents], or *Oomaaahsowaiksi* [their grandparents].) However, protocol restrictions apply to *Aawaaahsskataiksi* [those elders that are approached for everything from advice to conducting ceremonies]. They don't have "blanket privileges." For example, they can only participate in and conduct ceremonies they have gone through themselves and can only advise on certain matters as their experiences (actual participation) dictate. All other societies have similar structures.

Kaamotaan – Survival, "survival [from all perils]."

Kaamotaani – "Survival from all perils". Said with the wishes for long life used in reference to kaamotaan.

Kainai – The Blood tribe. (Also see: *Kainawa*).

Kainaikoan – a Blood Indian. Used for a male. A female person is referred to as *Kainaki*.

Kainawa – Third-party reference to *Kainai*. Pronounced "Gkai-na-[exhale "wa" from chest]." Exhale is in part a result of the release of air held at glottal stop prior to "w."

Kainawa Ot Akokatssoowai – *Kainai*, their sundance.

Kakyopissin – Meditation.

Kakyosin – The English terms "to align" and "to balance" refer to the *Siksikaitsitapi* understanding that there is an order of things or pattern that we can discern if we are observant (*Kakyosin*). We can see this in animal behaviour, weather cycles, etc. Through *Kakyosin* we align ourselves with these patterns and are thus capable of achieving the same things the observed beings can. To give an exaggerated illustration: If we behave like a cat, think like a cat, etc., we eventually become cats. This is the idea behind alignment, alliances, and *Kakyosin*. We are adopting the order of things observed to such an extent that we may even become it. Some of *Siksikaitsitapi* people were instructed by animals in what they should do to help themselves (*Iikimma*). For example, one time a man was starving, and he had nowhere to turn. He eventually came upon a decomposed carcass of a *Ksinna'oi* (not to be confused with *Omahkokoiyi* – George First Rider says that no one really knows what they are today). The man understood that these were small animals compared to the buffalo. As small as they were, they could bring these huge animals down with their teeth only and without weapons. When he slept, the spirit of the *Ksinna'oi* came to him and spoke to him in song. It gave the man these songs and his pelt (for use as a "disguise" while hunting buffalo) as a gift. He told him in detail how he should conduct a ceremony around these gifts. He was told always to conduct it before using the pelt and the knowledge. We can interpret this story as understanding (*Kakyosin*) gained by the man about the order of things as far as the life of the *Ksinna'oi* (its ways, skills, etc.) is concerned. With this knowledge, the man was able to transform into a *Ksinna'oi* and have the same success in hunting. This brief version of the story explains the importance of alignment, alliances, and *Kakyosin*.

Kakyosin isstaokakitsotsp – "Observation gives us intelligence knowledge and wisdom."

Kan – Reference to a collective; always used in combination with other world particles, never stands alone.

Kana'kaaatsiiks – Any one of the Societies, Horns, Maotokiiks, etc.

Kana'tsomitaiksi – The Brave Dogs or Brave Horses Society. This society has been called Brave Dogs for some years now; however, some people claim it is a mistranslation. They say it means "Brave Horse." Whatever the correct term is, *Kan* is a reference to a collective. *A'tso* comes from *matsisski*, meaning "brave," "courageous," "daring." *Iimitaa* = "dog" or "horse." "Dog" is *iimitaa* and "horse" is *poonokaamita* [elk dog].

Kano'tsisissin – All-Smoke Ceremony. This is a night ceremony. It is attended by past and present members of the various societies, past and present bundle holders, past and present medicine pipe holders, and others. (The common link is that all in attendance have had sacred transfers, *Iipommowai*, at one time or another). They are invited to bring their pipes for a night of praying, singing, and smoking of sacred pipes. This also a time to recount exploits. The recalling of the exploits is also the giving of the power of that event to the person who sits holy, *Aawaatooopi*. The prayers are also blessings bestowed to help that person, *Aawaatooopi*, or whomever he is representing in that position. It begins at sunset and ends after the sun rises. These ceremonies usually take place during the winter when the nights are long.

Kanohsin – Convocation; meeting.

Katoiyiisiks – Lit: "Sweet Pines." "Sweetgrass Hills" is a mistranslation of *Katoiyiisiks*.

Kii Nai'tsistomato'k Ai'stamma'tso'tsspi – Embodying or being the knowledge you have been given; making knowledge part of our body.

Kiipaitapiiyssinnooni – "Our way of life," and our connections with our ancestors; the *Siksikaitsipoyi* lifeworld that we seek to understand.

Kiitomohpiipotokoi – Role and responsibilities; "what you have been put here with." The assumption of responsibility comes with it.

Kimmapiiyipitsinni – Values; same as *kimmotsiisinni*. Compassion.

Kimmotsiisinni – Values; same as *kimmapiiyipitsinni*. This and the next term "mean kindness, caring, and including generosity." They are values within *Siksikaitsitapi* society. It is one of, if not the most, important value (see *Kimmapiiyipitsinni*).

Kipaitapiiwahsinnooni – (Dialect variation of *Kiipaitapiiysinnooni*) Our way of life. Also components of our way of life.

Kitssksah kominnooni – Geography.

Ko'komikisomm – Moon.

Koitapiiisin – Gift. There are other related words regarding gifts but in different contexts. *Koitapiiisin* is the best for overall use.

Kommo'tsisstapi – A round/cylindrical rawhide case.

Ksahkomma aatsimapiwa – "Earth is sacred."

Ksahkomma iikatsimapsiwa, aawatsimihkasatawa – "The Earth is sacred; our relationship is sacred."

Ksinna'oi – An animal similar to the coyote but it is said to no longer exist. See *Kakyosin*.

Ksiskani'kanna'soiyi – Morning star, literally "morning sparkling."

Ksissksta'kyo – Particle meaning "of the beaver type."

Ksisskstaki – Beaver.

Ksisskstakyomopisstaan – Beaver Bundle; pl. *Ksisskstakyomopisstaanistsi*.

Ksisskstakyomopistaiksi – (Collectively) the ones that have beaver bundles.

Ksisskstakyomopistawa – (Specifically) the one that has a beaver bundle.

Ksisstapsi – Ghost, literally "no real source." *Ksisstapsiiiks* pl. Cf. *Stao'o'wa*
   also ghost (pl. *Stao'oi'ks*); used when people have no ambition or are
   doing nothing of any use.

Ksisstsi'ko'm – Thunder.

Ksokoisin – Kinship alliance, for relatives in family structure.

Ma, mo'ta'k – The Spirit.

Maa Iimopisstawa – The person that has a bundle.

Maanistapaisspi – Behaviour, "the way [that a particular person is
   behaving]." Usually behaviour is referred to with qualifications (just
   as in referring to his attitude). The specific behaviour is described,
   e.g., *Sayikihkihsiwa* is a person who can't settle down including in
   relationships; *Piksiwa* is restless. *Siksikaitsitapi* language, for the most
   part, has no abstract terms. Words generally describe actions or what
   is being observed. These actions are then described to indicate what a
   person is like, what the attitude or behaviour is, or how the person is.

Maanitapiwa – The young people, the new people, our children.

Mahksinaamahkaan – Intention to acquire coup(s).

Makatowapsis – "If the person is going to have a sacred ceremony or take
   part in one."

Maohksiipssiiks – Red Belt Society.

Maotoki – Buffalo Women's Society member.

Maotokiiks – Buffalo Women's Society. Term comes from the buffalo
   pound/corral. A source indicates that the buffalo pound or corral is
   Annai Maotokowa, "that is the *maotokowa*." So *Maotokiiks* comes from
   Maotokowa. The *Siksikaitsitapi* origin legend of the *Maotokiiks* gives
   some clarity to the term *Maotokowa*.

Matoohpoiskiiit – "Go get your face painted."

Matsapsi – Brave, no regard for personal safety.

Matsisski – Brave, courageous, daring.

Miistsipiskaan – Wooden corral.

Miksinnitsi – Buffaloberry; red [baked] berry; thorny buffaloberry
   (*Shepherdia argentea*).

Misommahkoyinnimaan – Long Time Medicine Pipe, lit. long time pipe.

Misommipaitapiiyssin – Long life.

Miyohpo'koiks – Plieades, or bunched stars.

Mo'ta'k – A person's spirit; literally his or her shadow, the manifestation of the person's spirit.

Mokaksin – Knowledge, intelligence, and wisdom.

Mopisstaan – Bundle; literally "bundled [object]"

Naaahs – My grandparents (both genders – grandmother and grandfather) ceremonial or otherwise. My mother-in-law or my father-in-law.

Naaahsiks – My grandfathers. Ceremonial, biological, or extended family grandparents. Contextual usage determines definition, i.e., in the context of ceremony, they are past bundle holders, and in the context of family, they are simply grandparents of the common context.

Naamaahkaan – Coup; requires the physical and *Iiyikitapiiyssin* [bravery] characteristics to which *Niitsitapi* men aspired; complements the mission of balance, integrity, and bravery. The term "coup" means "blow" (Grinnell 1962, 245), and "to take a trophy from an enemy" (Frantz & Russell 1989, 347); it is attributed to the French traders and trappers. A direct translation of the *Siksikaitsitapi* word is "to strike the enemy." The Blackfoot term "*Naamaakaan*" means literally "to take a weapon." *Naamaa* = weapon.

Naamaahkaani – Referring to *Naamaahkaan*.

Naatosi – "Sacred power" = Sun. Also one who has sacred powers.

Naatowa'po'ksist – The [female] bundle holder prior to present holder(s), i.e., holy mother of the present bundle holders. *Naatowa'po'ksist* [holy mother] is the woman who transferred the bundle to the present bundle holders.

Naatowa'po'n – Holy father of present bundle holders, the man who transferred the bundle to the present bundle holders.

Naatowapi – Ceremony, literally "of the sacred nature," covers any ceremony. Ceremonies all have different names. Collectively, they are called *Naatowapiistsi*. If a group is going to have a ceremony, you would say, *Aaak Atowapsiyawa*, literally "they are going to be of the sacred nature." *Aaak Atowapsi* is "the person is going to have a sacred ceremony." *Aawaatowapsi* is "the person is having a sacred ceremony." *Atowapsis* is "when the person has had a sacred ceremony." *Makatowapsis* is "if the person is going to have a sacred ceremony." *Aawaatowapsiiksi* is "those people that have sacred ceremonies." That which is sacred or holy.

Naatowapo'kos – Children, i.e., holy children of the previous holders of the bundles.

Naatoyii – Power that is in the universe (according to some scholars).

Naatoyinnaiysin – Sacred songs.

Napi – Old Man; hero. Exemplifies dark powers of humanit. See English–*Siksikaitsipowahsin* glossary for explanation.

Natoa'pi – Sacred science; cf. *Naatowapi* – that which is sacred or holy.

Natowa'po'ksist – Holy mother.

Ninna – My father. Also: leader. A leader is seen as father to his followers.

Niinaimsskaahkoyinnimaan – *Niinaimsskaan* Pipe. The Thunder-pipe proper. Medicine pipe in general is *Ahkoyinnimaan*.

Niinaimsskaan and Niinaimsskaahkoyinnimaan – Said to refer to the pipe as being so expensive that only *Ninnaiksi* [Chiefs or leaders] could afford them. The transfer payments (*Sikapistaanistsi*) could run very high, but that is not always the case. *Niinaimsskaiks* also had a lot of authority (*Ninnayawa*/Were accorded a lot of respect), so "*Ninna*," is likely the source of the term *Niinamsskaiksi*. *Niinaimsskaiksi*, *Niinaimsska*, and related terms have "*Ninna*" as a prefix. See also *Ninnaa*.

Niinaimsskaayahkoyinnimaan – Variation of *Niinaimsskaahkoyinnimaan*, Thunder-pipe proper. (Sometimes referred to as leader pipe.) Pipe in general is *Ahkoyinnimaan*.

Niinaimsskaiksi – The term used commonly for the "Medicine Pipe Holders." It is not a literal translation. If translated, it would roughly be "leader possessors." More properly, the "Thunder-pipe-holders," as the pipe originally came from Thunder, *Ksisstsi'ko'm*. Beaver and thunder bundles were opened according to certain natural occurrences, i.e., the thunder pipe bundle is opened when thunder is first heard. The beaver bundle holders have the songs for the *Ookaan* and perform other duties as well in relation to the Sundance. Their presence is desired and the *Niinaimisskaiks* were said to dictate the camp movement. Unless there was an *Ookaan*, the beaver people were not involved to any great extent. Similarly, the *Niinaimsskaiks* were not always involved to any great extent (however, they do have ties to other, less easily noticed, activities).

Niinaimsskaipasskaan – Medicine Pipe Dance (Potvin 1966, 56–57).

Niinohkanistssksinipi – This is the way I know it to be (speaking personally).

Niipaitapiiwahsin – (variation of *Niipaitapiiyisinni*) The life or lifeworld of *Niitsitapi*.

Niipaitapiiyssin – Way of life, constant motion of breath; together with *ihtsipaitapiiyo'pa* identifies the meaning and purpose of life; to teach the way of life.

Niit – Real, as in *Niitsitapi*; from *Niitsi*, truth; cf. *Niitapi*

Niitaikso'kowammootsi'opi – Social structure, "how we know our relationships to be," "how we are related to each other."

Niitaoni'pii Kitao'ahsinnooni – Geography; "How we recognize our land (through geographic features)."

Niitapitapiiysinni – Live with integrity, i.e., live according to the teachings of *Niitsitapi*.

Niitap Ototamapiwa Issksinnimatstohksinni – "Education is of great importance."

Niitapaisso'pi – Refers to the way *Niitsitapi* people are, their *Niitsitapi* beingness. The particle *apais* is the part that refers to one's way of being as part of actions. *Apais* means "your actions," "the way you are moving."

Niitapi – The way it is, it is real, or it is true.

Niitsi – Truth.

Niitsi'powahsinni – Language; *niitsitapi* talking; language that carries the breath of spirit; speaking *niitsi'powahsinni* is experiencing spirit.

Niitsikso'kowammootsi'opi – "How we are related to each other," social structure.

Niitsipoyi – "Real people;" language speaker(s), sg. and pl.

Niitsitapi – Generic term for real people or all Indian, Aboriginal, or Indigenous peoples, including those that have Blackfoot as their language. *Siksikaitsipoyi* are specifically those Native people who have Blackfoot as their language; the term means "Blackfoot-speaking real people."

Niitsitapi Oopaitapiiyssoowaiyi – The lifeway of *Niitsitapi*.

Niitsitapiipaitapiiyssin – The life or lifeworld of *Niitsitapi*.

Niitssksinnipi omahtanistaissihpi – Philosophy. Literally: How we come to know how the [universe] works. (Understood only in appropriate contexts.)

Niksist – Mother (my mother).

Ninna – My father.

Ninnaa – Man; leader; a person that is accorded a lot of respect, and lately "tribal chief or councilor."

Ninnaiksi – Chiefs or leaders (plural).

Ninnaistako – Chief Mountain.

Ninnayawa – They are [leaders] to be accorded a lot of respect and authority.

Nitainaawa – Lone Chief.

Nitaisstammatsokoyi – What I have been taught (teachings).

Nitsitsihtaanists – My intentions. Sg.: *Nitsitsihtaan*.

No'ta'k – Spirit.

Noo Kainai – Here at Many Chiefs (Here at *Kainai*).

Noohtsspommowawa – I helped.

O'ohkowaipstssinni – Clan-ship. See also *Tso'ohkoway'sinni*.

O't'otamaaahs – The main elder [grandfather] or most important elder [grandfather].

O'to'tamsiwa – The most important person.

O'tsisstapi – Generic term for "bundle." Rawhide case holding the contents of the bundle, i.e., *Kommo'tsisstapi* = a round/cylindrical rawhide case. *Pokotsstapi* = small rawhide case. Also: *Mopisstaan*, which literally means, "bundled [object]."

Omaaahsowaayi – The sacred Horn Society's sacred grandparents.

Omahkitapiiks – Elders or old people, in general.

Omahkohkanakaaatsiiks – The big all comrade [individuals].

Omahkohkanakaaatsiisinni – Big All Comrades; see *Iitsskinnayiiks*. In the past most people would not refer to the Horns, *Iitsskinnayiiks*, by that name out of reverence and sometimes fear. They would just say *Omahkohkanakaaatsiiks* [the big all comrade, i.e., an individual], or *Omahkohkanakaaatsiisinni* [the Big All Comrades Society, i.e., a group]. Possibly meaning the "Ultimate All Comrades." Some of the societies were made up of older individuals, which also explains the "*Omahk*" in the word, which means "old," as in *Omahkinnaa* [old man].

Omahksspa'tsikoi – Literally "the big sand," "the Sand Hills."

Ookaan – The ceremony surrounding the building of *Ookaoyis* [the Sun-lodge]. It is initiated by a vow made by a holy woman who hosts the ceremony. Collective reference to the whole sundance ceremony and activities. The term "*Okaan*" originated from lashing together the wooden beams of the lodge with *apiss* [rope or rawhide strips], as in roping cattle.

Ookaoyis – Sun-lodge proper. Sun-lodge in the context of *Aokaawa*, the woman sponsoring the *Ookaan*.

Oomaaahsowaiksi – Their grandparents.

Oopaitapiisoowaiyi niitsitapi – The lifeway of *Niitsitapi*.

Ootai – Weasel in brown summer phase.

Ootohkoi – Usually in reference to yellow [sacred] paint.

Ootohkoinatsii – The color yellow. Literally, "yellow-looking."

Otaawaaahskatawaiksi – Those that they get as their grandparents. Elders.

Otsiitsitapiinihkasimmowaistsi – Their real people names.

Otsisstapiists – Bundles.

Otsitsihtaanists – [That person's] intentions. Sg.: *Otsitsihtaan*.

Paapaokaan – Dream.

Pahtsiipissowaasi – Mistaken-for-Morning-Star; Scarface's other name besides *Paiyo* name. See: *Ipissowaasi* for clarification.

Pahtsiipissowaasi – Scarface.

Paitapiiyssin – The processes of our way of life, lit. up[right] life, as in up and living, alive as a physical being walking around.

Paiyo – Scarface; see English–*Siksikaitsipowahsin* for all the names by which he is known.

Piikanaki – Peigan woman. *Pikanaki* is a variation of the same.

Piikanikowan – Peigan man.

Piksiwa – Restless.

Piskaan – Buffalo pound.

Pitsi (particle) – Means the person has the trait the rest of the word makes reference to.

Poiskinnaksin – Face painting.

Poiyawa – One of the names scarface is known by.

Poko'tsstapi – small rawhide case. Also: *Mopisstaan.* which literally means, "bundled [object]."

Pomma'ksinni – Transfer. Pl.: *Pommaksiistsi.*

Pommaksinni – Reference to *pomma'ksinni*/transfer.

Pommaksiistsi – Ceremonies which transfer knowledge.

Ponokaomita – Horse; lit. elk-dog.

Pookaiksi (singular), Pookawa (singular), Pookasin (collective) – Child, children (Also see *Naatowapokoos* and bundle holders.)

Pookawa (singular), Pookasin (collective) – Child, children.

Poowaksski – Scarface, Also known as *Paiyo, Pahtsiipissowaasi.*

Pisstahksin – To give tobacco.

Saam – Medicine; can also be translated as "food" (*Iisaami* = has medicine, or, acquired food).

Saitamsin – Breathing, breath of air.

Sao'otsistapapi – Mystery, some thing that doesn't make sense or incomprehensible.

Sayikihkihsiwa – A person who can't settle down including in relationships.

Siimohkssin – Cautioning, advice.

Sikapinaki – Blackeyes Woman.

Sikapistaan – An offering/payment: to elders for advice; to those that are transferring bundles to you; to those that are healing you; etc. Pl.: *Sikapistaanistsi.*

Sikapistaanistsi – Transfer payments.

Siksika – The Blackfoot tribe.

Siksikaitsipowahsin – Blackfoot language.

Siksikaitsipoyi – Those who speak the Blackfoot language.

Siksikaitsipowahsiistsi – Blackfoot language words.

Siksikaitsitapi – All Blackfoot speaking tribes; the term means "Blackfoot speaking real people."

Siksikaitsitapiipaitapiiyssin – Blackfoot way of life.

Skinnii-piikani – North Peigan (or *Aapatohsipikani*). The name Peigan may be the Anglo-cised version of the *Siksikaitsitapi* word *Pikani*, meaning "poorly dressed" or "torn robes" (Ewers 1958, 5) or "robes that are worn and thin from wear." *Skinnii* refers to the place that they occupy. It means to live at the edge, referring to the mountains. *Pikani* likely has been the tribe's name prior to contact.

Sokoisskitsipahpahsin – "Good heart."

Sooyiitapiiks – Water Spirits.

Staaapsiwa – A person of [that] laziness.

Stao'o'wa – Ghost (pl. *Stao'oi'ks*); used when people have no ambition or are doing nothing of any use. Cf. *Ksisstapsi* – Ghost, literally "no real source." *Stao'oi,* singular; *Ksisstapsiiiks,* pl., are both variations of the same.

Taapiimsin – Relationship. This is only the fragment which addresses relationship. Prefixes and suffixes would address the type of relationship. But usually of the physical being kind.

Tatsikiiyakokiiysinni – The centre tepee.

Tsi'ki – Address used to refer to a younger person than the speaker.

Tsihtaanist – Intentions. Sg.: *Tsihtaan.*

Tsisskaan – Sweat lodge.

Tso'ohkoway'sinni – Tribal alliance in the sense of relationships, as in clans, family, etc. Variation of *O'ohkowaipstssinni* – clan-ship.
Waa to'si – Powerful.

English–*Siksikaitsipowahsin*

The reader is advised to read some of the longer explanations of glossary entries in the *Siksikaitsipowahsin*–English glossary.

Align – see *Kakyosin* in *Siksikaitsipowahsin*–English glossary.
All-Smoke Ceremony – *Kanotsisissin*.
Altar – (place of smudge) *Iitawaamatosimmopi*.
Ancestor – *Akaitapiwa*.
Ancestors, the old people that lived before us – *Akaitapiiks*.
Attitude – *Maanistapaisspi*, see *Siksikaitsipowahsin*–English glossary for explanation.
Authority – *ninnayawa*, i.e., to be accorded a lot of respect, authority.
Balance – *Aawaatsimihkaasatai*, we can think of it as a return to balance for taking or undertaking rebalancing and harmonizing actions to return to the same, to counter every action and/or word that affects that balance and harmony.
Balance – *Aohkannaistokawa* = "Two of everything;" polar opposites such as: male and female; good & bad, etc. No specific term for balance.
Beaver – *Ksisskstaki*.
Beaver Bundle – *Ksissksta'kyo* usually used as a prefix indicating "Beaver type." As in *Ksisskstakyo Mopistaan* = "Beaver" Bundle.
Beaver Bundle Holders – *Iiyaohkiimiiksi*, literally translated to, "The-ones-that-have-water." Beaver Bundle holders are said to have no fear of water. The power of the bundle is also related to water. These are collectively the Beaver Bundle holders, *ksissksta'kyo mo'pisstaiksi* (Beaver Bundle is *ksissksta'kyo*).
Behaviour – *Maanistapaisspi*.

Behaviour (sacred) – *Aatsimihkasin*, (From where *Aawatsimihkasatawa* is derived) means "sacred way of behaviour, actions, acting."

Being – *Paitapiiyssin*. The processes of our way of life, lit. up[right] life, as in up and living, alive as a physical being walking around.

Being of good heart – *Aatsimoyihkaani* is performed from the source of a good heart. *Sokoisskitsipahpahsin* – Good heart.

Big All Comrades – *Omahkohkanakaaatsiisinni*; see *Iitsskinnayiiks*.

Blackfoot language – *Niitsi'powahsinni*, i.e., *Niitsitapiwa* talking; language that carries the breath of spirit; speaking *Niitsi'powahsinni* is experiencing spirit.

Blackfoot language words – *Siksikaitsipowahsiistsi*.

Blackfoot way of life – *Siksikaitsitapiipaitapiiyssin*.

Brave – *Matsisski*, meaning "brave, courageous, daring." *A'tsapssi*, meaning "brave" or "crazy."

Bravery – *Iiyiikitapiiyssin*.

Breath – *Niipaitapiiyssiin*, i.e., way of life, constant motion of breath; together with *Ihtsipaitapiiyopa* identifies the meaning and purpose of life; to teach the way of life.

Buffalo pound – *Annai Maotokowa*, "that is the *Maotokowa*," meaning "buffalo pound" or "corral." *Maotokowa* is also a washout or gully, natural formations that were often used as a pound or *piskaan*.

Buffalo Women's Society – *Maotokiiks*. Term comes from the buffalo pound/corral. A source indicates that the Buffalo pound/corral is *Annai Maotokowa* / That is the *Maotokowa*. So *Maotokiiks* comes from *Maotokowa*. The *Siksikaitsitapi* origin legend gives some clarity. See entry Buffalo pound.

Bundle holder – *Naatowa'po'ksisst*, i.e., holy mother of the present bundle holders; *Naatowa'po'n*, i.e., holy father of the present bundle holders; *Naatowa'pokos*, i.e., holy-children of the previous holders of the bundles.

Bundle holders, former – *Aaahsiks*, beginning with two generations back (*Naaahs* [my grandparents], *Kaaahs* [your grandparents], *Kaaahsinnooniksi* [our grandparents], *Oomaaahsowaiksi* [their grandparents].

Cautioning – *Siimohkissin.*

Ceremonialist – *Aawaatowapsiiks.*

Ceremony – *Aaopaatoom* (pl.).

Chief – *Ninnaa*, also: man; leader; a person that is accorded with a lot of respect; and, lately tribal Chief or Councilor. *Ninnaiksi* (or leaders) plural.

Children – *Naatowa'pokos*, i.e., holy-children of the previous holders of the bundles.

Clan-ship – *O'ohkowaipstssinni.*

Cognizant – *Akaaotsistapi'takyo'p*, i.e., to be cognizant and to discern tribal connections; sacred science; knowing as experiential knowing.

Coming to know – *Iissksiniip.*

Coming to know your heart = indigenous epistemology – *Aistomatoominniki.*

Compassion – *Kimmapiiyipitsinni.*

Consciousness of the natural order – *Aotsistapitsihk Maanistsihp* – Literally "when we understand how it is," "how the universe is with its natural laws," or "how the order of all things is." Consciousness of the natural order. Cf. *Ksinna'oi* story under entry "align" for an illustration. In it the man was shown what the order of things was for the *Ksinna'oi*, therefore he was able to emulate them to achieve the same things. He understood how it was, he had consciousness of the natural order of things.

Constant motion of breath – *Niipaitapiiyssin*; way of life,; together with *ihtsipaitapiiyo'pa* identifies the meaning and purpose of life; to teach the way of life.

Convocation (meeting) – *Kanohsin.*

Corral – *Annai Maotokowa*, "that is the *Maotokowa*," meaning "buffalo pound."

Cosmic alliance – See *Kakyosin* in *Siksikaitsipowahsin*–English glossary.

Cosmic order – See Cosmic universe.

Cosmic universe – *Ihtsipaitapiiyio'pa*, i.e., sacred power, spirit or force that links concepts; life force; term used when addressing the sacred power and the cosmic universe; Source of Life; sun as manifestation of the

Source of Life; great mystery; together with *Niitpaitapiiyssin* identifies the meaning and purpose of life. (I use the term "cosmic universe" to reference *Siksikaitsipoyi* understandings of reality emanating from *Ihtsipaitapiiyo'pa*, the Source of Life). *Ihtsipaitapiiyo'pa* is that which causes or allows us to live. The term natural law does not have a direct *Siksikaitsipowahsin* equivalent, however it is through *Ihtsipaitapiiyopa* that all "natural laws" are governed. It is *Ihtsipaitapiiyo'pa* that orchestrates the universe. Its laws govern the universe and including human life. *Ihtsipaitapiiyo'pa*, literally translates to "That which causes us to be alive." This force can also be called on to put things in your mind that will help you figure things out – to understand. It is very similar to what the Lakota call: Wakantanka, The great mystery. We don't really know what this force is. It is a mystery yet we know it exists to allow us to live and also is a great orchestrator of all life and the universe. It is intelligent and wise. It is not a direct translation of "cosmic universe."

Cosmic world – See Cosmic universe.

Councilor – *Ninnaa*, also: man; leader; a person that is accorded with a lot of respect; and, lately tribal Chief or Councilor.

Courageous – *Matsisski*, meaning "brave, courageous, daring." Related word: *Iiyiikitapiiyi*.

Crazy – *A'tsapssi*, meaning "brave" or "crazy."

Crazy Dogs Society – *Kanatsomitaiksi*; the Crazy Dogs or Brave Horses Society. This society has been called Crazy Dogs for some years now; however, lately many people have insisted that it was a mistranslation. Some now say it means Brave Horse. *Kan*, is reference to a collective. *A'tso*, comes from *matsisski*, meaning "brave, courageous, daring." Dog is *Iimitaa* and Horse is *Poonokaamita* (Elk Dog).

Daring – *Matsisski*, meaning, "brave, daring, courageous."

Discern – *Akaotsisstapi'takyo'p*, i.e., to be cognizant and to discern tribal connections; sacred science; knowing as experiential knowing.

Dog – Iimitaa. Sometimes you will only have the fragment *oomita*, can be understood as "dog." A Blackfoot speaker though would understand it is "horse" in the context it is used.

Dream – Paapaokaan.

Earth, sacred – Example: *Ksahkomma iikatsimapsiwa, aawatsimihkasatawa.* "

The Earth is sacred, we perform sacred acts to return our relationship to its sacred balance [whenever we upset that balance]."

Economy – Isstatsimihkasatawa, literally "we give tobacco." Economy does not equal *Isstatsimihkasatawa,* which means: to act in a sacred manner. The particle "*atsim,*" in the word comes from, *Aatsimapi,* which means holy or sacred. The rest of the word speaks to performing that sacred act. This act is intended to reestablish good relations with people, *Ihtsspaitapiiyo'pa,* animals, the earth, etc. (whichever has been affected by your actions). Usually done after you offended someone, but it can be done even if you are not the offender. If we take a plant we give tobacco to earth to reestablish your good relationship and maintain a balance, and harmony – sacredness. Elders say *Itsinohtatsimihka'so'p.* Meaning for any action you perform you should also perform an act to restore balance, harmony and sacredness. It is done all the time. If you hunt and kill an animal, "*Kitakatsimihkaas/*you will perform a sacred act [to restore the sacred balance and harmony]." Just think if we all did that with every act we perform. There would be less gluttony when it comes to natural resources and polluting the environment, etc. Just imagine the amount of *Aatsimihkasin* you would have perform to set things right today. Not only do we have enormous financial debt, but we also have an astronomical moral debt. We are easily morally bankrupt. Also: *Ksahkomma Aatsimapiwa,* which means, "Earth is sacred." We give it tobacco to restore the sacredness.

Elders – Aawaaahsskataiksi, i.e., those that are approached for everything from advice to conducting ceremonies. Elders are also *Omahkitapiiks.* The distinction is *Omahkitapiiks* are "old people" in general. *Aawaahsskataiksi* are those that have rights to advise on sacred matters. The right is acquired through having gone through transfers themselves. They must have passed those rights on too.

Epistemology – See *Ai'stomatoominniki.*

Experience – *Ihtsistototsp,* meaning "what we have been put through." In context it means "you have experienced it."

Experiential knowing – *Akaaotsistapi'takyo'p,* i.e., to be cognizant and to discern tribal connections; sacred science; knowing as experiential knowing.

Face painting, getting one's face painted – *Poiskinnaksin* – Face painting. *Aohpoiskinna* – (person) is getting face painted. *Ao'ohpoiskinahki* – When (person) has had face painted. *Matoohpoiskiiit* – Go get your face painted.

Force – *Ihtsipaitapiiyo'pi,* i.e., sacred power, spirit or force that links concepts; life force; term used when addressing the sacred power and the cosmic universe; Source of Life; sun as manifestation of the Source of Life; great mystery; together with *Niipaitapiiyssin* identifies the meaning and purpose of life. See: Cosmic Universe for explanation.

Generosity – *Aahsapsi* – Good, of the. *Aahsitapi* – [Of the] good person. The assumption is that a good person is a generous kind person.

Geography – *Kitssksah Koominninooni,* literally "our Land." *Niitaoni'pi Kitao'ahsinnooni,* meaning "How we recognize our land (through geographic features)."

Ghost helper – *Aiyiikinaan.*

Gift – *Koitapiiisin.* There other related words regarding gifts but in different contexts. *Koitapiiisin* is the best for overall use.

Giving – *Isspommotsisinni.* Giving and sharing.

Giving (giving and sharing) – Giving – *Matsiskahtaksin.* Sharing – *Isspomihtaan. Isspomihtaan* means "helping." You share to help people. If you give something to some one you would "*Noohtsspommowawa* / I helped [that person] with [the item]." The older word, which we hear rarely is *Iikawa.* Most people would not understand it when it is spoken especially not if they read it.

Good heart – *Sokoisskitsipahpahsin.*

Good heart, being of good heart –*Ikinniiyoihkitsipahpahsin*, meaning "soft-heartness." Cf. *Aatsimoihkaan* for further discussion.

Grandfather – *Kaaahsinnoon*.

Grandfathers – *Naaahsiks* = My grandfathers. Either ceremonial, biological, or extended family grandparents. Contextual usage determines definition, i.e.: In the context of ceremony, they are past bundle holders and in the context of family, they are simply grandparents of the common context.

Grandparent – *Kaaahs*, your grandparent. Ceremonial and otherwise. Also: Your mother or father-in- law.

Grandparents – *Aaahsiks. Oomaaahsowaiksi* – Their grandparents.

Grandparents – *Kaaahsinnooniksi* – Collective term for "Our grandparents." The term is understood properly in context. When the "Common" *Niitsitapi* (Real People), *Niitsipoyi* (Real people language speakers – specifically Blackfoot in this case) say *Kaaahsinnooniksi*, it is understood that they are referring to Grandfathers and Grandmothers in the family structure sense. When members of the various societies or individual bundle and pipe holders say *Kaaahsinnooniksi* they are more than likely mean previous society members, bundle holders, pipe holders, etc. These ceremonial people use it for previous "bundle/ pipe holders" who were holders two generations (transfers) before them. The set up is the same as in a family structure. The present members are the "*Naatowa'pokos*/Holy-children" of the previous holders of the bundles. The previous holders prior to present holders are "*Naatowa'po'n* and *Naatowa'po'ksisst*/Holy father & Holy mother" of the present holders. All those former holders beyond these two generations are *Aaahsiks* (*Naaahs* [my grandparents], *Kaaahs* [your grandparents], *Kaaahsinnooniksi* [our grandparents], *Oomaaahsowaiksi* [their grandparents]). However, protocol restrictions apply to *Aawaaahsskataiksi* [those elders who are approached for everything from advice to conducting ceremonies]. They don't have "blanket privileges." For example, they can only participate in and conduct ceremonies that they have gone through themselves and can only advise on certain matters as their experiences (actual participation) dictate. All other societies have similar structures.

Grandparents – *Naaahsiks* (plural), my grandparents (both genders – grandmother and grandfather), ceremonial or otherwise. My in-laws. Genderless term.

Great mystery – *Ihtsipaitapiiyopa*, i.e., sacred power, spirit or force that links concepts; life force; term used when addressing the sacred power and the cosmic universe; Source of Life; sun as manifestation of the Source of Life; together with *niitpaitapiiyssin* identifies the meaning and purpose of life.

Healing powers – *Aato'si* – To have sacred power, i.e., healing powers.

Heart, being of good heart – *Iikiniioihkitsipahpsin.*

History – *Inahkotait sinik a' topi*, meaning "[what] we pass on through the generations, through storytelling."

Holy father – *Naatowa'po'n*, i.e., the man that transferred to the present bundle holder.

Horn Society – *Ihkanakaaatsiiksi.*

Horn Society – *Iitsskinnayiiks*, Horn Society members; also: *Omahkohkana-kaaatsiisinni* – "Big All Comrades" (possibly meaning the "Old All Comrades," because, older men and women usually joined this group in the old days. It could also be "Ultimate All Comrades" because the Horn Society would be at the top if societies were arranged in a hierarchy. Other age grade societies ultimately led up to the Horn Society. Thirdly and likely the most accurate theory is that they are so named because four all comrades societies came together to avoid extinction after epidemics to create one big/unified all comrade society).

Horn Society – *Omaaahsowaayi.*

Horse – *Ponokaomita* (lit. elk dog).

Incense – *Aamato'simmaan.*

Indigenous epistemology = coming to know your heart – *Aistomatoominniki.*

Intentions – *Tsihtaanist*. My intentions = *Nitsitihtaanist*. [That person's] intentions = *Otsitsitsihtaanists*. Singular would be: *Tsihtaan*, *Nitsitsihtaan*, *Otsitsihtaan*, respectively.

Kainai (Many Chiefs) – *Aakainawa*.

Kindness – *Kimmapiiypitsinni*.

Kinship alliance – *Ksokoisin*, for relatives in family structure. *Tapiimihsin* are those you have a relationship (alliances) with.

Knowing – *Akaotsistapi'takyo'p*, i.e., to be cognizant and to discern tribal connections; sacred science; knowing as experiential knowing. The moment or the occasion you come to know is *Ao'tsistapi'takyo'p*. *Issksiniip*, i.e., knowing is active participation with the world, integrating experience through reflective meditation. Knowing is the ability to make reference to past experiences, contextualizing them in a system of meanings to make sense of present experiences and formulate, the basis for decision-making.

Knowledge – *Aissksinihp*, we know it to be like that.

Knowledge – *Kii Nai'tsistomato'k Ai'stamma'tso'tsspi*. Embodying or being the knowledge you have been given), making knowledge part of our body.

Knowledge, spirit of – *Kakyosin*. This word means "to observe." Literally *Kakyosin* can be seen as the "essence of knowledge." The term is related to *Mokaksin*, which is what comes from observation and connection with the universe. *Mokaksin* is knowledge, intelligence and wisdom.

Leader – *Ninnaa*, also: man; a person that is accorded with a lot of respect; and, lately, tribal Chief or Councilor.

Leaders – *Ninnaiksi* (or chiefs) plural. Also literally: "*Aaotoomakiiiks /* Those that [walk] first."

Life – *Niipaitapiiwahsin* or *Niipaitapiiyssin*, i.e., way of life, constant motion of breath; the life or lifeworld of Niitistapi; together with *Ihtsipaitapiiyopa* identifies the meaning and purpose of life; to teach the way of life. Life force – *Ihtsipaitapiiyopa*, i.e., sacred power, spirit or force that links concepts; term used when addressing the sacred power and the cosmic universe; Source of Life; sun as manifestation of the

Source of Life; great mystery; together with *Niitpaitapiiyssin* identifies
the meaning and purpose of life. See other discussions on life.

Lifeway – *Niipaitapiiwahsin*, way of life, constant motion of breath;
together with *ihtsipaitapiiyopa* identifies the meaning and purpose of
life; to teach the way of life. Our life ways = *Kipaitapiiwahsinnooni*.

Lifeway – *Niitsitapi Oopaitapiiyssoowaiyi*. The lifeway of *Niitsitapi*.

Lifeworld – *Niipaitapiiwahsin*, i.e., the life or lifeworld of the *Niitsitapi*.

Lone Chief – *Nitainaawa*.

Long life – *Misommipaitapiiyssin*.

Long Time Medicine Pipe – *Misommahkoyinnimaan* = long time pipe.

Love – *Aakomimihtaan*.

Man – *Ninnaa*, also: leader; a person that is accorded with a lot of respect;
and, lately tribal Chief or Councilor.

Many Chiefs (Kainai) – *Aakainawa*.

Medicine Pipe Dance – *Niinaimsskaipasskaan*.

Medicine pipe holder – *Niinaimsskaiksi*, term used commonly for the
"Medicine Pipe Holders." It is not a literal translation. If translated it
would be roughly "Leader possessors." More properly the "Thunder-
pipe-holders," as the pipe originally came from Thunder, *Ksisstsi'ko'm*.

Meditation – *Kakyoopissin*. In ceremonial language it could be
Aatooopissin = sitting holy.

Moon – *Ko'kommikisoom*.

Morning Star – *Ipissowaasi*. This is Morning Star's name. The term does
not mean morning star. But we refer to the morning star as *Ipissowaasi*.

Mother – *Niksist* (my mother).

Mysterious power – *Ihtsipaitapiiyo'pa*.

Mystery – *Pissatapi* = some thing that doesn't make sense or
incomprehensible. *Ihtsipaitapiiyo'pa*, i.e., sacred power, spirit or force
that links concepts; life force; term used when addressing the sacred
power and the cosmic universe; Source of Life; sun as manifestation
of the Source of Life; great mystery; together with *Ihtsipaitapiiyo'pa*
identifies the meaning and purpose of life.

Observation – *Kakyosin*. *Kakyosin isstaokaki'tsotsp* / observation gives us intelligence knowledge and wisdom.

Offering – *Ikitsstaan* = an offering to the sun or other entities. Related term: *Sikapistaan* = an offering/payment: to elders for advice; to those that are transferring bundles to you; to those that are healing you; etc.

Old Man – *Napi* (hero, exemplifies dark powers of humanity). *Napi* is representative of the fallibility of man. He reminds us that to do things that are wrong will result in negative consequences. He is the subject of our legends in which he is always getting himself into difficult situations because he doesn't do "the right thing." If something bad or humorous happens as a result of our in-attention, etc., we might say, "That is *Napi*, he is all around us."

Old people – *Iipommowaiksi*. Old people, those who have been transferred (initiated ceremonialists).

Ones-that-have-water – *Iiyaohkiimiiksi*. Beaver bundle holders.

Ontology – No term. However, much of *Niitsitapi* Life is spent in the process of trying to understand the spiritual existence etc. and all that is related to ontology.

Original responsibility – *Kiitomohpiipotokoi* = What you have been put [here] with. Anything we are "put here with" is our responsibility.

Payments – *Sikapistaanistsi*, i.e., transfer payments.

Pedagogy – *Issksinnima'tsstohksinni* = education in all forms.

Philosophy – *Niitssksiniipi omahtanistaissihpi*. Literally: How we come to know how the universe works (understood only in appropriate context).

Piikani, male – *Pikannikowan*.

Pipe – *Ahkoyinnimaan*.

Pipe keeper or medicine pipe holder – *Niinaimsskaiksi*, term used commonly
for the "Medicine Pipe Holders." It is not a literal translation. If translated it would be roughly "Leader possessors." More properly the "Thunder-pipe-holders," as the pipe originally came from Thunder, *Ksisstsi'ko'm*.

Power – *Aato'si* – To have sacred power, i.e., healing powers.

Power (sacred) – *Ihtsipaitapiiyo'pa*, i.e., sacred power, spirit or force that links concepts; life force; term used when addressing the sacred power and the cosmic universe; Source of Life; sun as manifestation of the Source of Life; great mystery; together with *Niipaitapiiyssin* identifies the meaning and purpose of life. *Ihtsipaitapiiyo'pa* is a sacred power that gives/allows life to exist.

Powerful – *Waa to'si*. Has the power of *Naatoyii*. Connected to *Naatosi* – the Sun – and its power.

Pray – *Waatoyinnayi*. *Aawaatoyinnaiyi* refers to the singing of sacred songs and also when a bundle is "taking care of" your home. Pray = *Aatsimoihkaan*.

Prayer – *Aatsimoyihkanni*. Praying should be done only while "being of good heart."

Real People language – *Niitsi'powahsinni*, i.e., *Niitsitapiwa* talking; language that carries the breath of spirit; speaking *Niitsi'powahsinni* is experiencing spirit.

Reality – No directly equivalent term. Only: *Aanoo Iitapaitapiiyopi* = Here, here we are living (physically).

Red Belt society – *Maohksiipssiiks*.

Relationship – *Isskanaitapstsi*.

Relationship – *Taapiimsin*. This is only the fragment which addresses relationship. Prefixes and suffixes would address the type of relationship. But usually of the physical being kind.

Relationship, sacred – Example: *Ksahkomma iikatsimapsiwa, aawatsimihkasatawa.* "The Earth is sacred; our relationship is sacred."

Respect – *Ainnakowa* = to respect a person or thing.

Respect – *Inna'kotsiiysin*.

Respected person – *Ninnaa*, also: man; leader; a person that is accorded with a lot of respect; and, lately tribal Chief or Councilor.

Responsibilities – *Kiitomohpiipotokoi* (or role). *Kiitoomohpipotokowa* – "What you have been put here with" – This comes with the assumption that what you are put here with is what you are responsible for.

Role – *Kiitomohpiipotokoi* (or responsibilities). See responsibility for explanation.

Sacred – *Aatsimapi.*

Sacred – Example: *Ksahkomma iikatsimapsiwa, aawatsimihkasatawa.* "The Earth is sacred, our relationship is sacred."

Sacred medicine powers – *Aatosin.*

Sacred power – *Ihtsipaitapiiyo'pi*, i.e., spirit or force that links concepts; life force; term used when addressing the sacred power and the cosmic universe; Source of Life. Sacred power, i.e., Sun is *Naatosin.*

Sacred science – *Akaotsisstapi'takyo'p*, i.e., to be cognizant and to discern tribal connections; knowing as experiential knowing. Also: *Natoa'pi*, that which is sacred or holy.

Scarface – *Poowaksi*, a.k.a. *Poiyawa, Paiyo, Ihspowakssk, Pahtsiipissoowasi.*

Sharing – *Isspommotsisinni* – Giving, support and sharing.

Smudge – *Aamatosimaan.*

Social structure – *Niitaikso'kowammotsiiyo'pi*, "how we know our relationships to be."

Social structure – *Niitsikso'kowammootsi'opi*. "How we are related to each other," social structure.

Society – *Kana'kaaatsiiks*, i.e., any one of the societies, Horns, Maotokiiks, etc.

Song – *Naatoyinnaiysin*. Sacred songs.

Source of Life – *Ihtsipaitapiiyo'pa*, i.e., sacred power, spirit or force that links concepts; life force; term used when addressing the sacred power and the cosmic universe; sun as manifestation of the Source of Life; great mystery; together with *Ihtsipaitapiiyo'pa* identifies the meaning and purpose of life.

Speakers – Sg. & pl.: *Niitsipoyi*, real people language speakers. This is how we address our Blackfoot people.

Speaking – *Saitamsin*. Through the breath of speaking.

Spirit – *Ihtsipaitapiiyo'pa.*

Sun – *Naatosi.*

Sun-lodge – *Ookaoyis.*

Sundance – *A ko'ko' ka'tssin* (lit.: circle encampment). *Ookaan*, specifically the vow made by holy woman who hosts the ceremony.

Support – *Isspomotsisinni*. Sharing and support.

Survival – *Kaamotaan* meaning "survival [from all perils]."

Survival – *Kamotaani*.

Sweat lodge – *Tsi'sskaan*.

Teacher – *Aisksinnima'tstohki*.

Teachings – *Nitaisstammatsokoyi*.

Teepee – *Tatsikiiyakokiiysinni*. The centre tepee.

Thunder – *Ksisstsi'ko'm*.

Thunder pipe – *Niinaimsskaahkoyinnimaan*, the Thunder-pipe proper. Medicine pipe in general is *Ahkoyinnimaan*. *Niinaimsskaan* and *Niinaimsskaahkoyinimaan* are said to refer to the pipe as being so expensive that only *Ninnaiksi* (Chiefs or leaders) were the only ones that could afford them. The transfer payments (*Sikapistaanistsi*) could run very high, but that is not always the case. *Niinaimsskaiks* also had a lot of authority (*Ninnayawa*/Were accorded a lot of respect), so "*Ninna*," is likely the source of the term *Niinaimsskaiksi*. *Niinaimsskaiksi, Niinaimsska*, and related terms have "*Ninna*" as a prefix. *Ninna* is the term for "man," "leader," "a person that is accorded with a lot of respect," and, lately "tribal Chief" or "Councilor."

Tobacco, to give – *Pisstahkssin*.

Traditional knowledge – *Kipaitapiwahsinnooni*. The Blackfoot term for life encompasses a lot of things. Our traditional knowledge is part of it.

Transfer – *Ai'pommootsp*, meaning when we have gone through a transfer.

Transfer – *Pommaksiistsi*. Ceremonies which transfer knowledge.

Transfer payments – *Sikapistaanistsi*.

Transfer, went through a – *Iipommowa*.

Transformational consciousness – *Ao'tsistapitakyoki*.

Transformed – *Aistommatop* = when we have embodied the knowledge, we are the knowledge, the knowledge is us.

Tribal alliance – *Tso'ohkoways'inni*, in the sense of relationships, as in clans, family, etc.

Understand – *Aotsistapitakyop*.

Values – No generic term. See *Kimmotsiisinni* for a central example of one of the *Siksikaitsitapi* values.

Way of life – *Niipaitapiiysiin*, i.e., constant motion of breath; together with *Ihtsipaitapiiyo'pa* identifies the meaning and purpose of life; to teach the way of life.

Way of life, Blackfoot – *Siksikaitsitapiipaitapiiyssin*.

Wind – *So'poi*.

Words in the Blackfoot language – *Siksikaitsipowahsiistsi*.

Vow – *Ahkoooomohsin*. *Ookaan* is specifically the vow made by the holy woman who hosts the Sundance ceremony.

Younger person – *Tsi'ki*. Address.

Bibliography

Adams, H. 1995. *A Tortured People: The Politics of Colonization*. Penticton, BC: Theytus Books.

Ani, M. 1994. *Yurugu: An African-Centered Critique of European Cultural Thought and Behavior*. Trenton, NJ: Africa World Press.

Ashcroft, B., G. Griffiths, and H. Tiffins. 1989. *The Empire Writes Back: Theory and Practice in Post-Colonial Literatures*. London and New York: Routledge.

Bastien, B., J. W. Kremer, R. Kuokkanen, and P. Vickers. 2003. Healing the impact of colonization, genocide, missionization, and racism on indigenous populations. In: S. Krippner and T. McIntyre, eds., *The Impact of War Trauma on Civilian Populations*, 25–37. New York: Greenwood Press.

Bastien, B., J. W. Kremer, J. Norton, J. Rivers-Norton, and P. Vickers. 1999. The genocide of Native Americans. *ReVision: A Journal of Consciousness and Transformation* 22, no. 1: 13–20.

Battiste, M., and J. Barman. 1995. *First Nations Education in Canada: The Circle Unfolds*. Vancouver: UBC Press.

Bolaria, B. S., ed. 1991. *Social Issues and Contradictions in Canadian Society*. Toronto: Harcourt Brace Jovanovich.

Boldt, M. 1993. *Surviving as Indians: The Challenge of Self-Government*. Toronto: University of Toronto Press.

Brizinski, P. 1993. *Knots in a String: An Introduction to Native Studies in Canada*. University of Saskatchewan: University Extension Press.

Buckley, H. 1992. *From Wooden Ploughs to Welfare: Why Indian Policy Failed in the Prairie Provinces*. Montreal: McGill-Queen's University Press.

Bullchild, P. 1985. *The Sun Came Down: The History of the World as My Blackfeet Elders Told It*. San Francisco: Harper & Row.

Cajete, G. 1994. *Look to the Mountain: An Ecology of Indigenous Education*. Skyland, NC: Kivaki Press.

Capra, F. 1982. *The Turning Point: Science, Society and the Rising Culture*. New York: Bantam Books.

Chrisjohn, R. D., S. L. Young, and M. Maraun. 1994. *The Circle Game: Shadows and Substance in the Indian Residential School Experience in Canada*. A report to the Royal Commission on Aboriginal Peoples.

Clarke, J. N. 1990. *Health, Illness, and Medicine in Canada*. Toronto: McClelland & Stewart.

Clignet, R. 1971. "'Damned if you do, damned if you don't': The dilemma of colonizer-colonized relations." *A Comparative Education Review* 15, no. 3: 296–312.

Cohen, D. 1996. *The Secret Language of the Mind: A Visual Inquiry into the Mysteries of Consciousness*. San Francisco: Chronicle Books.

Colorado, P. 1988. Bridging Native and Western science. *Convergence* 11: 49–67.

Cushman, P. 1995. *Constructing the Self, Constructing America*. New York: Addison-Wesley.

Davis, R., and M. Zannis. 1973. *The Genocide Machine in Canada*. Montreal: Black Rose Books.

Dion-Buffalo, Y., and J. C. Mohawk. 1994. Thoughts from an autochthonous center. *Cultural Survival*, Winter, 33–35.

Dossey, L. 1985. *Space, Time, and Medicine*. Boston, MA: Shambhala Publications.

Duran, E., and B. Duran. 1995. *Native American Post-Colonial Psychology*. Albany: State University of New York Press.

Ewers, J. C. 1958. *The Blackfeet Raiders on the Northern Plains*. Norman: University of Oklahoma Press.

Fanon, F. 1963. *The Wretched of the Earth*. New York: Grove Press.

Frantz, D. G., and N. J. Russell. 1989. *Blackfoot Dictionary of Stems, Roots, and Affixes*. Toronto: University of Toronto Press.

Freire, P. 1996. *Pedagogy of Hope*. New York: Continuum.

Frideres, J. S. 1974. *Canada's Indians Contemporary Conflicts*. Scarborough, ON: Prentice Hall.

Gilbert, H., and J. Tompkins. 1996. *Post-Colonial Drama*. London & New York: Routledge.

Gonzalez, E., and J. W. Kremer. 2000. The Maya shape of time. *ReVision: A Journal of Consciousness and Transformation* 23, no. 2: 24–37.

Goodman, R. 1992. *Lakota Star Knowledge, Studies in Lakota Theology*, Sinte Gleska University, Rosebud, South Dakota.

Grinnell, G. B. 1962. *Blackfoot Lodge Tales: The Story of a Prairie People*. Lincoln: University of Nebraska Press.

Harrod, H. L. 1992. *Renewing the World*. Tucson: University of Arizona Press.

Hildebrandt, W., S. Carter, and D. First Rider. 1996. *The True Spirit and Original Intent of Treaty 7*. Montreal: McGill-Queen's University Press.

Indian Association of Alberta. 1987. *Child Welfare Needs Assessment and Recommendations*. Edmonton. Unpublished document.

Kehoe, A. B. 1995. Introduction to the Bison Book edition of C. Wissler and D. C. Duvall. *Mythology of the Blackfoot Indians*. Lincoln: University of Nebraska Press.

Kremer, J. W. 2000. Shamanic Initiations and their Loss – Decolonization as Initiation and Healing. *Ethnopsychologische Mitteilungen* 9, no. 1/2: 109–48.

Kremer, J. W. 1996. Indigenous Science issue introduction; Evolving into what, and for whose purposes? Reading Bateson. *ReVision: A Journal of Consciousness and Transformation* 18, no. 3: 2–5, 27–36.

Kremer, J. W. 1994. *Looking for Dame Yggdrasil*. Red Bluff, CA.: Falkenflug Press.

Kremer, J. W., and M. E. Gomes (eds.). 2000. Prophecy and historical responsibility. *ReVision: A Journal of Consciousness and Transformation* 23, no. 2.

Knudtson, P., and D. Suzuki. 1992. *Wisdom of the Elders*. Toronto: Stoddart.

Lincoln, B. 1986. *Myth, Cosmos, and Society*. Cambridge, MA: Harvard University Press.

Men, H. 1990. *Secrets of Mayan Science and Religion*. Santa Fe, NM: Bear and Co.

McClintock, W. 1992. *The Old North Trail: Life, Legend and Religion of the Blackfeet Indians*. Lincoln: University of Nebraska Press.

Peat, D. 1994. *Lighting the Seventh Fire*. Secaucus, N.J.: Carol Publishing Group.

Potvin, A. 1966. *The Sun Dance: Liturgy of the Blackfoot People*. Ottawa: University of Ottawa, Department of Religious Studies. Unpublished thesis.

Reason, P. 1994. *Participation in Human Inquiry*. London: Sage.

Royal Commission on Aboriginal Peoples. 1996. *People to People, Nation to Nation*. Ottawa: Minister of Supply and Services Canada.

Sharpe, K. 1993. *David Bohm's World: New Physics and New Religion*. London: Associated University Presses.

Taylor, F. 1989. *Standing Alone: A Contemporary Blackfoot Indian*. Halfmoon Bay, BC: Arbutus Bay Publications.

Titley, E. B. 1986. *A Narrow Vision: Duncan Campbell Scott and the Administration of Indian Affairs in Canada*. Vancouver: University of British Columbia Press.

Urban, G. 1991. *Pedagogy*. Austin, TX: University of Texas Press.

Wissler, C., and D. C. Duvall. 1995. *Mythology of the Blackfoot Indians*. Lincoln: University of Nebraska Press.

Wolf, F. A. 1991. *The Eagle's Quest*. New York: A Touchstone Book Published by Simon & Schuster.

Wub-e-ke-niew. 1995. *We Have the Right to Exist: A Translation of Aboriginal Indigenous Thought*. New York: Black Thistle Press.

York, G. 1990. *The Dispossessed: Life and Death in Native Canada.*
London: Vintage U.K.

Youngblood-Henderson, J. 1992. *Algonquin Spirituality: Balancing the
Opposites.* San Francisco: California Institute of Integral Studies.

Zukav, G. 1979. *The Dancing Wu Li Masters: An Overview of the New
Physics.* New York: Bantam Books.